PENGUIN BOOKS

LONG PLAYERS

Peter Coviello has written about Walt Whitman, Mormon polygamy, Steely Dan, the history of sexuality, queer children, American literature, stepparenthood, and Prince. This work has appeared in *The Believer*, *Frieze*, *Avidly*, *Raritan*, and the *Los Angeles Review of Books*, as well as in several books. In 2017–18, he held a fellowship at the Institute for Advanced Study in Princeton, New Jersey. He lives in Chicago.

PETER COVIELLO

Long Players

A LOVE STORY IN EIGHTEEN SONGS

PENGUIN BOOKS

PENGUIN BOOKS

An imprint of Penguin Random House LLC
375 Hudson Street
New York, New York 10014
penguin.com

Library of Congress Cataloging-in-Publication Data

Names: Coviello, Peter, author.
Title: Long players : a love story in eighteen songs / Peter Coviello.
Other titles: Love story in eighteen songs
Description: New York, New York : Penguin Books, [2018]
Identifiers: LCCN 2017037330 (print) | LCCN 2017037788 (ebook) | ISBN
    9780525504313 (ebook) | ISBN 9780143132332 (pbk.)
Subjects: LCSH: Coviello, Peter—Relations with women. | Men—United
    States—Biography. | Popular music fans—United States—Biography. |
    Man-woman relationships—United States.
Classification: LCC HQ1090.3 (ebook) | LCC HQ1090.3 .C677 2018 (print) |
    DDC 306.7—dc23
LC record available at https://lccn.loc.gov/2017037330

Printed in the United States of America
10   9   8   7   6   5   4   3   2   1

Set in Arno Pro
DESIGNED BY KATY RIEGEL

Penguin is committed to publishing works of quality and integrity. In that spirit,
we are proud to offer this book to our readers; however, the story, the experiences,
and the words are the author's alone.

for SFD and EFD

She was vigorous enough to have borne that hard night without feeling ill in body, beyond some aching and fatigue; but she had waked to a new condition: she felt as if her soul had been liberated from its terrible conflict; she was no longer wrestling with her grief, but could sit down with it as a lasting companion and make it a sharer in her thoughts. For now the thoughts came thickly.

—GEORGE ELIOT, *Middlemarch*

Long Players

IT MUST HAVE been in the eighth or ninth song. I'd lost count by then, the way you do, even if it's a band like this one, a band you treasure. There in the press at the front of the crowd I was just then beginning to give myself over to that weird abandon that comes over you in unfamiliar places, where you have no friends, no connections, no social responsibilities of any kind. (This was Madrid.) What happened next took up about four minutes and thirty-four seconds. That, anyway, is how long "Dalliance" takes on the record. But somewhere inside the dilated time of that performance—and "Dalliance" is a slow-blossoming bruise of a song, one that broods over a woozy guitar riff and ascends finally toward a huge uncoiling blast of sound—somewhere along that way, aflail in a way only someone generous-hearted would call "dancing," it came to me. I knew it, right there, without words and well beyond the possibility of contradiction: *It is better to be doing this, exactly here, exactly now, than any other human thing.*

There isn't much unusual about these strobe-lit bodywide rushes of conviction. You will have enjoyed some of your own, I imagine, and so will know they are not unique to the concert hall, the dance floor, the bar. Not at all. The whole bright delirium of sex, for instance, might be described in just these terms. Who hasn't known the feeling, in the midst of those few hours stolen away from the weary day, that you've stumbled for that sheltered moment into the right world? The world whose content is surprise, delight, self-forgetfulness, and self-reclamation? The world whose chief currency is joy? Who doesn't know that sensation: the inflooding belief in the possibility of being alive and being delighted, of being different and being you? This is some of what it means to say that sex—in a phrase I once read that always lingered with me—is "an always available idiom for dreaming."

But it's not the only one. We find our way to other idioms. Dreaming, you could say, speaks in other tongues.

I swear to you I encountered exactly that feeling, that sense of elated certainty wedded to a welcome susceptibility to transformation, there at a show by a band called the Wedding Present, at around eleven p.m. Madrid time, the thirteenth of November, near the end of the first decade of the twenty-first century.

IT HAD BEGUN that morning in the café. I'd arrived groggy and spiritless the night before, coming into Madrid from, of all unlikely points of departure, Norwich, in the east of England, where I had passed the previous week. Consult your nearest maps and you will see that Norwich is the metropolitan center of a region of England called East Anglia. I can tell you that it is a town that saw its heyday in about the mid-1400s and, to the underinformed visitor, appears to have been in a steady, unhurried decline ever since. Of course, this is hardly fair. In Norwich you will find a major university, Norman churches of evidently high distinction, and, once you make your way past the dismal car parks and retrofitted malls, miles of slow-rolling fields reaching up to a mild chalky sky.

Norwich could claim, too, just then, one couple very dear to me indeed—friends of my twenties, the both of them Irish born, whose lives had deposited them once more among the exasperating English. I was there because they were there. I was there because of the volume of postadolescent hilarity that had passed so fluently between us and that had, over the years, broadened and solidified into what all three of us would have just called love.

I was there because I was in flight. Unluckily for them, my brokenness and I—that wearisome pair—had washed right up at their door.

They did what they could. They welcomed me. With an unstraining deftness of touch, they cared for me. At night we drank, and talked, and launched ourselves into three-body dance parties in their underheated front room. Every morning, before Anne went to work, Donal would make us all eggs and sausage in an enormous silver fry-pan, the sight of which always reminded me of the Joni Mitchell song: *"The bed's too big, the frying pan's too wiiiiiide."* I'd croon it to him in the warming and close little kitchen, and feel a brief restorative rightness in the world.

Then one afternoon a few days into my visit, because it seemed like just the thing to do, because nothing could be safer than this little nest in the east of England, I played them "All My Friends" by LCD Soundsystem, a song I thought we three might dance to and delight in. And before I could prevent it happening there it was: that familiar, enveloping awfulness.

A queasy weightlessness. A little rising plume of fear.

A small voice sidled up to me. *Get ready,* it said. *Get ready. Get ready.*

It occurred to me I was not well.

THAT NIGHT I wrote a friend back home, who knew the shape of these episodes. She sympathized, and reassured, and encouraged. She told the kinds of jokes that aren't really only jokes.

("The thing about you," Dana said, as she had said before, "is that you go a few months without having sex with anybody and you start to catastrophize your life." And I remember thinking, *Yes, LIKE EVERYONE ELSE IN THE WORLD*.) Maybe what I needed right then, she suggested, was care in a different, more immediately bodily mode. "Get out of England," she advised. "Now. They are the unsexiest people on planet Earth."

And so, a few days and much train travel later: Spain.

But there in the bright café morning, at my table for one, Madrid seemed better in the abstract than in fact. Have you ever been to Madrid? Here are some of the basic and curative things it was rumored to possess: warmth, in many senses; a nightlife of almost polemical excess; small fried foods in unlimited supply. What was there to dispirit? And yet from the start nothing was quite kicking my way. Implausible rain, a botched hotel reservation, and a misapprehended order had dented my already fragile sense of traveler's competence. (*"I asked for water,"* Elvis Costello sang into my headphones, *"and they gave me rosé wine."*) Postcards littered the table in front of me, but what could I write? "In Madrid, awash in the tourist's sense of isolation, ineptitude, and foolhardy conspicuousness. Send help."

I picked from out of my bag a battered copy of *The Portrait of a Lady* by Henry James, a novel of youthful promise and blighted happiness that in just those unsteady days it would perhaps have been wise not to peruse. I was reading it cover to cover, again.

But then, there it was.

Inside the doorframe was the familiar collage of posters: announcements, advertisements, solicitations multilingual and in bright array. I thought: "That's a poster for the Wedding Present."

And: "They're playing in Madrid."

And: "They're playing *tonight* in Madrid . . . a block away from my room on Gran Via."

Well.

≈

IT ISN'T THE CASE that I'd reached, either that day in Spain or back in England, a pinnacle of despondency. That had come earlier. Some thousands of miles away the terms of it all, of that terrible and unforeseen dissolution, were being haggled over by bored, prosperous attorneys. But the implosion had come almost exactly a year before, the detonating announcement. I marked it in the journals I so fastidiously kept in those days, the way you do when you are convinced that what you're doing, and where you are, and how you spend your days, matters to a vanishingly small set of people. There in Madrid I was yet suffering from what you could call a failure of imagination. In a thousand lifetimes I would not have believed the previous year of life to be even remotely possible. That, really, continued to be the problem. It was so shattering and ugly but also, inescapably, so commonplace. A bit of unexceptional private cataclysm. Some part of me must have known this. And yet it felt like a daily immersion in incomprehensibility. I was in the midst of an experience, unyielding and actual, that I could not quite *imagine*. Reality outran apprehension. And there was I.

So a pervasive lowness of spirit had settled over me, and persisted, even in the warmth of Spain, in the freedom of travel, in the luxury of uncommitted time. I found to my dismay that I couldn't quite talk myself into the enjoyment of that freedom and that luxury. When my inner ear wasn't clamoring with the sound of all the work I wasn't accomplishing, monitory quotations from some long-abandoned moment of scholarly diligence would come bounding over the sill of consciousness: "Quicksands of leisure!" the poet James Merrill at some point despairingly proclaims. Or worse, from a character in Hawthorne, who speaks of "the vague wretchedness of an indolent, half-occupied man."

Meanwhile, from Maine to New York, and then from Italy to England, from the tranced air of libraries to the clatter of foreign speech in far-flung bars, I moved in a haze of undispersing grief. Everything, then, was a kind of trip wire. I'd look too long at a stranger's curling smile, or I'd linger too unguardedly in the pages of a book, and there'd be these terrible flashes of memory. A bright day. A shared joke. Fragments of a lost self, a despoiled life. I walked around feeling like nothing so much as my own puzzled ghost. Out one cloud-congested Parisian morning on a mopey stroll, I wandered past a playground, a tumult of children speaking rushes of words I did not understand. And there, in an instant, with day-derailing clarity, a vision rose up before me. I saw two little girls on a schoolyard in Maine—sisters—standing inside a crowd of classmates in the clamoring minutes before the first bell. And one of them, the oldest of the two, is looking at me, and then to one of her little grade school friends, and then back to me.

"Oh, that's Pete," is what I heard her say. "He's my stepdad."

For a long tremoring moment, it held me, that vision.

Mine was a wretchedness becoming daily less vague.

BUT THERE'S THIS BAND, you see, and they're called the Wedding Present.

The Wedding Present, I should say, is a British postpunk outfit, anchored by a singer named David Gedge, who, in a thin unpretty voice—honestly he sounds less like a vocalist than a middle manager being interviewed on BBC 2, with a backing of frantic guitars—sings about the humiliations, defeats, weirdnesses, and occasional errant delights of grown-up romance. I like to think of him as the great guitar-rock poet of the romantically aggrieved postadolescent. You know the type (and, perhaps, *are* the type): junkies for the turmoil, the high-blooded anguish, of those vibrant years of teenaged fumbling and ardor.

More or less every Wedding Present song makes the argument that rock and roll and love are, in most all the ways that matter, exactly alike. Both of them carry us down Persephone-like into selves we may sometimes fear have abandoned us, left us to wander the colorless deserts of adulthood. But that descent is also a kind of renewal, because those putatively outgrown selves, ridiculous though they may have been, are awash in these undiminished intensities of feeling.

If you like arguments made mostly of enormous distorted sound, guitars up and vocals down, you may well like the Wedding Present.

I like the Wedding Present. I like especially a record called *Seamonsters*, from 1991, that high season of my youth, on which "Dalliance" appears, track one, to tell you exactly where the record is going. "Dalliance" is a rock song built around the smallest of reversals. You know the long tradition of songs about the Other Woman, about her deferrals and duplicities and inevitable disappointments? For its part, "Dalliance" tries out a rival proposition: pity, for a moment, the *other man*. Sung in the voice of a man whose lover has, after fully *seven years* of illicit intimacy, given him up at last, it takes its title from the concluding lines, where, with bitter ironies rebounding in every direction, the singer wonders, *"Is that what you call . . . a dalliance?"*

For a nervy few minutes, though, the song swoons a bit, over-brimming with questions this singer can't quite bring himself to ask. What kind of sorrow is *that* lover entitled to? What *is* jealousy, and what can living inside it feel like, for a man who has himself been so much the cause of someone else's dread? Our singer, all wounded petulance, has no kind of answer. What it proves he does have, though, arrives in the layered upwelling of furious noise to which the song, in its final moments, at last surrenders itself. I mean nothing denigrating at all when I say it sounds, when it happens, exactly like the '90s. Or rather, it sounds exactly like guitars in the '90s were so good at sounding: like some huge exhilarated anger—cleansing, ecstatic, very probably unearned—finding for itself a livid vital form.

If you tend in your relation to music even a little toward the obsessive, there is a moment I'm going to bet you know. It's the moment when, after years of living with a song floating around the rafters of your consciousness, it snaps into a startled, intricate clarity—when the words you've spent years singing recombine somehow into new and cogent form, alive with density and irony and crosshatched meaning. Inside the normative frame of daily life, this is a happy enough microevent, one of those small-scale disturbances of the dulled surface of things that make the world seem to flash, for a bright instant, with unexpended possibility.

Imagine this, then, unfolding inside the battering cacophony of a live show. There, it feels a good deal less like dawning clarity than like a deeply pleasing species of *assault*—a siege on sense, played out on the fine responsive instrument of your whole body. Stand in front of a wall of shuddering amplifiers and, as they resonate in your sternum and along the bones of your face, tell me this isn't true.

So I shook and sang and shouted. I leapt; I clenched and unclenched. And at some point, maybe around the second verse, the clinging grip I'd been keeping on my misery must've begun to weaken. Because then, deliriously, like every teenager ever, I found myself you could say *comprehended* by this song, hailed by it in a way that would have been eerie and unsettling were it not so stupid—I had never been anybody's other man—and, also, so hugely, so inarguably, so radiantly fucking pleasurable.

"Do you know," the man on the stage shouted, *"how much I miss you?"*

And my heart, my bruised and seized American heart, sang back: I DO KNOW IT, DAVID GEDGE, I DO.

And then he sang the next lines: *"It's not fair, after all we've done / That I'm so . . . I still want to kiss you."*

I SHOULD SAY that I had, at this point in that year of free-fall terror, expended many thousands of words in letters never to be sent, each one saying the rosary of my losses, and written, it seems to me now, in the dismal hope that some proper torque of grammar, some untried flight of syntactic complication, might wrench it all into a manageable intelligibility. You'll have to trust me when I say that I do that dire outpouring no injustice in suggesting that it is diminished very little, and probably not at all, in its rendering in these words, and these words only: *It's not fair. I still want to kiss you.*

And yet all that grief, that wild self-pity and imbecile rage: it came back to me, as I shouted out these words in a crowd of strangers an ocean away from my friends and my ex-lovers and my family and my stepdaughters, as an exhilaration so jolting and remainderless I swear I may have starting laughing out loud. (Laughter, says the philosopher Henri Bergson: "a momentary anesthesia of the heart.") And you can say it was the ordinary delirium of loud frenetic music. You can say it was the familiar ecstasy of communal immersion and stranger-intimacy. You can call it juvenile. No one will say you're wrong. But I will tell you this: the sense that this was misery, *and that misery could take form as joy,* sang through me like voltage.

If what I felt then had words, they might have been these: *That you are here, and not anywhere else, is the luckiest thing in the world.*

In November of that terrible year, there was, for me, no thought as profoundly unlikely. I stood there, sweating and grinning a probably frightening canine grin, and the odd fact that I was not dead, that I was indeed *very much not dead,* came flooding through me in a great dumb rush. I enjoyed a brief reprieve from the stupefied misery that, to my horror, had come in that year to fill quite completely the space between me and being alive. In an unfamiliar city, in a bar, as I surrendered to pleasures that at thirty-seven I was long since supposed to have aged out of, something shook loose. A plank in sorrow broke.

I'D LIKE TO BE ABLE to tell you that was the end of the story, or of one long section of it. I'd like to be able to say that *perseverance* and *restoration* followed *loss* the way *verse* and *chorus* follow *bridge*. Nothing would please me more than to tell you a story of blossoming serenity and achieved contendedness, at the center of which is the unlocking magic of loud, propulsive music.

That's not quite how it goes, though.

But Madrid is where I started to figure something out, something I'd been carrying around with me long before I met Evany, long before we made a little family in Maine with two small girls—my sudden stepdaughters—and a little house, and a garden tucked behind a stand of pine trees. It was around then, I think, that I began to contend with the possibility that, despite a career devoted entirely to books and talking about books, and despite spending virtually an entire life in the company of bands and records, I did not have quite the language I needed to say just what it was I thought songs did, or why I believed in them in the needy, devoted, not entirely defensible way I did.

It wasn't that I had no language. I'd grown up to be a *critic*, a person who made a kind of living getting into states of wordy animation about novels and poems and other such "slight, useless things" (to lift a perfect portable phrase from Robert Lowell). As friends and exes might've told you as readily as editors, the availability of words was never my problem. As much as I liked to read I liked to *talk*. I liked to talk the way some people like to run, say, or to eat. I liked talking the way some people could be said to "like" breathing.

So I knew there were lots of useful ways into songs. You might understand them as solacing, or galvanizing, or humanizing, three-minute rehearsals for the disciplines of empathy and understanding. Conversely, you might regard them as anodynes and bourgeois opiates, the cheapjack consolations offered up by a hypercapitalized global marketplace for the miseries it induces, cannot cure, and wishes only for you to misrecognize. There's a lot to both of these positions—a good library's worth, in fact—just as there is to the impulse to sidestep both banal heroicizing and lazy dismissal by hearing in songs the density of historical unfolding itself, of contradictions and clarities straining toward resolution in the available idioms of genre, form, style. I knew this too. You do not grow up a boy of my enthusiasms and *not* read Greil Marcus.

But what happened to me in Madrid seemed involved in all these ways of addressing songs without being grasped by any of them. Brokenly, which was the way I was doing everything then, I started thinking about that. I started thinking about the objects we devote ourselves to, some of us, with such weird implacability. I started thinking about how songs and things like them (slight, useless) had made but also—maybe, maybe—unmade me. Why was it that I could not quite imagine, *except* through these noisy word-drunk rituals of devotion, how to make friends, hold intimates close? Or for that matter how to be a boyfriend, a lover, a stepparent—and, now, it seemed, of all mystifying things, an *ex*-stepparent?

Like about ten million other people—perhaps like you—falling for things like songs had taught me an alarmingly large amount of what I knew about love.

Was that strange? *Wrong?* It seemed, just then, a thing worth figuring out.

I suppose I should confess that, if I turned in those long

lonely days toward songs and their intoxications, I did so not solely in a spirit of neutral inquisitiveness. It was also another kind of flight: a way to escape from something significantly less thinkable, something larger, looming, a puzzle presenting itself to me daily in new and unworkable configurations.

I just mean the terrible fragility of the wish to be alive.

What do you do when you find yourself abandoned by that elemental desire, staggered by some ordinary grief into a grave uneasiness about the prospect of "continuing to live," as Philip Larkin puts it in a bleak poem I long ago committed to memory—an uneasiness that, some days, sharpens toward antipathy and fright? How do you live in the ruins of a life you loved? What makes a scene of intractable sorrow somehow habitable, perhaps only for moments but, possibly, not only for moments?

Some people, surely, could answer questions like these without reference to the world's array of slight, useless things. I was not one of those people.

I WENT HOME from the show to an empty room above the Gran Via, jangled and body-sore, a cooling film of dance floor sweat clinging to my skin. I smoked one or two furtive cigarettes out the cracked-open window, and the city beneath me pulsed and glowed. It seemed alive with a buzzy sort of late-night serenity. So I sat down and wrote a little letter to my stateside friend. I still have it. Dana, I said, my dear. Tell me: have you ever, in a state of unanswerable sorrow, turned to a novel, or a song, or a poem, or whatever, and found there enough of something—affirmation, recognition, unforeseen joy—to sustain body and soul through another unavailing day? Maybe not. Not everyone turns to songs and books in this childish, hungry sort of way. But oh, my dear, if you *have*?

Listen, I've got a story for you.

Part One

HALF-AWAKE

There is an element of positivity in the visible world, and in color particularly, that totally eludes the historicity of language, with its protocols of absence and polarity. The color red, as an attribute of the world, is always there. . . . The branch upon which the blossom hangs may be long or short, rough or smooth, strong or weak according to our expectations, but the redness of the blossom is irrevocable, and the word "red" tells us next to nothing about it.

—Dave Hickey, "Pontormo's Rainbow"

Once, in the first violent spasms of love for the woman I was to marry, from whom I was just then separated by travel, I saw a famous cathedral in Barcelona. I'd been wandering around to no determined purpose, moony with longing, finding my way down blind alleys and elegant thoroughfares. And then, abruptly, there it was: Gaudí's soaring masterwork, uncompleted still, scaling every sight line straight up to the sky. Everyone had told me about the splendor of it, that dream of exaltation that somehow took form as stone and brick.

But no one told me about the fruit.

There, at the top of the spires, are enormous, sculpted, tumbling baskets of fruit. And, like the rest of the city the cathedral graces, they are painted. Lush bluey reds, yellows curving toward a ripe green. I looked at them and looked at them and looked at them. And then, as I stood reaching for words I suddenly didn't have, these lines I'd read in a book of art criticism came shotgunning back to me. "When color signifies anything," it went, "it always signifies, as well, a respite from language and history—a position from which we may contemplate *absence and death in the paradise of the moment." Staring straight up, I felt a meaning working itself loose. Never before had the delirium, the outrageous fucking plenitude of color been made so vivid to me, or so real. This was, I realized, about the most joyous physical thing I had ever stood before.*

And though it may have been as much my own heart-strickenness speaking to me then as any of the intentions of Gaudí or his army of masons, what I saw before me, I felt certain, was a vision of the world as conceived in love: fecund, abundant, overflowing with an awesome sensuous vitality that was easily the equal of any conceivable grief.

I was young.

I can remember spending the rest of the day wandering around half-lost and not caring, carrying these thoughts around with me through the city like an armful of bright flowers, and also—and honest to God this is true—singing, under my breath, to myself, song after song after song. These were the last black days before you could fold one thousand records into your shirt pocket. Which meant that access to the solace and exhilaration of songs was limited to the errant mercies of bars and cafés. And, oh, I wanted the solace and the exhilaration. I wanted, as quickly as I could have it, some confirmation that my dim and growing intuition was right: that there was, in the irrefutable positivity of sound, some resonant echo of what I'd just seen, a like riposte to the stern orders of absence, loss, death. That was the shape of the world I wished to believe in, and if that meant producing a belief so vehement it actually called that world into being, I was ready for it. I had an archive. "You can never get too sad," I'd once told a school friend, unforgivably, who was at the collapsing end of a love affair. "There's just so many novels and records left to love." A decade later and an ocean away, I still believed it. There were so many songs. So I whispered and hummed them, one after another. I think of them now as making up the soundtrack to these, my early middle years, the pax humana, the long-playing days of edgy bliss.

1

Be Still for a Second

ON THE WAY to what would prove to be the last of these, driving with Evany up the coast of Maine toward an anniversary getaway, I found myself crying.

This was not unusual.

I had spent, by then, nearly two decades shedding sudden tears over pop songs. In my twenties, in the isolation of graduate school, this happened most often in the shower. I'd have some rusted-out boom box perched on a towel rack, and be listening for the fourth or eighth or eighteenth time to a mix tape, hoping in this way to steel myself against the unforeseen inanities of the academic day. And then some track would come abruptly to life, deliver its quick little knife to the heart. Maybe I'd be missing someone. Maybe the key change in a Jawbreaker song would unlock from its chamber some minor, unforgotten sorrow. Or maybe the inclusion of a Cheap Trick song, or "Going to California," or Theodore Roethke reading "A Rouse for Stevens," would set off a microburst of happiness, reminding me of the nearness to my life even of people no longer close by. And so I would find myself, half-shampooed, one eye asquint with the sting of soap, enjoying a brief surrender to tearfulness.

I will not lie to you and say that this ritual diminished much in frequency as the waters of adulthood began more and more to rise around me. In the shower, on subways, and most especially in the car—the private theater of emotional extravagance that is the car!—the strange visitations continued. I had no objection to them. Even at my most sedate I have always tended toward what you might call an effusiveness that, at least in the metrics of the WASP-y New England where I eventually came to reside, was forever being read back to me as something between extravagant and alarming. How surprising was it that a certain vulgar loudness—which I preferred to call *enthusiasm*—would have as its counterpart an easy susceptibility to watery eyes, a hitch in the breath? The way I looked at it, Freud was right: people were, in the tumult of their emotional lives, far, far too much for themselves. There would always be more entailed in being a person—more conflict, more fear, more desire, more joy, more sorrow—than you could ever quite wrestle into stasis or unruffled serenity. Because of what being a person *is*—conflictual, overabundant—you would always be in some real senses a kind of mystery, even to yourself. So if pop songs managed to open this little space inside you, where you might actually stand for a moment in the presence of some of your more occult and turbulent emotions without being just pulverized by them, then God bless pop songs, was my feeling. As a mode of contact between you and your sharper conflicts, your impermissible excesses, you could do a lot worse.

So my mistiness, that early morning in the high flower of midsummer, was really just a part of the texture of things. We were listening to the anniversary mix I'd made for her—yes, I had made her an anniversary mix: I was quite entirely that guy—and had come to a song that, all of a sudden, seemed to distill into shimmering clarity the whole atmosphere of our busy, besotted, married-people happiness. I can remember looking across at her as I drove, at her half smile and her legs bared for summer, and in an unsteadied voice saying something like, "I want this all to go much, much slower."

The song was called "Apartment Story," it was from a record called *Boxer*, and it was by a band called the National.

FOR A LONG TIME after its swift, startling implosion, people would ask me about what my marriage had been, that I would grieve it so implacably, and so long. In the worst of it friends would say that the time had come, *now*, to gather up all the ambivalences about married life I had incubated in those long years of coupledom, and turn them to use. "Take advantage of them," they would say. "They will save you." The unhappy truth was that I had nurtured far too few of them.

I met Evany when I was in my late twenties, new to the state of Maine, and overspilling with the kind of excitement about things—this new job, these new friends—you find in people not yet tested too severely by the more unmerciful parts of life. There is this moment, early on in *The Portrait of a Lady*, that's both sweet and a little mean. Of American ingénue Isabel Archer, James says, in a phrase that always stuck with me, "she had a fixed determination to regard the world as a place of brightness." If there's something unforgivable about the naive will to believe the world nothing more than a great scene for the staging of your own private happiness, James treats it, here, with a sympathetic tenderness. I think now of my own unballasted eagerness, my own bright determination, and try to be as kind.

Evany, meanwhile, was a person inhabiting altogether different latitudes of life. She was older, had until recently been married, had two very little girls, treated me with a friendliness I measured against the somewhat scorching quality of her humor, was imposingly, even imperiously beautiful. I'd come into her orbit at all because she was the curator of the museum of art at the college where I'd somehow found professorial employment, and she specialized, friends informed me, in "contemporary art." Had I been told she was a runway model, or a jewel thief, it would've struck me, then, as not a lot less suffused with exotic glamour.

I had not long before broken up with my graduate school girlfriend, and that sentence says about all you need to know about the piteous, the embryonic state of my achieved adulthood in relation to this tall striking woman with a career, a little house, children—*children!*—and a crumbling marriage.

So when, at the back end of a very pleasant night in late May, she sat across a bar table and, looking at me with an unblinking directness, said she wanted to take me home, my response was to sit a moment in frozen silence, to blink back and say, "Excuse me?" That could not have been a sentence I heard correctly. Not from this woman, spoken across these vast gulfs of sophistication and beauty and lived-in worldliness, to me.

For years, we laughed about that small hiccup of time, when the world I inhabited held its breath, pivoted, and became wholly new.

I am tempted to say of the summer that followed, "All at once we were madly, clumsily, shamelessly, agonizingly" and so forth. It was that sort of summer, the kind for which words like *besotted* and *enraptured* were coined. (Also, probably, *insufferable*.) But not those words only. The grad school girlfriend with whom I'd split some months before had said, I felt unkindly, "You say you love me, but really you don't." Standing sex-drunk and exhilarated at the bright center of this sudden cyclonic passion—I speak the strict truth when I say that we had more sex that summer than I'd had in all my previous years of life—I remembered that ex's words and thought, *Oh. Oh, no.*

Of course, she was right.

But a marriage, as everybody knows, is not an affair. A long-coupled friend once said this indelibly great thing to me. "Oh, *marriage?*" she offered, in response to a question I didn't remember asking. "I'll tell you what marriage is." This was after a few drinks, at some dinner party, and we didn't know each other that well. "Marriage is a daily reckoning with the intractable otherness of another person." It was a sentence that dropped into me with a rattle, like a coin into an empty jar. You don't stay coupled very long without learning, in cartographic detail, the many regions of your lover's intractability. Or, for that matter, your own. Had you not imagined yourself as a person who regarded dishes left unwashed in the sink as both moral outrage and calculatedly *personal* affront? Now you know.

So a marriage is not an affair. Unless, also, somehow, *it is.* Because on that summer morning nearly a decade later, what I heard in the thrumming insistence of this one luscious National song was exactly that: a reminder of the way that, through all the domestic tedium and marital irritation of our unbroken years of cohabiting togetherness, the sensation of being inside our initial summer—of feeling lovestruck and amazed, giddy with the vastness of my good fortune—was never far from me. The least thing could call it back all in a glow. This look, that touch, some four-minute burst of gauzy pop loveliness. I used to think that's why marriages *had* to start in these blazing affairs. It was the fuel you burned forever, the pilot light that never went out.

LOOK, I ADORE the National—if we were in a bar I would tell you I fucking love the National—and I say that in full knowledge of the fact that you might fairly say they're the straight *bougiest* of rock bands imaginable, party music for the NPR set, soundtrack to the lives of indie-rock kids aging into mortgage payments and online stroller shopping. My friend Mark has a great phrase for the Saucony street shoes he and I like to wear—"aging hipster slippers," he calls them—and the National, with their often gorgeous blending of the postpunkish and the

orchestral, might without grave injustice be described as their aural equivalent. ("When will they go all in," Mark once texted me,
"and make concept album about difficulty of getting kids into
Park Slope Montessori?") They make stately, medium-rock-y,
atmospheric songs, mostly charting the shifting inner microcli-
mates of romance. Some are dirty, some are sexy, most are tinged
with a nervous sadness, an ambient dread: a fine calibration of
mood, in all, for the American middle-aughts.

And some songs are just fucking fantastic. There's a track on
Alligator, their first truly great record, called "All the Wine," and if
you want to hear a transcription, into the idiom of the rock song,
of the hilarious, swaggering elation of those first rushes of crazily
impassioned love, let me recommend it to you. *"I'm put together
beautifully,"* the singer says, and, God, his *voice*, that dreamy resonant baritone. He has a voice, I like to say, that sounds like a thing
made of air, testosterone, and oak. And then, and then, in perfect
deadpan, he drawls out the next line:

"I'm a perfect piece of ass . . . like every Californian."

I read a lot of poetry, but it isn't clear to me that I know a better depiction of the charmed and half-ridiculous sense of being
desired, of falling in love and knowing your beloved is falling in
love with you.

I can remember hearing clearly for the first time one line in
particular—*"I'm so sorry but the motorcade'll have to go around
me this time"*—and breaking into this huge idiot grin. By the
time I'd heard it, I knew the feeling.

And maybe just because of how well I knew that feeling, and
how much I adored it—how great my determination was to see
the world as a place of love-lit brightness—I did not at first take
all these humming tracks for what I now think they are. Were it
up to me, were the fates to conspire such that I would be assigned
the task of titling some National compilation record of the future, I would not hesitate.

Love Songs for Ugly Times. That's what I'd call it.

This is not, in truth, much of a stretch. The name of the first song on *Boxer*, from 2007, is—wait for it—"Fake Empire," which I admit does not require overmuch in the way of decoding. *"We're half-awake / in a fake empire,"* goes the refrain, and anyone who remembers the Bush years will remember well the world to which it refers.

But love songs, protest songs: it is not entirely easy, on these records, to tell them apart.

Take "Apartment Story," the track that for years I cherished with such undiminishing devotion and would include not just on mixes for Evany, but on every CD I made for *everybody*. It is a song of honeyed, voluptuous bliss, all glassy melodic guitars and midtempo thrum. The whole atmosphere it conjures is one of dreamy insular delight: the lazy joy of retreating to a handful of rooms and filling them up, floor to ceiling, with your happiness. It starts with the singer leaning in to pin flowers for his lover to wear, and there we are, in the midst of this sweet two-body closeness. When in the chorus the singer recommends they maroon themselves indoors for uninterrupted days at a time, sheltering there with only the TV for vigilant witness, he speaks in the very voice of a dazey, blinkered besottedness.

Listen to this in the right mood—while in radiant love, say— and it just *kills* you.

"All things are well," he says, layered indie-rock gorgeousness compounding all around him. *"We'll be alright."*

Jesus, those lines. I'd wait for them, and they'd come, and still I'd be unprepared. Who knew coupled life could transpose itself into song, and so gorgeously?

And yet.

It's abashing to me now, how little to the contrary of this love-lit vision of the song I was able to recognize then. *All things are well!* the singer says. *We'll be alright!* Believe me when I say it would be years—*years*—before I would hear in these lines even the first faint traces of something *not* blissed out, something rather faltering, and fearful, and cowed—some straining attempt at self-soothing. *No, no, really, everything is fine, do not be afraid, we are well, it's fine, really.*

Staying inside and doing whatever it is the TV tells you to do: could it be that this was, despite the cocooning atmosphere of serenity and sex, an actually quite terrible image of frightened acquiescence? A scene of beaten-down surrender, dressing itself up as coupled exaltation?

It took me, alas, an awful lot of life before I could manage even to allow myself the thought that the actual drift of "Apartment Story," and of all the National records I adored, was not toward the surprising joyousness of ordinary grown-up love. One after another these records were saying something else, not that I noticed the first two hundred or so times I listened to them. They were insinuating instead that twenty-first-century American bliss, however you might swoon to it, was a thing so interfused with these habits of dug-in insularity—this will to misperception, self-mystification, and retreat—that you don't finally know what to call it. Unwakefulness? Unknowing? Amnesia? Happiness? Love?

IN THAT SEASON of the later Bush years, driving up the coast, tears and summer on my face, I could have told you precisely none of this. It's not a mystery why.

All I can tell you is that I loved Evany then, with a want of uncertainty that now makes me embarrassed, sad, and proud. I loved her even after our years of coupledom with the stupid fervor of some heartsick new boyfriend. And I was in a like kind of blinkered, wide-eyed love with the whole of our little world, the minicosmos, we had somehow elaborated into being, with our devotion, our bodies, our words.

Here is the rough and unlovely fact of the matter: even then, in some only barely nonliteral sense, I understood Evany to have *invented* me. I could never puzzle out exactly how, but she had looked at the twenty-nine-year-old I had been—a good person, I would have said, who had been well loved, and who carried around with him an undented capacity for joyousness—and had somehow seen things he could not then have quite dared to believe, selves living on the very outer edges of his capacity to imagine them. She saw someone who could write books and maybe could *excel* as a professional person (rather than feeling all the time just dumbly grateful to be employed). She saw, I knew, a person not just "nice" or "smart" or "sweet" but genuinely fucking *carnal*, and this was a recognition I felt flaring through me as daily astonishment. She saw a person who might allow into her life a quantity of happiness she had hungered for enough to untangle herself from a bad marriage, but had not yet had. She saw a person who might bring her relief from the darknesses, the inward-turning passages of sorrow, that had marked so much of her adolescence, and then, her adult life.

In the unspeaking privacy of my own heart, I got to christen myself *that* person: the emissary of happiness. The defender against darkness, the harbinger of joy.

But this, even all this, was not the whole of it.

I remember how, in our very first months together, we would meet sometimes at the playground where Evany took her little girls after day care or on weekends. This was long before the days when I'd meet up with the three of them for lunch or, later, for dinner or, later still, for a night over, long before I became anyone Lucy or Amelia would've recognized as a factor of much importance in their little lives. Evany and I would meet, really just out of the buzzing impatience to see one another again, to touch however furtively, and there they were: two utterly ordinary little girls, more or less indistinguishable to me from their peers, scrabbling over kid-sized climbing towers and play sets with something of the unloosed energy of puppies, or squirrels. Had you asked me to describe them to you then I would have been able to say not much more than that they seemed to fit, securely enough so far as I could tell, inside the genre named CHILDREN.

They were smallish, grubbyish, "cute," by mystifying turns noisy and silent, wearing funny little smocks and miniature sneakers.

Soon enough, of course, they would come at least a bit clearer. Here was Lucy: the oldest, big-sister bossy, full of insistence and self-assurance and an ever-growing fund of words for the world. If you told her a joke, turned a funny phrase, she would after a moment erupt into cackling gap-toothed laughter—though not before eyeing you for a beat or two, wary, surmising, as though you might be trying to pull something over on her. And here was Amelia: the baby, two years younger, less chatty than her sister and readier in these preschool years to hide behind her mother's knees but also so beguiling in her aspect, so bright-eyed and smiling, that strangers would often stop Evany on the street—I saw this happen, more times than I could count—and say, *Oh, what a lovely little girl!*

Before I quite knew any of this, on those playground afternoons, Evany and I would sit together, hip to hip, as much touching as we could risk, and we'd watch them weave in and out of ramps, slides, ladders.

Moooooooom, look at me!

They'd wander over toward us, scamper away, drift back.

And then, with that neutral heart-stopping directness of gaze proper to children, they would regard me.

Remember, sweetie? This is Pete.

A nod, a little half-shy shuffle.

Hi, Pete. Would you push me on the swing?

And, oh, God, that look, those faces: so free of anxiousness or mistrust or anything but an eager and immediate wide-openness.

Hi, Pete. You wanna catch me on the slide?

And there was I, gone rigid with fear, on a bench in a playground in Maine. Some deep-down part of me commenced exclaiming, *WHAT THE ACTUAL FUCK?*

Why—truly, why—would I be entrusted even momentarily with these funny, frightening, infinitely strange little blurs of brightness?

Somewhere inside me, though, I knew.

I was there because of Evany. I was there because Evany had looked at me—at *me*—and thought, *Oh, you, sweet man, will be good at loving these precious little persons.* I was there because Evany, through some unexampled miracle of vision, saw something infinitely beyond me then: she saw a person who could be someone's partner, someone's husband, and even—and here was amazement proper—someone's father.

Believe me when I tell you Evany had, in truth, invented me. Being in love with her made me feel, in a way both ordinary and astounding, ampler, richer, *larger*, improbably beautiful and infinitely lucky.

I'm a perfect piece of ass, like every Californian.

All I could do was believe in her. Which, with an aching vehemence that I assure you felt nothing like unknowing or a catastrophic failure of foresight, I did.

So I steadied my breath. I put a hand on Evany's tanned leg. I straightened up and watched the road. I let the song fill in the details, the colors and shades, of my elation.

All things are well, the speakers said. *We'll be alright.*

After that, things began to move pretty fast.

2

Find Me

IN A LOT OF WAYS, things had been moving unaccountably fast from the start, though maybe not by the mark of clock time.

I had asked Evany to marry me on an unremarkable Maine night in late December, silent and vast and glinting with cold, and by that time we'd already been together better than a year and a half. I suppose it was in my character to be undaunted by the obviousness of rote gestures because, despite that long stretch of time already together, I did each and all of the formulaic things. I kept it a secret. I made sure there were logs ready to be lit in the fireplace. I conspired to buy on my own a ring that, though crowned with a stone one would not call ostentatious— a diamond not easily visible to the naked eye—Evany might nevertheless find artful and elegant enough to delight in. And still I was *nervous*.

Maybe this was just because it was, at that late stage, so preordained and obvious. Or maybe, contrarily, it was because of the wild, only marginally diminished dauntingness of the prospect of a life not only near but actually *with* children. I had by this time moved in, and the most mundane of things—Lucy's sometimes obstinacy or periodic crying jags, Amelia's bouts of

clinging neediness—still could rattle me into an all but humiliating discomposure. I experienced myself as failing at patience,
forever fumbling with stepparental incompetence. But I was
working on it. *Every day,* I told myself, *you're working on it.*

Or maybe it was because the shadow cast by Evany's previous
marriage, which had not been long on ritual or romance, had
filled me with the determination to make of all our milestones
something purely dazzling, occasions somehow both compensa-
tory and utterly our own. Escalating this impulse in me, too,
were Evany's ongoing entanglements with what she sometimes
called, with companionable familiarity, "my depression"—by
which she meant the bouts of spirit-deadened coldness that
could come over her, those iterations of darkness she had worked
so, so hard to leave behind her, along with the stagnating unhappiness of her first marriage. They were tremendously frightening
to me, these periodic seizures by unforgotten pain. They were
like an obscure menace, flashing out over the horizon, to the
happiness I was so busy trying to make around us. Her trying
adolescence, her postpartum miseries, her long-running struggles with a sort of barbed self-dislike that was always so much
a mystery to me—"But you're the *most* lovable!" I'd insist,
stupidly—sent tremors of disquiet all through me. My instinct
then, I remember, was to try to make our happiness a thing so
radiant, so glittering and capacious, that old grief would seem
dull by comparison, unscary, small.

She'd smile back at me that singular, crooked grin, the one
that made pain into the punch line of some joke I hadn't heard,
didn't get. "Okay, sweetie," she'd say, patient, tolerant.

To be honest, though, it was just as likely none of these things.
Maybe my worked-up nerviness was simpler. Maybe it was just
the obvious gravity of what, between us, had happened.

In the anxious days before the day, one scene flashed back to
me a lot, a little totemic memento I'd rub and rub. We were on

the couch at the end of a summer Saturday. It was absolutely usual. The girls were off with their father. There had been some coffee, some ocean, sex, a garden, a drive. I lay there with my legs across Evany's lap while she turned over the pages of a magazine and a greenish light glowed around the window edges. And then, swimming up from some depth of self with which I had never been in correspondence, there came a thought unlike any I'd had before. *The moment I die,* a small voice said, *I want Evany beside me.* I remember she turned to me with her off-kilter smile and a furrowed look. It should have been such a strange and morbid thought, but it wasn't. Not then. I read it as plainly as the face of a clock.

You'll just know, people always say. I knew.

And so there we were at last, huddled against the December cold, Evany and I and my heaving heart. Winter night, ring, *kneeling,* and what I would later describe as the briefest of fireside Q&As. I'll forever hold a place in my heart for Evany's father, who, when she called later on and said, "Dad . . . I'm getting married!" responded merrily, "Oh, that's great! So who's the lucky guy?"

And then it was *another* year and a half before we actually got married. "I'm a woman of careful virtue," Evany would say when asked about the long engagement, shifting Amelia on her hip.

And yet there truly was something rapid and impetuous about it all that gave these long months the feeling of being swept downstream. If you'd known the person I was only a few years before you would not have seen many paths leading to this, the very most conventional of outcomes. I wasn't so much unconventional as unlikely—and from the looks of me, maybe a little militantly so. Here is a sheaf of photographs. Observe the guy on the left of that trio of boys outside a Chicago bar, with the stringy hair falling in limp curls down to his shoulders and not quite distracting you from the disaster of his goatee. The one with the yellowing WE CAN DO IT! T-shirt and the oversized jeans torn open at both knees, as if for ventilation? Him. He will not sell you drugs, this young man, though he will regard you politely when you ask since, looking as he looks, he is used to it. There he stands, offering every last stylistic tic you might have hated about the '90s, gathered in one place for ease of consumption. You could be forgiven for looking at that person and thinking something other than, "Yes, let's give him a couple of little girls to raise."

"Marriage is a noble daring." John Dryden said that sometime in the seventeenth century and when I think of that line now (which is not infrequently: we wrote it into our wedding vows) my mind appends to it immediately something my friend Jennifer likes to say, which is this: "Sex makes us stupid." It is a sentence for which there are lots of human occasions. My own more Pollyannaish version says that the feeling of being lovestruck, that cracked-open exhilaration, can induce us to believe extravagant, unlikely, possibly counterfactual things about ourselves. Being in love with Evany made me feel gorgeous and wise, superheroic, like the protagonist in every love song I had ever heard. (Today, I'd put it like this: *"Before you came into my life, I missed you so, so bad."*) I was not, then, much equipped to mistrust this richness of sensation, what Neko Case, in a song of which I would come to be very fond indeed, calls "that teenage feeling." It seemed to me true north, the realest possible thing, a beacon to steer toward whatever the surrounding seas.

But the truth is I was not so altogether unprepared as you might've thought, despite the mute eloquence of the story told by my closet full of ill-fitting flannel and unrepaired denim. Even that guy knew some things. My heart was not a long blank page. Even then, I had some ballasting experience to draw on, if I needed to persuade myself that what I was proposing to undertake was, let's say, feasible, and not some messy calamity waiting to unfold. I had practice, I mean, in loving things a lot, and in turning ungoverned ardor into habitable worlds. I was *prepared*.

I'd been listening to records for a long time.

COLLEGE, FOR ME, was like coming over the ridgeline of adolescence and discovering, in one long exultant gulp of perception, that I'd lived unknowingly for years in the outer suburbs of a glittering Oz-like metropolis, except instead of witches and emeralds there was French cinema and birth control. Some people get to school and discover politics or drugs or group sex or any of the other intoxicants of spirit you encounter once removed from parental stricture. Not me. (My adolescence, though it had some of these, would've been improved by more.) I did the predictable things. I read, with dumb astonishment, a great many books, and I listened to an even greater number of records, and these I talked about with the florid intensity of undergraduate devotion. It is only barely not true that most of what I learned in school I learned by listening to Van Morrison's *Astral Weeks*, again and again, more or less uninterruptedly, for four years. You misjudge me a lot if you think that's a complaint.

I met a boy there, early on, called Mark, and he had a talent, enviable and unfaltering, for making Theories. Pick any handful of objects frozen just then in amber of your cultural consciousness: metal bands, *Bonanza*, the early poems of Hart Crane, Patsy Cline. It didn't matter. Without overmuch effort, and following whatever the cascading stream of talk, he could extemporize a narrative linking them into this cracked, kaleidoscopic cohesion. It would be fluent and fast and unserious and for me, eighteen and new to college and all but vibrating with happiness about being there, pretty fucking joyous to behold. He had an oversized concert T-shirt embossed with the cadaverous image of Robert Smith, in which he would sometimes sleep. It was he who first played me tapes of Lyle Lovett, Dinosaur Jr., Nancy Sinatra, Ornette Coleman, the Replacements. He'd read books by people with names like Roethke and Coover and Rukeyser, though he could talk as readily about Guns N' Roses' *Appetite for Destruction* with the offhand familiarity of accidental expertise. ("So you see, Alec"—deadpan—"Slash is a player of *many moods*.") He was also about the least self-aggrandizing person you were likely to meet within the egotropic climates of collegiate sociability, and he made you feel, when you were talking to him, that whatever he said was somehow half your invention.

A long time before I had words for it I knew I loved him.

This, along with the decision that he was the funniest person I had ever met, is one of not many judgments I made in the late '80s that I stand by utterly.

From the ages of eighteen to twenty-two, that passage of maximal male insufferability, we weren't much apart, and this was a blessing and a mercy. (It's hard to imagine how much worse I would have otherwise been, though it's clear I would have been worse.) What this meant was that we lived for a while among a set of Theories on deep rotation. These included: The Theory That Clifford Brown Was Better Than Miles Davis. The Theory of the Inevitable Return of Madonna's Repressed Italianness. The Theory of Grace Kelly's Entrance. None of them was, finally, a great deal other than stupid, by which I suppose I just mean clever, insular, designed to do not much more than entertain each other and whoever was around.

The greatest of these, the brightest star among lesser lights, was the Theory of *Astral Weeks*.

LIKE MANY OF THE OTHER THEORIES in vogue with us then, the Theory of *Astral Weeks* followed a basic grammar: What you think of as one thing is, actually—ha-*ha*!—something else.

You might think of *Astral Weeks* as a collection of gorgeous songs, neither hippie folk nor psychedelia nor rock 'n' roll—a record so extravagant and weird, and of such enchanting unlikeliness, you hardly knew what to call it. But you would be wrong. It was my friend's insistence that the secret of *Astral Weeks* was that it told, in fact, a sprawling broken story. Once you recognized this, each song, and then the album itself, became a new thing, strange and dense but also, in a delectable way, *explicable*. The thing to do, if you were listening with this kind of Talmudic devotion, was to make sense of the story.

If you've heard *Astral Weeks* you'll know this is not a simple task, though it is exactly the kind of work to beguile young people looking for reasons to procrastinate, or get high, or just keep talking to each other. The record commences in a tangle of words and sounds that, the first time I heard them, seemed to address me from some location considerably removed from the conditions of my small teenage life:

> *If I ventured in the slipstream*
> *Between the viaducts of your dreams*
> *Where the mobile steel rims crack*
> *And the ditch and the back road stop*
> *Could you find me?*

The blank-wall impenetrability of these opening sentences was, for me, matched only by a reverence for them I wished I could better explain. I remember another friend writing them out in black marker on the pull-out tablet of his dorm-room desk, and if after doing so he had any greater sense of what the fuck Van was talking about he did not share it with me. It seemed a great rush of high-flown hippie mysticism, tricked out with some beautiful particulars and buoyed along by Richard Davis's outrageously virtuosic bass line, carving impossible figures around the melodies and countermelodies. Listening to it was like listening in on some stranger's private language, some fully elaborated cosmology tethered just enough to the shared human earth to make it legible in fugitive glimpses, the occasional bright flash.

But then, all of a sudden, it was something else. I can remember Mark sitting across from me at some ridiculous piece of institutional furniture and, with gentle persistence, explaining over and over again one point. He's saying, "They're at a wake." I am all vacant unresponsiveness. "They're showing slides of whoever's dead. They're pointing at him, at the singer, because he's in the picture." Nothing. "Do you get it? The singer's the person who's dead." Blink. "It's the singer of the song and he's imagining whoever it is he's in love with, and, and . . . he's asking what she'd do if he was dead. Dude. *Listen*."

And Van is singing, *"Would you find me? Kiss my eyes? Lay me down in silence easy?"*

Branching mythologies would follow, until we had it, a theory, a story. Here was a record that starts out at this imagined wake, and then for most of the rest of its duration tours exultantly through the stations of a youthful love affair, only to end back where it began, in the contemplation of death, with the singer conjuring up an eerie shrouded figure. (*"Slim slow slider,"* he says on the final track, *"horse you ride is white as snow."*) But then came the largest fact, the claim that made everything resonate on another frequency altogether: *Astral Weeks* ends like this because the death with which the record contends is not, as in the opening, imaginary. *It is not the singer who is dead.* The record is sung to, and for, and about a lover who has died. *Astral Weeks*, for all its enveloping gorgeousness, is a memorial, an eight-song edifice of grief. It is the sound of a young man contending with the blank fact, obvious and all but inconceivable, that those we love will die, quite independently of the force and implacability of our love for them. It finds the singer unleashing these cascades of joyous sound because it's all he has by way of bulwark and pro-test. It offers noise as life, cacophony against dying.

It was college. It was talk like that.

I assume that at some point you'll have made a similarly ba-roque liturgy out of your love for some like object. Young people in particular excel in making rituals of their devotion. And I cer-tainly was devoted to *Astral Weeks*. But I will say that in the midst of all that juvenile veneration what struck me most force-fully was not the record's interfusion of joy and annihilating grief. No. All my wonder was saved instead for the quantity of *work* just a few swift sentences, properly placed, could do. For quite a long time I could have told you staggeringly little about what you might call the substance of *Astral Weeks*. Love it though I would surely have said I did, the record itself was for me really not much more than a radiant atmosphere, a wash of sound whose sum was this giddiness of spirit it produced in me. And that was fine. I won't say this felt inadequate, or like a deficit of pleasure, because it did not. But once touched with the wand of just a handful of words—a crackpot narrative, a theory—the re-cord found itself transformed into a different kind of thing, something alive with sex and love and the strange, mostly ab-stract sorrows of adulthood.

For years, that transformation was most of what I'd hear. Play a track and I'd be dropped back into that long-ago moment when a friend I loved wrote this piece of quasiscriptural revelation back into the world for me, and made it a thing we might talk back and forth about, in words anybody could use. And I'll tell you: this was, for me, an estimable and ramifying joy. It occurred to me that you could set even this record's flights toward the mystic, its weird exhilarations, down amid the ordinariness of your daylit life and they would, in the exchange, shed not a bit of the glowing otherworldliness for which you fell in love with them in the first place. You could turn your experience of dumbstruck delight in a thing into something else—theories, words to trade—and it would *lose nothing*. It might in fact be said to gather into itself a new kind of density and brightness, something lit from within by the presence of other people, and your love for them, and theirs for you. This is what I meant when I would say, as I did say many years later as he stood beside me on my wedding day, that Mark had given me my first glimpse of what criticism could be, and why you might want to make a life out of it.

I SHOULD PROBABLY be more embarrassed by those aimless hours-long disquisitions than I am. Instead I find I'm very loyal to them. It was that talk, as much as any seminar or visiting lecture, that gave me my first real exposure to the reckless joy you could find in the ordinary transformative act of interpretation. I'm grateful for that, without question. But something else was happening.

So much of the joy of listening to *Astral Weeks*, then and later, came from the clear sense I had of *collusion*. I just mean that thrilling, half-conspiratorial sense of finding in the pleasures of things you love a testament to the intimate and densely layered histories that had brought them, in the first place, into your hands. Not much made me happier in those years than participating in the talk that condensed around the objects people loved most. It came to me after a while that that was what friends did, that this was *how* friends came to love one another, and to nourish that love. If we taught each other anything worth learning in those years it was just that falling in love with people might be deeply involved in the making together of a *language*—a language of veneration and disparagement, of criticism infused with joy—about the things in the world you found captivating or disquieting or thrilling or otherwise in need of transformation into urgent, overheated exchange.

Isn't this what you do when you're young, especially if you are tending toward a life in proximity to one or another kind of critical enterprise? You gather around you, by affinity and good fortune, a little gang of coconspirators who out of the sheer abundance of their enthusiasm find themselves inventing these intricate little codes and idiolects, these semiprivate vocabularies with which to distinguish, say, Yeats's politics from the Pogues', an early Clash song from a late one, or Sam Cooke's version of "Bring It On Home to Me" from Van Morrison's. You turn your ardors and delights, your disgusts and devotions, into this special kind of melody—this funny sort of love song—and then, year after year, you sing it back to one another, refining and inventing as you go.

What could school possibly be for, if not for this?

SO YOU SEE, I was not so catastrophically unprepared for life as I might've seemed, supersized flannel and goatee notwithstanding. By the time I found myself kneeling in a living room on the coast of Maine, these were songs I knew how to sing.

IT DIDN'T MUCH OCCUR to me to be concerned that my model for family was friendship, and not the other way around. If there was meant to be a sharp contrast between these ways of imagining the worlds you make out of your loves—between the private and the sociable—nothing about the life Evany and I were conspiring to build around ourselves made it apparent. We lived in a little house in Maine, and it was noisy and full, with art hung in frames on the walls, a shower with a radio in it, and a bed that was not a futon, with a curving white metal headboard. We had jobs and friends and schedules, a great density of those pleasures and commitments proper to what even I would've called adulthood.

And, of course, we had these little girls. We had Lucy, stricter now with the strictness of the older sibling, tidy, stretching daily toward coltishness, and beginning, too, the period of her un-apologizing adoration for each and every iteration of the school-yard joke. (Between the ages of eight and eleven Lucy responded to every even remotely plausible inquiry—"Who did you play with?" "What was on TV?" "Where's your homework?"—with the unfailing response, "*YOUR MOM.*" It tracked from funny to exceedingly not funny, back to a purely slaying kind of funny.) And we had Amelia, her sister's sometime rival but more fre-quent coconspirator, making rules up as she went, growing into a sweet sort of wildness—she used to stroll out into the garden to pluck dill out by the handful and eat it right there—but still, inexplicably, exasperatingly, coming awake in the middle of the night and needing her mom and only her mom to tuck her back in. There she'd stand, lit by the winter moonlight, a little night-time spirit beside the bed.

The startlingness of it, the unlikeliness of my place here, had never quite evaporated.

I remember one bleary morning, after all of us had been awake for more of the night than was ideal, finding Amelia sit-ting by herself on the side of the bed. I looked at her, fumbling with something, and did a kind of sputtering triple take.

"Hey, uh, sweetie? Hey, what are you doing there?"

Amelia had retrieved from its spot under the bed Evany's vi-brator, the venerable Hitachi Magic Wand, and was turning it off and on, rolling the tennis-ball-like top of it over her kneecaps.

Bzzzzz. Bzzzzz. Bzzzzz.

"Oh!"—bright-eyed, at her ease—"I'm using Mom's *massager.*"

Jesus, I remember thinking, caught up in the standard parental way, stumbling between hilarity and stupefaction. *Jesus.* They were, these two girls, busy, bright, confounding, exhausting: daily reminders that, however prepared I may or may not have been for the adventure of loving Evany, being an actual stepparent—which, evidently, I was—was undiscovered country, all thickets and wilds, steep slopes and blind drops.

Adult life pulsed all around me and I was fucking *in it*.

And yet nothing about the life I'd somehow found for myself had demanded I surrender even a little of my unoutgrown attachment to those loud, word-made socialities.

With the amazement proper to our long-belated recognitions, it came to me: for all its dysfunction and rivalrousness, its saccharine aggrandizement, family, too, if you were lucky, could be another site of exuberant language-making. You could fall, as I had, blindingly and marginlessly in love with a person, you could by the grace of some merciful god *marry* that person, and still be left with ardor enough for new kinds of love, and for the nurturing of the old ones.

And that, probably, is a lot of why I'd come awake on these impossibly bright and frigid coastal mornings, and even before the ordinary annoyances of consciousness could shape themselves into thought, there would ripple straight through me this quick steep rush of hilarity.

The name for this, I suppose, is gratitude: elation's domesticated twin.

3

Easy

LIKE ALL PEOPLE not wholly destitute of heart, when I hear the opening of "ABC" by the Jackson 5 I experience the familiar jolt of pop elation—that swift brightening of spirit that comes of being in company with a human thing that is also so pure a distillation of joyousness. This was true before I had kids—before, say, I'd propped their rubbery and squirming little selves on my hip and swung them in woozy circles around a living room in Maine singing *"That's how easy love can be!"*—but it was a lot more true, and a lot differently true, after.

Of course I did not, in point of strict fact, "have" kids, not by the measure of any number of authorities. I was married to a woman who, when we met, had two very little girls. I was not their father. I'd moved in with them eventually, after many months spending days and then dinners and then nights and mornings with them, in expanding microcalibrated doses of time. But how should they refer to me, the girls wanted to know, at school, in day care, on the playground? Together, at home or in the world, I was just Pete. Lucy liked to say, during the long period between our engagement and our actual marriage, "Pete's my semistepdad." *Semistepdad!*

The world is not overfull with designations for these errant, uncharted sorts of love.

Over months that stretched into years, the four of us shared a little house near the coast and together made our way through the mazy and ordinary complications of improvised family. It was hard—for me, still a youngish man who had little experience with kids and even less with little girls, it was *very* hard—but it was also, this sudden new life, a daily adventure in ingenuity and invention. How do you live with children who are and are not yours? What does a little tribe like this *do* with itself, day into night and after? These questions, I promise you, were in no way abstract.

Among the rituals we devised for ourselves in the early years, in our hunger for forms that felt all at once familial and our own, was that of the prebedtime dance. (When the girls were very little, this was also often the postbathtime ritual, and so was appropriately named "Naked Dancing," a scene that gave me a new standard for little-kid joyousness. *"Naked dancing!"* they would squeal in delirious unison, then bolt from the bathtub, where they'd been splashing together like slippery little seals, to the living room.) We would dance to two or, maximally, three songs, and then Evany would take them upstairs for pajamas and books and good-night kisses, and I would clear the table, do the dishes, maybe catch a few innings of a Red Sox game on mute. Sometimes it was the Cure, sometimes it was the Magnetic Fields, sometimes it was, in deference to their mother's tastes, the B-52s.

"ABC" was never not among the selections.

So we would, the four of us, caper and twist and jump. The girls would take turns being twirled around, and we'd gather them up and sing, *"C'mon, c'mon, c'mon, let me show you what it's all about!"* I can remember on one particular winter night finding myself looking at Lucy, our oldest girl, the one whose rigorous devotion to familywide *fairness* even then broke my heart a little ("We like Mom's car and Dad's car *exactly* the *same*," she would remind Amelia, with her big-sister sternness), and then, as she gave herself over to three or so minutes of unclouded and full-bodied joy, feeling this shock of helpless, undefended love for her.

LET ME CONFESS: I was not, in those early years, as open to these bright flares of ardor as I ought to have been. In the slow-moving accretive way of such things, I was learning, day by domestic day, much that I had not known about the rigors of life with children, and in fact had not so much as suspected. Here is what I can tell you, now, about stepparenthood: it's like a tango on a balance beam. You want so much to be *parental*, to share the often incapacitating labors of care with your spouse. But you want to be mindful, too, that these children *have* fathers and mothers, whom you never want them to feel you are trying, even in the most implicit way, to supplant. These are on the easiest days delicate geographies, and all the other things of grown-up life—envy, money, anger, sex, loss—conspire to intensify their fraught, fractal complexity. The quick-shifting uncertainty about whose role was whose, and what its parameters were, could play a quiet kind of havoc with your couplehood, and because of the stunned passion with which I'd fallen in dumbstruck love with the girls' mother, all uneasinesses around the scene of my marriage put me on edge. There could be some shift in the climate of the day, some small domestic disquiet, and I'd find myself straining against sulkiness or worse.

I know it pained Evany, these coldnesses in me. I loved people so capaciously! she'd say. On weekends without the girls, we went off to see far-flung friends, to whom devotion had not wavered. We had dance parties as large of scale, as drunk and drugged up and raucous, as you were likely to find among grown-ups in a sleepy college town in coastal New England. Because I delighted in parties, I loved these occasions. In my very first year at the college, when I was less a professor than a green kid figuring it out class by class, I threw a party for my friends, my colleagues, really anybody who wanted to come. The occasion was the fifteenth anniversary of the release of Prince's masterpiece—or rather, his *first* masterpiece—*Purple Rain*. Every year thereafter I tried to have what came to be referred to as "the Prince party," which seemed to me a fine ritual to have inaugurated in small-town Maine.

Evany had come to that first-ever Prince party, on a frigid night deep in the Maine midwinter. She was hard not to notice. She wore what I then understood to be a dress of outrageous slinky stylishness, though I won't now vouch for my discernment. I know it was intricate and blue and frankly disobedient to the demands of the arctic season. In the staid, preppyish world of the New England college, her art-world fashionability was an everyday token of refusal: a small private flag of noncompliance. "So," she said as I took her coat, ushered her in, "is this where the *young people* come to dance?"

I laughed and laughed.

Later I'd say, *You walked in. I woke up.*

But the greater wonder was that Evany, who had never loved the indiscriminate sociability of parties with the heedlessness I had, found in time that she had come to enjoy them, to enjoy ours, quite as much as I did. The messy camaraderie, the delightedness, the humanizing respite from the sometimes choking pretense of academic life: all of it was for her a new-dawning pleasure, and a relief from the habits of uneasiness and mistrust that a trying adolescence, and then some horrible years in graduate school, had made for her. If you had met her in our early years she might've impressed you as friendly but also a bit standoffish, reserved, with a certain veiled intensity crackling in the space around her. It was there in the wicked arch of her brow, the caustic quickness of her deflating laugh. In time I came to see this was not unkindness so much as a complex sort of guardedness, the expression of a vigilant mistrusting alertness to the ways the world might, all at once, turn on you, bring you to sudden hurt.

With me, she liked to say, she'd found in herself a new set of tolerances, something maybe akin to these sweet recalibrations of self that came with having the girls, but less private, less inward. We had figured out together how to make our marriage not a retreat but something turned *toward* the world, a staging ground for larger kinds of togetherness—and this was a thing we'd said, from the first, we so much hoped to do.

I remember blinking through the weak light of one morning-after, stuffing red plastic cups in the trash and feeling half-pleased with my postdancing achiness as we recapped the night's choicer absurdities, and there was Evany lining up empty bottles in rows across the counter and flashing me her quick crooked grin.

"Sweetie," she said, all those caustic impulses held in sweet abeyance, "you make everybody feel so *welcome*."

I loved every throb of my hangover right then, and I loved that she saw in me the thing I most wanted to be true. But I could hear, too, even through the fine element of that happiness, the unspoken sentence that hung in the air between us.

Why is it so hard to be like that with the girls?

This was and was not a fair question. Our circumstances were not the simplest, and what I experienced as the incurable fecklessness of the girls' father helped not at all. Oh, the wasted hours contemplating pickup times, schedules, and calendars, their variables shifting like integers in an equation always a little too advanced for my comprehension. "Custody": Is there a word that speaks more cheerlessly of failure? Of the translation of love into obligation, of joy into administration, of "grim things produced in court," as Henry James puts it? But every time the girls' father, back in those early years, changed plans abruptly; every time he resisted what felt to him like the unduly "binding" force of regularized schedules; every time he announced at the last moment he had someplace he needed to be and he *could* get a sitter for the girls, unless we wanted to take them?—every time he would propose some such impossible choice to Evany I'd find myself feeling inconsolably angry and slighted. Of course Evany wanted the girls. It is the condition of sharing custody *always* to want your children when you don't have them, even as you live in the enjoyment of the different sorts of freedom their absences afford you. A strange and wrenching mixing of devotions is the order of every day.

Had I been able to summon a little more feeling for Evany's wretched position, wanting the girls and wanting me not to feel so wounded, I'd have been less broody and recessed than I was. But I was young, and loving Evany made me braver than smart. We'd cancel our plans and I'd feel stymied and disregarded, full of a dull rage. Why should I pay with my life for the way his love for the girls, which was never in doubt, kept such easy company with capriciousness? Evany was obviously more afraid of her ex-husband's flights of mood than she was concerned to forestall my minor disappointments, and if this was inarguably proper it was also, on my end, a small but real heartbreak. On terrible days I'd say I was afraid her ex was poison in the well of our happiness.

You will have noticed that sullen resentfulness is not much prescribed as a key ingredient for deft parenting. There is good reason for this.

BUT BENEATH THESE SURGES of anger were, I'm afraid, uglier currents. There were, to begin with, the ordinary kinds of turbulence that come from several people, differently tuned, endeavoring to live together in one space. Lucy's swervings from easygoing to implacable, for instance, never quite lost their power to unnerve me. *Be patient!* I'd tell myself, as once again I failed at patience. And then there was the bewildering fact that the girls were—ha-*ha!*—*not identical to one another,* in character or need. Whereas Lucy was keen on structure, neat, and mostly tractable, Amelia, the baby of the family, was untidy and largely uninterested in being otherwise, not so much rule averse as rule indifferent. With the Machiavellian incisiveness proper to *all children everywhere*—or so I was coming to learn—she was not above playing to her mother's nostalgia for the lost years of her babyhood, and so shielding herself from any too-stern punishment or rebuke. They made together in this way, Evany and Amelia, a kind of two-person weather system, from which I could sometimes feel a pang of exclusion, as I never quite did with Lucy. Evany thought of Amelia as her baby, in need of her protection, and so this scene of withheld severity would disquiet Lucy, and me.

How strangely these garden-variety disequilibriums of birth order, discipline, and familial intimacy shook and shook and shook me! How easily I could find myself inhabiting one child's resentments or the other's needs!

Another way to say it: how pitiably *childish* I could find myself becoming, when called upon to be a fucking grown-up.

"Amelia," I would hear myself saying, with a sharpness in my voice that was unneeded, unhelpful, and unaccountable. "*Clean. Up. Your. Room.*"

Or maybe not unaccountable. Because beneath all this were currents dimmer and uglier still. For instance: With no encouragement whatsoever, I had over the accumulating years nurtured this one idiot fear, which seemed to lie in wait for me behind every even faintly testy exchange, every delicate moment of coparenthood. It was simply that Evany, in some subterranean and unspeaking part of herself, felt a coldness toward me, a nothingness, because she had had her children, these so beautiful girls, *with someone who was not me.*

Do you remember that shattering moment at the end of Joyce's beautiful story "The Dead"? The protagonist Gabriel is looking at his wife, who has wept herself to sleep because a song—of course: *a song*—has recalled to her a tragic youthful love. And it occurs to him, in one of the least merciful phrases in the whole of the story, "to think how poor a part he, her husband, had played in her life"? Like an obscure, elaborate curse, that line haunted me.

Or it would all be more mundane. One free Friday we went to the movies and saw some stupid rom-com, and there at the end, before the rolling of the credits, there was this lame marital montage: stills fading one into the next of scenes of pregnancy, and then of labor, all culminating in a dewy mother cooing over husband and swaddled babe. My heart, my stupid cringing heart, began to heave and jerk, and my breath stopped. Evany had had this, and— oh, God—I had not been there. How would she ever forgive me?

I'd form the thought, and think, *That is wholesale fucking insane.* But I couldn't quite unform it. It hovered around the rooms of our life.

And maybe that was what gave point to all those lesser struggles, the ordinary give-and-takes of parenthood, sharpened at their edges by my somewhat qualified status. I was susceptible, you could say, to feeling a bit second-string: when a kid falls off her pogo stick in the driveway, her first startled cry is not likely to be for her stepdad, no matter the breadth of his care.

It tells you a lot about the person I was, the nominal adult, that I had room, back then, to feel a bit hurt by this.

So, WITH THE RESOURCES of my considerable sense of unearned marital good fortune to draw on, I did what I later learned all parents did: I improvised. I kissed them good night and walked them to school. I made Lucy laugh and with Amelia, Evany's baby, I tried to find some inner reserve of calming patience, or to invent one. I was beaten without pause or mercy at word games, board games, and approximately 375,000 games of crazy eights. ("Sorry, Pete," Amelia would say with a pleased glinting grin, "but pick up two. Aaaand *last card.*") I told them jokes that tipped toward the adult, and these we repeated to one another until they became worn in, a blanket to wrap around us. I spoke to them always in my grown-up voice and tried never to call them by nicknames, besides *sweetie* and *love*, because I'd read that this was a way stepparents insinuated an intimacy they had not earned. Raised as I was among doting and disciplinary people, I slipped almost without knowing it into the role of the Strict Parent, the keeper of clocks, the minder of manners, the policeman of tone.

I took my peculiar place among the spectators at ball games, dance performances, and chorus concerts and learned there are more soccer games being played by the bourgeois children of America than there are blades of summer grass.

"Hey, sweetie, you having fun?" I asked in the middle of one of those marathon afternoons under the great autumnal skies of Maine.

Lucy, impassive, her shin pads and bright socks reaching up above her knees, gave a little distracted nod. And then, lucidly, "Does Mom have my water bottle?"

I thought a lot of what my dear friend Henry had said to me, after I confessed to being frightened of the kind of stepfather I might prove to be. Henry, a colleague, was a ruddy-cheeked, sweet-natured, occasionally filthy-mouthed Englishman; I often described him as looking like Christopher Robin gone delightfully to seed. He had two kids the girls' age, so I took him seriously when he said he knew, beyond doubt, that this was something I could do.

"But there's one thing that's always going to be awful," he said, "and there's not a fucking thing you're gonna do about it."

This was alarming.

He leaned in close: *"Other kids' parents."*

A strange true fact: in the town where we lived I counted among my intimate friends not one stepparent. Divorced parents, queer parents, adoptive parents, single parents, yes. But I could scan the horizon and find no other semistepdad. But then, as Henry was suggesting, the horizon was pretty near. I used to pick the girls up sometimes from gymnastics—a sweetly comic spectacle of little kids scrabbling like squirrels over mats and carpets in "routines" that were always collapsing into knots of frantic disorder. The classes took place in a barn out in the country and you'd stand in the airless little waiting area for parents that in the wintertime felt like nothing so much as the back of an overfull Greyhound bus, though without the luxury of seats. No one was unkind, exactly, or even especially impatient, but I remember trying to explain to Evany the sourness of the atmosphere, the vivid sense of incubated unhappiness.

She was unimpressed. "That's just what happens," she explained, "in a room full of people who've given up on sex." And then, a limber sidelong grin.

WHAT I HAD TO OFFER this world was not always clear to me. How's being a parent? people would ask, maybe not masking the note of incredulity as completely as graciousness would dictate. I had a line that became dulled with overuse. About the only genuinely good parental thing I bring to our house, I'd say, is the example I provide to the girls, by being so radiantly in love with their mother, of how *they* deserved to be loved. I think I mostly believed this. I had so little fluency in the world of little girls, of crafts and make-believe, dolls and dresses. For one of Lucy's birthday parties Evany had staged in our living room a "spa night," complete with homemade avocado face masks and cucumber eye patches, for what I later described to Henry as a group that seemed like two dozen, and was probably closer to five, grade school girls.

Birthdays proved a kind of blessing for me, though. I found there a foothold.

A few years earlier, just around the time computers started to make such things possible, I began assembling for the girls what we called their birthday mixes. These they could play on drives with us or on the little player in their room, and they were by and large uncomplicated little affairs, not much involved with that careful curation of resonances and interimplications that goes into mixes you make for friends or lovers. They were instead mostly offhand combinations of what I knew they liked already and what I thought might hold their attention, if not at just that moment then in some nearish future. It was wonderful, how little you could know in advance what would stick. I tried, I promise you I tried, not to be too prescriptive about it, since there isn't much sadder, or for young people less useful, than middle-aged men offering them maps to the byways of Cool. In the effort to cultivate the ass-kicking feminists I suspected they'd someday become, I did, it's true, seed them with tracks by Chrissie Hynde and Missy Elliot, Aretha Franklin and Liz Phair. (How they loved Liz Phair!) Was I pleased by Amelia's affection for the Magnetic Fields? (Parenting tip: "Chicken with Its Head Cut Off" is a surefire winner for the under-seven set.) Did I exult a little when Lucy could be heard in the shower singing, *"Well it's white noise and wishes that held us together, I know!"* from the Superchunk B side? Not in an *unseemly* way. But yes. Very much yes.

But then, in a happy way, this accumulating litany of songs worked their way into the patterns and habits of our days, became as much a part of the fabric of our togetherness as our dinners, our rules, our repeated jokes. To this day I cannot hear "In Between Days," that sparkling anthem from a lost '80s youth, and not be returned to a February snowstorm, with Lucy in the backseat as we inch our way home to dinner after ballet. She's telling me how it stacks up against other songs on the Cure's *Greatest Hits*, which is a record that for some reason I'd thought she might like. (For the record: she ranked "In Between Days" as better than "The Lovecats," the equal of "Just Like Heaven.") And like it she did. She had a lot to say about it.

I'd hear the song somewhere in the tumult of a regular day, spinning up on shuffle or in some playlist squeaking through my tinny office speakers, and I'd feel the familiar warm buoyancy. But the nearnesses it brought with it weren't Mark's or Evany's or John's or Pam's in England or Beth's in California, or for that matter that of my own adolescent self. They brought me nearer to Lucy, to Amelia.

I THINK NOW that they helped me, those little mixes, to encounter something that I was for no good reason—or, I suppose, for the always good reason, which is *titanic fear*—hiding deftly away from myself. Because even I, even then, wasn't *so* stupid not to recognize a blessing when I saw one. Whatever the turbulence and tedium of raising them—I had been totally unprepared for how much of the labor of child-rearing is an ecstatic, mind-scalding kind of *boring*—some part of me knew that these little girls, with their weird enthusiasms and slangy playground speech and sudden cloudbursts of tearfulness and hilarity, were a kind of astonishment.

I remember an afternoon when an aunt of Lucy and Amelia's was visiting, their mom's baby sister, and in the obligatory tour of rooms Aunt Charlotte noticed how pristine, how tidy and well arranged, Lucy's room was. And then, without special inflection, without the least indication she was saying anything even a little extraordinary, she let out brightly, "Yeah, I mean. I take after Pete!"

I remember it stopped my heart for a second, that offhand declaration.

I take after Pete!

But then, after a suspended moment, just one long breath later, my deft little minimizations kicked back in. I said to myself the same thing that, playing defense against my own fears and failings, I'd say over and over, to anyone who inquired after the girls, me, or my stepparental acumen: *The best I can do for these girls is love their mom.* Repeat, reset, repeat.

Still, I cannot pretend not to have had the dim sense that something else was being transacted between us. For all the impacted circumstances, for all my dumb guardedness—for all that I had permitted to stand between me and openheartedness—it was also, I knew, simpler, more elementary. I loved them.

But it wasn't just this. Because when we'd crouch down together and make a four-person huddle of jubilant noise there on the living room rug, when we'd start to soul-clap in the breakdown where Michael shouts out, *"Sit down, girl!"* and Lucy would jump up into my arms, all bright eyes and toothy grin and unrestrained silliness, even I couldn't stop myself from knowing what, with both wonder and not a little dread, I knew. *Oh, thanks, Aunt Charlotte! Yeah, I mean, I take after Pete.* It was right there, easy, like counting up to three.

She loved me too.

MARRIAGE IS A NOBLE DARING, the line goes, and if I'd been paying closer attention I might have caught the implication not only about bravery and tenacity, but about the omnipresence of fear. The girls' father made me incandescently angry, but that was probably just the inner lining of something much larger. I was afraid of something happening to the girls. I was afraid of something happening to Evany. I remember reading an essay about a photographer whose subject was her stupendously gorgeous children, and coming to a line that brought me up sharp. "The child is achingly beautiful," it went, "too precious not to dread losing." That was it exactly. I was only then coming into the sense that as your happiness scaled up and grew intricate and involved, so, too, in exact proportion, did the quantity of your life given over to dread.

Only a few months before Evany and I enjoyed our anniversary getaway up the coast, I joined her around lunchtime at the grade school behind the college, where both of the girls had gone. I think I understood myself to be going to a chorus concert. Or a play? An iteration of jump rope club? I'm not sure, but what it proved to be was a gymnastics show, in which the kids from that class in the barn performed their routines on sawhorses and mats laid out across the school gym. A sparse crowd assembled in the bleachers. The performing kids clustered together in one corner and pop songs blared in accompaniment, the vocals echoing toward indistinction up in the rafters. There was the mild clamor of grade school children released for a moment from class, a low-grade expectancy. You had the feeling of excitement, in one of its neutered institutional forms, set to transpire.

Implausibly, something did happen.

Evany and I sat together, nodding hellos at the friends who were there, and noting between us the funny distinctness of character you came to appreciate, at scenes like this, in kids you watched over years. That one's concentration. That one's irrepressible goofiness. That one's grace.

And then Amelia fell.

She was tumbling her way through a somersault and came

down wrong, with a hard thump. We watched it happen. In slow, articulated instants, you could see her face crumple and a startled cry set itself in her throat.

And then, across a small interval of time of which I have no account, I had her in my arms.

I'd come across the gym floor and had scooped her up, carried her a few steps to the side of the little mat, and held her there a second until it was clear she was fine. She was perfectly fine. She steadied herself, wriggled, and was gone.

I found myself, then, on a gymnasium floor, faintly puzzled about how I'd gotten there. With the music thumping you might've thought I'd picked her up like it was bedtime, just for a little swinging dance.

Exciting! At least as far as grade school performances go, but, in the scheme of childish things, a nonevent. I don't know that I'd remember it at all except for what happened next. Things wrapped up and before Evany and I made our way back to campus I found a little bathroom. I stood in front of a sink that barely cleared my knees and as I washed my hands I caught sight of myself in the silvered mirror. I looked unchanged, exactly like me. But suddenly it was as if Amelia's little shock had poured itself into me. I started to shake and, abruptly and irresistibly, from the pit of my stomach, to sob. There was another lost interval of time. As silently as I could, I let the little storm carry me up and, eventually, set me back down. I washed my face, then caught up with Evany and floated back along the stream of the day.

Those tears, all of them, they told one story.

It was no use pretending.

They had, these glinting and weird and irritating little creatures, become etched in secret into the obscurer places of my heart. There was Lucy, her big-sister assurance, her commitment to the silly joke, the glowing little core of imperturbable self that you could see in her, everywhere, all the time, as weeks together turned into months and years. There was Amelia, her watchfulness, her sometimes neediness, the menagerie of stuffed animals she would never pick up off the floor, and with it all her outsized, inborn, unconfected *sweetness*, every bit as disarming as her big sister's.

Pete, Pete: let's play crazy eights again! C'moooooon!

They could call me by whatever name they wanted. People could read me as their babysitter or their mom's boyfriend or as nobody worth noticing. It didn't matter. No amount of sulkiness or retraction or even, it seemed, incompetence could unwrite the fact that, somewhere in the stretch of small hours and unfunny jokes and dances danced, they had become mine.

Without question, I was theirs.

AND SO, JUST AROUND the time of Amelia's minor fall, Evany and I decided to try to have a baby of our own.

THAT WHOLE WINTER had been, in its way, momentous. Quite a bit to our surprise, I had been offered a job at a much bigger place, for a different sort of money, and all at once a new set of questions rose before us. Together, for a few months, we turned over in our hands the possibility of a life altogether different. It was a strange exercise. Everything around us, the house we filled but also the fights we fomented and the small-bore difficulties that from day to day worked themselves toward intractability, seemed for a dizzy moment something other than inevitable.

With great seriousness, we considered leaving. We took trips to the other place, looked at houses, met people. We talked and talked.

We decided to stay.

Because of the girls, because of the complications of blended families, because of the life we had made, and were yet making, and did love, we decided to stay. At a party we threw to celebrate making up our minds, and the relief of it, our friends came and drank and danced and the next morning we woke to find bright threads of carpet, little tangled piles of them, scattered in all the corners of the living room. I remember realizing, with a little burst of delight, that "cutting a rug" was a metaphor but it was also—who knew?—a *real thing*!

But unrealized possibility is a genie and it was out of the bottle. And so, in this season of momentousness, we made another decision.

The idea to have a baby of our own had come up before, but circumstances were never quite right. Near futures were pressing, complications presented themselves one after another, and in truth there were attractions to the arrangement we had, at last, jostled into place. The girls' father had recently consented to a regularized, recurring schedule. (The divorced among you will know what is signified by the sequence 2-2-5.) Lucy and Amelia were growing in independence. And though we came at it differently, and those differences could be difficult to navigate, still I think Evany and I both savored the doubleness of life that followed from joint custody. We were people with children, standing mannequinlike and laden with mittens and scarves and snacks among others like ourselves in humid waiting rooms . . . except on those days when we weren't. On those days our lives looked different. We got drunk or threw parties or went to Chicago or stayed in bed or just ate out.

We sat one night in early summer in the backyard and puzzled it through. *A baby?* What scared us? For me the answer was easy. It was the prospect of no longer walking through our days like double agents. A line I'd read in a Philip Roth novel long had hold of me. "You gave me a double life," says a married woman to her adulterous lover. "I couldn't have endured with just one." The ending of our own double life—that would be a lot of loss.

I have a picture of Evany from about this time there in the yard. (I was always, always, always taking pictures of Evany.) There's the unmistakable buttery light of the Maine summer gloaming. There's Evany, with a glass of wine at her lips, and she's looking sidewise at me, gray eyes cut but grinning in satirical tolerance. On a night just like that one, Evany told me she wasn't afraid of having a baby with me. Or, if she was, it was a fear less of having a new child to raise than of her *not* having a baby. It would be a kind of heartbreak, she said, to find here in her forties that she'd gotten pregnant when she had, with whom she had, but couldn't with the person she loved the way she loved me. She feared how much it might return her to the bitterness of her first marriage, or the swamping shame of her adolescence, to find she could not get pregnant, now, with me.

But then she reminded me of something. She told me again how *scared* she'd been when she was pregnant with Amelia, the youngest. It was not childbirth she was afraid of, or even the growing decay of her marriage. No. More than any of this, she said, she had been afraid that she would never, ever be able to love this new unmet creature with anything approaching the intensity, the comprehensive world-filling force, with which she loved Lucy, the baby she already had. It seemed an impossibility, stark and terrifying. And the fear of it renewed in her that old gnawing suspicion that she was consigned, was somehow malignly *fated*, to make disastrous decisions with her life.

But that, she said to me those years and years later, the summer gloaming diffusing in the trees, that was *all wrong*. Because there came Amelia, and with her the sudden radiant sense of being cracked open, possessed in a huge inflooding rush by the life-upending knowledge that love, that great bafflement, was not like that at all. "You just find out there's *more*."

It had been, she said, the happiest moment of her life till then. And she turned to me, her great gray eyes gone shiny and bright. "And then," she said, "I found you."

The low light settled around us. The neighbor's cat stalked into the uncut grass, in and out of pools of shade. It was the beginning of a very good summer.

The plan was not to have a plan. We wouldn't, we decided, medicalize the attempt. We would just live the regular lives of our bodies and see what happened. ("Oh," one friend said from afar, "you're just gonna pull the goalie.") In all cases, we would be fine. We divided the future into two likely possibilities. In one scenario, which we took to conjuring for each other mostly in the form of jokes ("Do *you* feel pregnant right now? I pretty much don't"), we would end up sleepless, creaking with age, and making room at the party for one more. Mornings we lay together and, in what was for me a scene of piercing joy, picked among the books that littered the bed. Fertility books. Books about giving birth after forty. One memorable volume of baby names.

And in the other scenario? The scenario of the failed attempt? In that version of our future, we had our girls, growing every day into rangier and funnier and more formidable versions of themselves.

In the meantime, then, we lived in the rituals we had made. At night we made dinner and sent them off to do their chores and disputed about this or that grave parental injustice. And then we'd gather them up and the music would go on and it occurred to me that what I heard in "ABC" was not the joyousness for which I initially fell in love with it. It wasn't even the sound of a damaged family, such as the Jacksons surely were, producing in seamless harmony a thing so purely jubilant, though that was there too. Michael would sing *"One, two, three, you and me!"* and the groove would shiver up the length of my body, and it would come over me that if the thing we were making together had a voice, that queer little love without legal title or proper name, it would speak in the voice of this song. It would sing.

IT WAS A VERY GOOD SUMMER. We traveled, we went to the beach, we watched the girls swim in the frigid little waves. We had all the sex, all the time. We took an anniversary trip up the coast.

4

Big Day Coming

ONE OF THE GREAT ongoing fights of my coupled life—and by great I mean bountiful and nourishing—was about female-fronted bands of the early '80s. It pitted the Go-Go's against the B-52s and I was playing, I believed, the much stronger hand. The idea that a band of such confected pop-rock splendor as the Go-Go's could be compared at all, let alone unfavorably, to so plainly lesser an outfit as the B-52s—this, to me, was strange to the point of incomprehensible. Because, I mean, *the Go-Go's*! They were the L.A. postpunk ladies-only Stones, all coked-out rock-star depravity delivered in the guise of winning girl-group tunefulness. Be serious! I'd hear a song like "Head over Heels," with its finger-exercise piano intro and oversized backbeat hooks, and be returned in an instant to adolescence, to the little civic pavilion right on the public beach where I grew up, where the town threw "teen dances" and where the bands my brother was in, and then the bands *I* was in, would play for fifty or so seventeen-year-olds stealth-drinking their way through a suburban summer in the 1980s. I can tell you that "Head over Heels"—like "Vacation" and "We Got the Beat"—was *excellent* fare for punkish bands of boys hoping to crowd the dance floor. Honestly, play me these songs and I could all but smell the Coppertone, the sour salt of Long Island Sound, and the sweat of thwarted teenage desire.

Not long after I met Evany I began saying that so far as I could tell there were three strong reasons for being alive, rather than not: sex, talk, and dancing. The Go-Go's were a pure-cut dose of at least two of these, so *come on*.

It was Evany's position that I had mistaken suburban nostalgia for cultural worth and, worse, that I had mistaken pop consumability for genuine quality, artistic heft, and lasting value. It was Evany's *further* position that since I was in grade school during the years in question, while she was busy seeing bands like R.E.M. and Let's Active and the Mekons in the basements and college bars of North Carolina, I should probably cede the floor to my wiser elders, who after all were in a better position to appreciate the force of queer innovation that was to be found in the B-52s.

Oh, how I loved this, our stage patter, rehearsed over years into an effortless fluency. Over dinners or at the sprawling late-night dance parties we'd throw to brighten up long Maine winters, it allowed me to burnish once more my theory of the '90s afterlives of the Go-Go's. (The Blake Babies were Dinosaur Jr. crossed with the Go-Go's; Veruca Salt was the Blake Babies crossed with the Go-Go's; Belly was Veruca Salt crossed with the Go-Go's. *Everyone was striving to attain a purer state of Go-Go's.* Etc.) It gave disagreement a staging ground. There was a line in a love poem by a writer named Mary Kinzie that often came back to me: "Even our quarrels," the line went, "bore the sly stamp of how to make them up." Ours had the virtue, too, of expanding the roster of songs cycling through our days. There was Neko Case and the National and the Jackson 5. There was the Beach Boys track to which we strode up the aisle, newly married and weepy, whose familiar opening strains, as they pealed through the

church, set off a quick surge of impious hilarity among the con-
gregants. (This was "Wouldn't It Be Nice," of course.) There was
the Gillian Welch song to which we swayed in our first dance
("Dear Someone"), and the Yo La Tengo number I *begged* Evany
to walk down the aisle to ("Big Day Coming"), to which she re-
plied, disappointingly but not wholly unreasonably: "I am not
walking into my marriage to the sound of wailing guitar feedback. I don't care how fucking 'orchestral' it is."

And for Evany there was the B-52s, another strain of devotion that spoke to the microgenerations separating us. In a way I
found beguiling, a lot of what my peers would have taken up as
retro pleasures were for Evany objects encountered more directly, and with much less in the way of ironic detachment. She
was fourteen when *Rumours* came out, pouring herself into
high-waisted denim and feathering her hair in upstate New York,
and she never got over her swoony delight in the slick West Coast
ardors of Fleetwood Mac. Sometimes she'd say she fell for me
because I had, in my longer-haired days, something of the look of
a young Lindsey Buckingham, which was all at once funny, flat-
tering, and strenuously false. "No, sweetie, it's true!" she'd say.
"You just need some more, like, peasant blouses." Then, too,
when I needed a countervision to draw myself away from the
tidal pull of some stupid domestic aggravation or other—some
spat over dishes or laundry or schedules—I had only to call up
the image of Evany driving the girls and me home one day and
singing her way through the lower ranges of that silly chromatic
chorus in "I Think I Love You" by the Partridge Family. In an
instant, my hardnesses of heart would melt away into nothing. If
she kept her love for me in any songs, it was as likely in these
prepunk effusions as in any of the Sleater-Kinney mixes I made
for her or the Sade record that accompanied our first vacation
together. This delighted me, and made me only too happy to
keep our differences circulating.

And so, one night early in the summer committed to our at-
tempts at getting pregnant, we had a dinner party of our own,
where the question of the Go-Go's made its eternal return. I can
remember the ordinary pleasures of it: the last-minuteness, the
thrown-together supplies, the sense of an opportunity seized. I
should say that by this point I had at last managed to surrender
the pretense that my life was being lived in brave opposition to
the narrowness of my suburban upbringing. (I was in fact raised
in the suburbs, though raised in a raucous and militantly loving
extended Italian family, whose holidays tended to feature meals
laid out for two-to-five dozen of us, typically stretching out over
the course of several cheerfully gluttonous hours.) Family was
fine, but *I* was a person committed to lateral kinships, the legiti-
macy of invented worlds, loves without name. And so forth.

With a patience I probably did very little to earn, Evany
explained to me over years of talking that a life of overcrowded
sociability, anchored in pleasure and delighting more in noise
than quiet, was if anything a *tribute*. ("Think of what Christmas
is like at your uncle's," she'd say. "Think, like, *for a minute*.") A
friend who'd known me forever observed that being with Evany
had given me a way back into my family and into a wider, less
brittle sense of how well loved I'd been. "She's curing you of your
adolescence," she said, "but in a really nice way."

Nice not least because this form of accommodation to adulthood did not require the putting away of those childish things
that never, really, struck me as all that childish. So on this one
night we ate, and sat around the living room listening to records
and drinking beer, and as the summer evening settled itself
around us we fought about the B-52s, indie rock, and the fractured legacies of the 1980s. That we could do this even with these
people, many of whom we did not know well, was its own kind of
pleasure. Just then the museum where Evany worked was in the

final stages of an enormous, hugely expensive, and for her immensely stressful renovation, and this work required the hiring of technicians and art handlers on temporary assignment from all up and down the East Coast. Evany had admired their work, and was coming to enjoy the atmosphere of deadline-heightened backstage camaraderie, and so wanted to have them round.

If I remember this all especially well it is at least in part because the satisfaction I took in our familiar semiscripted Go-Go's disquisition came, that night, from the contrast it made, its distance from the other scenes of couplehood unfolding around us.

There was one couple there, local folks actually, nearer Evany's age than mine, and they showed in their manner and conversation, and in the whole posture of their togetherness, the telltale signs of years of what a friend calls "attritional intimacy." Unhappy couples are a fine genre of partygoer. A lot of the time, they might as well be wearing Day-Glo jerseys: TEAM DOMESTIC IMMISERATION. Straining bonhomie came off these two in waves. It was not a surprise to learn they had married young, this arty, slightly hippieish, pleasant enough pair of fortysomething Mainers, still taking gigs where they came—he was working as an assistant to the museum preparator—and gamely laboring away at their art. She was smallish and slight, and beneath her cloud of frizzed unruly hair were a pair of bright and earnest blue eyes. He was the prettier, with a kind of alt-'90s pageboy haircut, art-school glasses, and an air of semistunned inarticulacy about him—something sweetish and wide-eyed but maybe, because of that, a little bovine.

We joked later about them, the way you do after parties. "That is the face of a dude grabbing for the rip cord," I said, stacking dishes in the sink, "and looking to parachute right the fuck out of his marriage."

Evany laughed. It was her kind of joke.

≈

THERE WERE FEWER laughs by the end of summer. In the last week of August, just before school was to recommence and our lives to be taken up once more in its tides, Evany believed she was, in fact, pregnant. We'd been trying, and she hadn't had her period, and for that bright suspended moment her pregnancy seemed an imagined possibility surging suddenly toward fact. Perhaps this was wishful, a bit of shared desire doing its transformative magic on what was in fact pretty limited evidence. It did not occur to me that the extraordinary pressures of Evany's summer, escalating as the date of the museum's grand opening neared, might be a proximate bodily cause. Or if it did it was a thought soon made inaudible in the midst of all the happier inner exultations.

Evany made a doctor's appointment. Mornings found me sitting in the bed, knees up, a book open across them, tracing a finger down page after page of these long lists of names.

A fluttery elation, childish and undiminishing—this is a lot of what set itself in my stomach in the weeks before Evany's appointment, and I can tell you it came as a surprise. I had never been a person who experienced a particularly strong desire for children, a *need* for them. This was still another of the ways I felt myself to be, if not at odds with, distinct from the scene of my upbringing, which at this point was crowded with parents. That I had stepchildren was surprising enough, to me but not only to me. The hunger for progeny had long struck me with the force of a kind of human mystery. I didn't disbelieve in others' expressed desire so much as I wondered at the failure of a like desire to appear in me. In grad school, in the midst of a night spent drinking for reasons I cannot now recover in a bowling alley bar, one friend explained that she knew she'd have kids because she wanted—and the phrase stuck with me—"to go on all the rides of life." Which caused another friend to reply that having kids seemed to be exactly the thing that would *prevent* you from going on all the rides of life. (Another conversation from that night swims back to me. "I want to have someone in my life who'll always love me, no matter what," the first friend said, prompting the return volley: "Oh. Tell me how you feel about your mother.") None of my indifference to these supposed inducements to reproduction had altered.

But it had begun to occur to me, in the accretion of years with Evany and the girls, that you might entertain other reasons. In little flashing glimpses, I began to catch sight of the idea that you might want to have a kid not so much to make some Frankensteinian version of you and your love blended in indiscernible sequence but to commence a kind of life-traversing labor, a project the two of you might devote yourselves to as another way of being together. There was this one night at dinner, a night of surpassing ordinariness. And yet with no especially good provocation we'd found ourselves, the four of us, passing around a dumb joke—some creaking, execrable pun, I'm sure—until it picked us up in a tornadolike embrace, and suddenly we were all gasping and teary with idiot, uncontrollable laughter. I remember looking at Evany, who was wiping her welling eyes, her smile gone as wide as Amelia's, and at the girls turning from their mom to me and back again, all dissolving hilarity, and feeling one of those long sweet rushes of recognition.

I swear to you that once I thought of having kids as at least a little like throwing a very long and largely boring party—a party Evany and I could conspire to stage together day and night, into the reach of years—I started to see into what had been, to me, the most mysterious of impulses in otherwise sensible people.

Also, of course, in the shameful and narcissistic way of men who should know better, it made me feel a delirious kind of wanted. Not even my fitful stepparenthood, my want of fluency and my failures of patience, had been disqualifying. I felt a lot of what I felt those years before: *She chose me.*

THE NEWS FROM THE DOCTOR was not good. It was, in its way, cruel.

The doctor told Evany that she was not pregnant and, more than this, that what had seemed like the dawning of this new possibility was actually the symptoms of something else. The doctor told her that she was in, and in fact nearer to the end of, what she called "early-onset menopause." This was why her periods had become intermittent.

Could it truly be that the indications of this, the end of years of fertility and its ceaseless management, were those of a pantomimic pregnancy? Yes, it could.

I can remember being jolted when she told me less by grief than by the terrible fucking gratuitousness of it. There wasn't much selflessness in this, really. What else was there to see, beyond the astounding cruelty, to Evany, of just this? I thought of her there in the office in the basement of the clamoring museum. I thought of all that she had loved, fucking *loved* about being a mom, how it made her feel renewed and enlarged, available in new ways to wellsprings of love. How it had tuned her to the world with a new quality of patience, of openheartedness, a readiness to believe being hurt by it was not her destiny, a haphazard fatedness. I imagined her there, not weeping but *smiling*—smiling that glinting crooked fatalist's grin—and turning back to her day.

I called my friend John in Chicago, who over the past months had been a gracious audience for the rehearsal of excitements and anxieties. He had a little boy, was about to be remarried, and could keep a secret. I knew I could count on his indulgence.

"I'm scared," I said. "Of all of it." I took a breath, and something else occurred to me, a small recoiling spasm. "I'm scared," I said, "about how sad I'm going to be about this."

And we talked about the peculiarity of this grief—for the loss only of possibility, a thing never real—but then he said, kindly but a little sternly, that there'd be time for that, more than enough, later. Now, he said, was the time to look after Evany. There was nothing imaginary or abstract about the losses involved for her. I remember thanking him and thanking him and hanging up and then, in a state of numb distraction, walking down to a coffee shop, where I sat by a tall window looking out at a scene of exceptional Maine loveliness, a river cascading down into the falls beside an old repurposed mill, and wrote Evany a little note. It said I was so sorry for the day's news. It said I was so sorry but that she was my radiant love, the most beautiful woman in every room she walked into, and so, so much a badass. Nothing could change that.

I sent it and she wrote back a sweet midday love note and we went home and the month rolled on and, sooner than you'd have thought, the demands of the rapid days of fall swallowed up what might've been a larger, more immobilizing grief. If there was sadness in the air between us we were, just then, too busy to feel it too acutely, and that was at least part of the point of making a world together so dense and involved, so thick with ordinary life. We had our girls. She had her beautiful new museum to open. I had books to write, students to teach, and this was a thing we tried once that didn't work. I wouldn't say we ignored it. Our lives together had grown spacious, and so had room enough for losses like these.

A COUPLE OF WEEKS after this Evany started fucking the assistant preparator.

≈

SHE TOLD ME, drunk, on a night early in November. "I've been unfaithful to you," was I believe the phrase employed. The world broke apart, huge jagged fragments of it coming unjoined and falling away into empty black space.

By the middle of the week I was on a couch in Chicago crying myself fetal. Poor John and Karen. On a few hours' notice I brought to their North Side apartment a spinning galaxy of terror and incomprehension. My body had started a violent revolt. The first thing I did, that night back in Maine, once the words Evany had spoken assembled themselves into meaning, was stumble to the bathroom, fall on my knees, and commence retching. It proved I could not stop throwing up. Whatever this was, whatever new and impossible condition of the real, my body was having none of it. *This will be expelled.* At the level of the organism, I said no, in convulsions.

Poor John and Karen. I wept and clung and heaved. I was suddenly more afraid than I'd known it possible for anyone to be, of anything. Surging fear seized all the mechanisms of consciousness. I spoke thousands of useless words. Had the previous months been especially strange, or hard? they asked. I mean . . . in their way, yes. But I had understood Evany's skittishness, her recessed distraction, to be a function of the monumental pressure of the museum's opening, coupled as it was to the undiminishing demands of motherhood. By way of congratulations I'd rented her a little cabin up the coast for a long weekend at the end of October, after the opening, where she might enjoy at last some replenishing solitude while I looked after our back-home life, the house, the girls. A private victory lap, I said. I even made her a mix for the drive up! (Of course I fucking did.) It was called "Escape" and featured not one, not two, but three early R.E.M. tracks.

Though I knew the answer, I asked Evany if the assistant pre-parator had joined her there, on the getaway weekend I had thought she might savor.

An image formed that, as I told John and Karen, would not stop insisting on itself. It was not the fucking, the turned eyes and opened mouths, the pornographic loop. No. There had to have been a moment when Evany knew he was about to arrive, and waited for him, at the window or on the edge of the bed or beside an opened door, in a state of nearly unendurable *anticipation*. There was no overstating how little I existed in that moment. There was no overstating how quickly the whole accretion of our life together could be made to vanish, exactly then.

I made this thought into a little chamber of torment, the dungeon beneath the castle, and locked myself inside.

Karen drove me to the airport a few days later. She held my hand in the drop-off lane as I tried to take regular-sized breaths. "Oh, Pete," she said. She offered me the wisdom of the once-heartbroken. "I don't know what's going to happen," she said, "but I do know you're going to lose a *lot* of weight." Which made me laugh exactly enough to permit me to leave the car.

I would try. Standing inside this hurricane of sudden fear, I told myself I would try. I replayed all that Evany had said. She hadn't meant what she had done. No, she absolutely had. She didn't want to be married to me anymore. Of course she didn't not want to be married to me anymore. She wanted everything to be different. She didn't know. She was paralyzed. Replay, replay. She was obviously in a state of terrorized anguish. The thing to do was not to abandon her to it, shame her, or boom at her.

The thing to do, then, was to love her through it. To stand fast in loving her, and the life we'd made together.

I would try.

I would try to give her the things she needed. This would be hard, not least because I could not *speak* to anyone—only these few friends afar and one in Maine but, in deference to Evany's privacy and the hope for an ongoing life, not my family or the world of people around us. And of course he worked with her, there at the museum, where he passed her every day. Still. I would, failingly, try. I would pay attention, and give her room, and be reborn as a new and more patient and less need-filled person. I would do what she needed. If what she needed was a few days here or there, away from me and the frantic need for assurance I could conceal only so much, I could do that. Of course I could.

The thought of what it would mean *not* to do so was too annihilating to pursue, and so I did not.

5

A Letter on a Lonesome Day

ON AN AFTERNOON of which I can tell you very little except that it was I *think* in April—some four or five plummeting months after Evany's announcement—I came home to find something amiss in our house, some obscure but insistent tremor.

"Our house": I should have said before that this was no longer the little bungalow we'd started out in, to which Evany took me home from the bar that late spring night in my late twenties. A couple of years before, after I'd gotten tenure, with the girls growing each day rangier and our lives together expanding laterally around us seemingly without volition, we decided to make a change. We looked and looked. We toured through houses new and old. (Of one beautiful nineteenth-century home that needed a gut renovation Evany's brother-in-law, an architect, opined, "Buy this and you will have, about it, roughly one hundred fights." We passed.) And so, having found nothing possessing anything near the plain sweetness of the house we were in, and with the pitiable unwariness of amateurs, we thought it'd be wise to build out an addition onto what we had. I can't tell you those were the most joyful months, what with the household chaos, the unrelentingness, the daily onslaught of microdecisions to be made,

each one of which seemed of such lasting and outsized consequence that it was all we could do to block from consciousness
the one thought that, in the midst of it all, must never be allowed
to form itself: *What the fuck are we doing?*

But for all that—all the delay, the money panic, the varieties
of negotiated truce—there was no denying it: it had come out
beautifully. It was elegant, and it was homey. Evany had a garden. I had a study, painted in a bright midsummer blue. The girls
had a bathroom of their own. For our first Valentine's Day there,
I bought Evany a pine green love seat for the sunroom, where,
with a cup of tea and an art magazine, she'd curl up at night and
look at the shadows of the moon in her flower beds. I cannot pretend to you to have felt, as night by night I took this all in—as I
told myself, *This is here because once we wrote some sentences*—
anything but the most pure-cut dose of bourgeois pleasure I had
ever known.

It was, that feeling, anodyne and unheroic and completely
intoxicating. When we were thinking about leaving Maine, leaving the college and the little life we'd made there, the accomplished loveliness of our new old house was strong inducement
to stay.

So it was into this space that there had come, I felt that afternoon, some small atmospheric disturbance, something invisible
but off-kilter.

But this was April. By then, the whole of life had grown quite
spectacularly off-kilter anyway. By this point several months
into what I understood to be the collapse of all things, that ripple
of disquiet could only have been an echo—or maybe a tiny-scale
model—of the altogether vaster awfulness that, since the fall,
had been creeping over everything. Early in a strange, beautiful
Iris Murdoch novel, a character whose marriage quite suddenly
shatters speaks, in regard to the first not quite comprehensible
pronouncement, of feeling "the first light touch of a nightmarish

terror." It was because of precisely that enveloping nightmarish-ness that I cannot, even today, remember much at all about the spring of that so catastrophic year, beyond the daily climate of frantic incomprehension and desperate, annihilating fear. The absences, those wide holes in consciousness, felt truly strange for a while—strange in the way it was strange for me to step daily into clothes that no longer fit, but draped off my shoulders as though on hangers—but I can't say I regret this particular patch of unknowing.

But I do remember this afternoon, with the tranced clarity of a horror film. I walked in the side door, through the kitchen and the dining room into the living room. There it was: an ugly un-canniness. The dreamlike sense of a scene of easy familiarity made somehow *wrong*. I stood in the middle of these, our ac-creted things. I looked. Moments pulsed by.

I drifted into the bedroom, sat on the bed. I must've thought to change shirts. And there, in my closet, stacked tidily, the mys-tery was solved. Here was what had been subtracted from our home, and the arranged texture of our life there. Someone had gathered up the pictures of me and Evany together that we had scattered around the house, from vacations and parties and wed-dings, including our own, each and all, and delivered them, in a neat pile, here, to me. They were a little hill of frames, mis-matched, wood and metal, tucked inside my closet and set atop a flat rectangular box that I did not need to open, since I knew it well. Inside it was a great sheaf, pages and pages and pages. These were love letters.

THERE ISN'T MUCH WORTH SAYING about these intervening months beyond that they were stupendously awful, mostly in the ways you would imagine. Indecision, untruthfulness, haphazard cruelty. A seesawing between passages of fragile optimism and a plunging hopelessness. The sense of holding to an entire world, its treasured past no less than its unwritten future, as it slews sickeningly toward destruction.

I won't belabor these days. Know that there were pledges and plaints, sudden reversals, terrible revelations, and clumsy deceits. Evany would decide to commit to "trying to think about staying together," reverse herself, drift among differently inflected states of paralysis. One evening I went to buy groceries for dinner and as I drove down the main thoroughfare and past the museum, there he was, with Evany, leaving the building and ducking with her into our car. Paying the phone bill I noticed an unfamiliar number, repeated over days, during a week I'd been away at a conference. On a memorable winter night I went off to teach a night class in Augusta for extra money and called Evany to say I'd arrived. And called. And called. And called. On breaks and at intermission. With no response, for all the hours I was gone. I made the long dark drive home, phone clutched in one hand, believing with focused certainty in the unsurvivability of each moment, and then the next, and the next. My mind was a scrambled signal pattern. A jet engine roar.

Imagine scenes like that, on repeat, between December and April. Imagine breathing is a thing your body periodically forgets how to do.

Or, if you want to know what the particular derangements of this passage of paralytic wretchedness truly feel like, imagine the transformation of all of your most cherished forms of shelter and replenishment—those pop objects that have long sustained you—into the carriers of a swift, blindsiding devastation. I don't at all mind confessing now that there was one song especially, one song of an altogether laughable demographic predictability, into which I had poured great quantities of my love for Evany. Men my age should not readily admit how much they're, like, *really into Dylan*, or how transporting the ginned-up dust bowl reediness of his folksy drawl had been to our teenaged selves, marooned out in the Great Mundane of the suburbs. But why pretend? I was exactly that boy and then, with minor refinements, became exactly that man, an integer in some marketing demographer's algorithm. When it came out on PBS, I'd watched the four-hour Scorsese biopic about Dylan, this piece of pure auteur hagiography, and found to my surprise I was *defenseless*. Reader! I *wept*. I couldn't understand how utterly it worked me over, but Evany did. "He was your hero," she said, simple as that, and this was the precise moment when I realized it was true.

So when I walked around Barcelona on a lonely trip back in the first days of our romance, uncomforted by an iPod on shuffle or the possibilities of a quick transatlantic Skype date and then so overexhilarated by the sight of Gaudí's Sagrada Família cathedral I thought I might levitate with the awestruck wonder of it, the song I found I'd hum to myself over and over, the pebble I rolled over my tongue, was none other than a ballad called "Boots of Spanish Leather."

Listen, listen: I know. Nothing excuses it. It is an indulgence that would have embarrassed, I don't know, Werther. It is a song that seems to have been created expressly to appear on PBS pledge drives of the future. I know, I know, I know. But there I was, a lonely one-man jukebox. I'd like to say my susceptibility to "Boots of Spanish Leather" on those Barcelona days was merely circumstantial: it is a song about absence, a song about letters, a song about *Spain*. Any of this might have distracted me from the fact that this was above all a kiss-off ballad, a song of a lover's callow pledges and misfiring devotion, and his eventual stinging rebuke.

In truth, none of this made much difference.

I was just then discovering something about how, as a kid, I had used songs like these, songs I listened to in the adolescent way, with repetitive and unwearying devotion. Nothing else produced for me such a fixed intensity of concentration. It was as though they contained the encoded secrets to an elusive grown-up world, one I might miss out on if I didn't pay the proper kind of fanatical attention. I had begun to piece together, in these lonely and contemplative European days in my still unripened late twenties, that what I'd found in songs was an irreplaceable kind of holding place. Like nothing else in the world of the near-to-hand, they made it possible to love things with an ardor that had no outer limit. They made it possible to love things, with ludicrous and consuming devotion, before there were things to love, or things that would love you back with an answering ardor. I listened to songs and bands like that, to Bob Dylan and Charlie Parker and every band whose lyrics I ever wrote in a spiral notebook, because they held open the possibility that there might be other objects—*possibly even objects who were persons*—to whom such unembarrassed and overheated love might someday be attached.

When people say, as they often do, *This song kept me alive,* I take this to be something of what they mean. They have in mind the way that songs can nourish in us what a writer named Adam Phillips calls "the sense of possibility upon which our lives depend." Grown-up people who continue to love songs in a way others call childish have not forgotten the anxious magic of that holding-open.

Until the year everything broke apart, I could not fail to hear even in the saddest of songs some murmuring undercurrent of affirmation, of a dim distant wish coming true. Every song, after Evany, was a love song to the world—a reminder of how much you could love something and how much love the world could hold. It was a solace greater than religion and even of literature and no fucking wonder I had sung myself elated and tearful to Bob Dylan songs, a dope in fraying hipster sneakers, as I walked alone through the crowds of Las Ramblas.

I remember this all as I do because I wrote it down, all of it, in the letters I wrote to Evany, day after day, a tremendous overspilling volume of words, written mostly in bars and cafés, longhand, in a yellow legal pad. Later we gathered them all together, that copious archive. We put them in that little box and stored them away.

IMAGINE ME, then, in these gasping, desolate days. Imagine staring into the likely revocation of not only all you cherish—your love, your life, your home, the world you have been making together—but, with them, the possibility of ever being solaced again, by any of the things that had nourished and in some not figurative senses *made* you. Later in that Murdoch novel, which is called *A Severed Head*, a character meditates on heartbreak. "To lose somebody," we are told,

> is to lose not only their person but all those modes and manifestations into which their person has flowed outwards; so that in losing a beloved one may find so many things, pictures, poems, melodies, places lost too: Dante, Avignon, a song of Shakespeare's, the Cornish sea.

Poems, melodies, places. I think now it could've been anything that unraveled me.

"I don't know when I'll be comin' back again / That depends on how I'm a-feelin'..."

All these poisoned joys, these despoiled memories.

Dylan would breathe through a harmonica into the air of some recording studio in the mystic 1960s, and I heard only a dire pronouncement: *This was your past, and your future—your only future—is to live in its ruins.*

"BOOTS OF SPANISH LEATHER" was hardly the only song that, over those stark clinging months at the end of things, had the power to shatter me out of my brittle performances of self-composure. It did, the Dylan ballad, work me over with an especially terrible magic, which I wish I'd been better able to resist. But *everything* was shattering: daylight, knives on a plate, a touch, the withholding of a touch.

Deep into a snowbound February my mother and one of her sisters found a pretext to visit us in Maine—a school concert, maybe? a dance?—and one night just the four of us had dinner. If it was strained it was not unmanageably so, and was if anything a small relief to have something between us, around the table, besides our stalemated anguish. There was food, and there was wine. At one moment Evany got up from the table to retrieve something from the kitchen, a bottle or a glass. And as she walked past, sliding between the wall and my chair, she managed to elude entirely all contact with my person. Not a hand on my hand, not a palm on my shoulder as she angled behind me, not the least grazing touch. Not any of the million steadying gestures of habituated intimacy, all of which say, in their small voice, *I am here, love.* There was only their absence, and to me the sense of invisible, violent rebuke. I felt the future start to crack and tumble inward and later, as I drove my mom and my aunt back to their hotel, between vast columns of piled-up frozen snow, the grip I'd been keeping on myself at last began to slip.

We idled in the car, beneath the entrance of the Comfort Inn, and I remember my mother saying to me again and again as I shook out dumb sobs, "Peter, tell us what's wrong, *please tell us what's happening."* And I said back, no less repetitively, I can't, I can't, I can't.

Through the winter and into the cold dawning of spring, I told no one I believed could not forgive Evany. I was committed to protecting our future. I held on to myself as best I could, and so for some time I could not keep myself from things that would produce in me far less succor, or even momentary reprieve, than elaborate torment. But how could I? How do you unlearn your deepest habits of self-sustenance?

None of this, finally, made any difference. In early April, after a season of confusion and terror, after pledges made and retracted, she told me I needed to get a lawyer, because she had one. It was one day after my birthday. That was the end.

BEWILDERED, UNHOUSED, quasipsychotic with inrushing grief, I reached the girls at last, by phone. Evany had, in light of that vivid quasipsychosis, kept the girls from me in the initial weeks after declaring us, truly, over. This was perhaps not as cruel as it seemed to me then, given the wreckage of the self I'd been, though that she had told them of our dissolution *without me there* seemed another inconceivability that I would just have to make room for.

Everything's okay, sweetie, I said to Lucy. *Nothing will ever, ever stop me loving you, and being proud of you. Nothing, ever!*

And Lucy cried. She cried and cried and cried. She cried as vehemently, as inconsolably, as I'd heard her cry since she was little.

Flashing up before me then, in the space between words, in the dim static of the phone connection, was every uncompleted hand of crazy eights, every appointed pickup and drop-off, every household annoyance—*"Pick. Up. Your. Room." "Fiiiiiiiine."*—every song debated, every pop icon scrutinized, every cramped hour of familial tedium. All of it now rushing away from us into darkness.

I'm so sorry, love, I kept saying. *Lucy, sweetie, I'm so sorry. Oh, love, I'm so sorry, I'm so sorry.*

"I know," she said. "I know. I know. I know."

AND SO NOW, a couple of weeks later, here I am back once more in Chicago.

I am back in Chicago and it is the week of John and Karen's wedding, at which I am to stand up with them. That is days away yet. At the moment I am in a coffee shop tucked directly beneath the elevated train tracks in a North Side neighborhood called Lincoln Square, where every few minutes the walls rattle and send little silver milk cups on twitching arcs across the tabletops.

But I am not much noticing the furniture, or the rumbling trains.

Unappeasable anguish—that's all that fills the day. I had thought a trip to Chicago would be somehow steadying, restorative. I badly want to be here, with John, whom I have loved since I was eighteen and who is somehow, in a way I can very nearly convince myself is not ungenuine, not ashamed of me. Right now, though, it is going very, very badly. Instead of restoration I have found myself on the losing end of a series of panic attacks, which I fear I've half talked myself into. God, they are awful: auditions, I would later call them, for your own death. But all these wedding details are recalling to me, with fierce clarity, my own wedding day, which had been about the most euphoric moment of my life. And overlaying that recognition is the lacerating sense of how amazingly little gravity that crush of memories can have had for Evany. The horror of it, of being thus derealized, is at this point more than I feel up to. The panic rolls across me in successive waves of seized breathlessness—making me think, inanely, unhelpfully, of sex with Evany, of her body as it grows taut and yielding and gives itself over to spasms of pleasure. *Oh,* my mind says, *this is like that.* But in the place of delight is a sorrowing fearfulness racing along the edges of all my nerves. *Wait, no,* my mind says. *This is like the* opposite *of sex.*

Crossing all of it is the desperate desire not to bring any of this to John, or Karen, or this week of convening and joy. No. The imperative is to keep it the fuck together.

But I am so broken open and can't stop thinking myself into frightened incomprehension. Remember, I tell myself, when next time you go about professing to classrooms about a dissolution of meaning in Melvillian wildness and chaos, a plunge into the terra incognita of a world suddenly stripped of the anchoring points of sense and legibility, remember *this.* This queasy terror-struck heartsickness. This is what it is like, and what it is. I have watched Evany vanish into trackless distances. I have watched her begin to look at me almost quizzically, with a recessed impassivity, as though I were a person she can *almost* place. This slow-settling vacancy of gaze, after the frantic sorrows of the previous months, has scared me more than anything I have ever seen. Words like *dissociative* and *derealization* have been offered to me by thoughtful professionals, though I have been unable to make much use of them.

Evany has said so much. Every word of it clings to me, and burns. She has said that I tell all the stories of our lives and she has none of her own. That she cannot thrive in relation to me. That she needs to be with someone—this was the very word— *creative.* That I am selfish. That I am grudging in love, and ungiving, and ungenerous. That I have never truly loved her. Or the girls. *Or the girls.*

I am battered by this, confounded. Right before I left for Chicago, I managed to say to Evany that there are lots of people who have loved me, lots of friends and intimates, and what she was saying did not square with what they believe of me, what they have told me. And Evany snapped back at me what is probably the most damaging sentence she would ever utter.

"None of them is married to you."

I am battered and I am confounded. What she has said bears so little relation to any of my own experience of her, of me, of our life. In that sense it can't be true. But it is Evany who has been saying it, and Evany, since I have known her, has carried around with her the wisest and brightest and *truest* version of me. In that sense it can only be true.

It is terrible terrain.

The problem before me, then, is how to manage it, how to compose this self—somehow *my* self—in the midst of this ecstasy of grief. I take all options seriously; I write them in a notebook as the trains rattle by. But I feel as I sit there so gawky and unlovely, so hopelessly remote from the possibility of other people's desire. Everything, everywhere, each person who fails to return my look, feels like redoubled rebuke. I turn in my seat and look at the bodies of the men and women, and they seem so strange, so *unlikely*, until I realize I'm scaling them all according to their failure to be Evany's. Oh, God, I think. I have made Evany—her beauty, her frailties, her needs and enthusiasms, her devotions and desires—the measure of all human things. Was that *not* the thing to do with your love?

And then, then fuck it all, then there's the sex, the great overspilling quantity of sex! I remind myself again that ours was all I could have hoped for by way of an intimacy sustained by an always kindling passion, an in-the-body mutual delight that felt year after year just fucking endless. It rises before me, not for the first time, though now as an intricate moving horror. The kitchen counter. The desk in my old apartment. The study at the Ransom Center. The room in New Orleans. Cambridge. Quebec. Ireland. The glance at the end of a dinner party. That field. To the degree that I have a body to which I feel any kind of sensually attached, to the degree that I am capable of thinking of myself as sexually adaptive, eager, avaricious, full of yearning and possibility, it is due to Evany. What kind of life is it, I wonder, to do without that?

And so, released from that shifting parade of visions, the rising panicky dread returns, and with it the sense of, you could say, a raising of the stakes of things. I am thinking, with forced concentration on the point, that if this is what life is to be, this pretending not to be shattered or ripped open or broken against a grief I'll never get myself to the end of, then perhaps "life" is not something I want to continue to do. It is an ugly and a desperate sort of feeling, though it does not for that seem to me like the opposite of reason, and at the moment it is very much upon me.

And it's here, picking my way among diminishing options but trying to hold it together, that a thought comes to me, a little black star rising in a pale sky. It occurs to me that if what Evany most needs at the moment is for me to vanish, then what she would be made most happy by is my disappearance from the face of the earth. Everything that has happened in these rushing weeks has told me a story—that she had not as she had long promised ceased sleeping with this person; that she had told the girls we were divorcing without me there, and without my knowledge; that she has begun having this man over to the house that she and I had made together . . .—and that story, I remind myself, is not unclear. She needs for me *not to have been.*

I give myself credit for recognizing, in some reptilian corner of consciousness, that I am beginning to approach a new precinct of grief. The look of things changes. I pack up and pay and walk north along Lincoln Avenue, back to John and Karen's place. I let myself in and put down my shoulder bag of unread books, and as I sink into the couch in the thinning daylight I decide to let these thoughts take up space with me for a while, here in the rooms of their apartment. We are alone together, these thoughts and I, and they begin to talk.

They are talking, but I am also remembering that, before I had begun to love the girls and our family, I had not quite known what dread could be. I am remembering all the time I spent frightened that something would happen to Lucy or Amelia. I am remembering all the time I spent frightened that something would happen to our lives.

I call Evany at work, and she picks up. There are stilted greetings. And then I ask her if she thought it would be better for her, for her life and the girls', if I was dead. There is a pause, the sound of which is like the rushing of emptiness between planets.

"No," she says.

Honestly? "No."

I hang up. I am on the couch at John and Karen's, in the apartment where only last summer we spent a weekend drinking Wisconsin beer and listening to Tom Petty, to Etta James, to Steely Dan. In the room with me, in the weak light, are all these thoughts, and they keep talking. I discover a new way of being afraid. I am frightened of something happening to my mind.

Something happened.

Part Two

SEX, TALK, DANCING

"Were you at the National show in Central Park last week?"

Something about the way she said this, with a smile a shade more genuine and—was it?—inviting than you usually get from your bartender, made me think better of taking my book and my beer to the shady back corner.

"Oh, I was!" I said. And then, out of some unsuspected reservoir of flirty competence, "Was that you sitting behind us? I recognize your curls."

I took a seat at the bar.

Somewhere in my inner ear a lyric clanged: "My mind's gone loose inside its shell."

≈

For a certain kind of person, and a certain kind of man, anger is a volatile quantity, fizzing with danger.

For much of your life you look around you for visions of how to be something other than, say, an asshole—a man who bullies and blusters, who takes his private sorrows for large-scale social facts, who lives out his disappointments in a series of ugly resentments, directed more often than not at proximate women. You expend a lot of energy devising ways of being something other than that guy.

Only later do you come to the realization that not being a bad guy is not the same—is not the same at all—as being a good man. Only later, and, I think, only if you have the good fortune to be surrounded by friends, and especially by women, who regard you with a fierce unexonerating love.

Before that, though, you consider your own capacity for anger with grave wariness, as if it were the seed from which something altogether malignant might be grown. It can be no accident that boys and men like that—boys and men like me—find themselves as captivated as they do by music that is loud, frantic, and concussive, filled with a thrashing propulsiveness. Here is a place where you might have your furies, and have them as something other than poisonous: as elation, perhaps, or as transport, or as scene-making joy.

But, again if you are very fortunate, you might discover something else along this way. Fall recklessly in love, anchor that love in your body and the body of your beloved, and you can find the world around you crackling into new constellations of itself. Sex, you may find, is other and better and larger than you had suspected. Because sex is where you get to encounter fugitive aspects of yourself—a frightening vulnerability, say, but also intensity, force—tuned to the note of a bodywide exhilaration. In sex you might find a way to live out an altogether ampler self than you'd imagine was available to you, one that comprehends your errancies, your fearful tendernesses, even your brokenness.

You can be forgiven, when you're just discovering the wild breadth of it, for thinking sex is a kind of miracle.

≈

When you lose everything—your home, your family, your lover—anger is, let me assure you, a volatile quantity. If in your deepest habits of being you mistrust what is violent and furious in you, and are fearful of where it might take you in your daylit life, then be prepared: it will live itself out, that rage, with or without your permission. It will, if it needs to, batten on whatever is nearest to hand.

Most commonly, of course, this is your own bruised self.

"Why aren't you angrier with Evany?" people would say. Because I was saving up all that venomousness for a better, a more convenient object: it was all for me.

But then an odd thing started to happen. In cities, at the homes of friends, in strange apartments, and in bars and in bars and in bars, I made a discovery that shocked me probably more than it will you. Evany, it transpired, neither invented sex nor exhausted its possibilities.

"Look," I said, in a voice I was surprised to find sounded a lot like mine, "I'm only in Brooklyn for two more days. This is my number. Call me if maybe you'd like to go out."

6

The Next Person I Meet

SANDY AND ILONA have arrived in Maine like Magi. They have come bearing gifts. There are oranges in a netted bag, chocolates, a book. Provisions for survival in the aftermath of disaster.

In the back of the car, Sandy is fumbling with something else, something unwieldy. He has brought with him CDs, a whole stack. It is a gift, he says, it is for me. He tells me it is a mix of songs and I swear to you it is the most prodigious thing of its kind that I have ever seen.

And listen: I fucking know from mixes. I have made them in delight and sorrow, in remembrance and expectation. I have made them for lovers, for friends, more lately for children. Years before, I scored the entirety of our wedding day, five hours of music plotted into meticulous arcs and crescendos, having put it all together the only way you could in those days, which was song by song, on a dual CD burner located at the college radio station, which I monopolized over the course of one obsessive-compulsive weekend without shame or apology.

But this is something else entirely. It is a mix like no other. It is, to begin with, *nine CDs long*.

We put it on as we drive and immediately there comes a blast of pop-rock voices, stacked and chorusing, and out of the high-gloss production one crystalline tenor steps to the front.

"*Starting now I'm—starting over,*" he sings, leading a band I'd never heard of, called the Format. And then, "*I'M GONNA SLEEP—SLEEE-EEEEEP—WITH THE NEXT PERSON I MEET.*"

It's a strong opening.

THE COUPLE OF MONTHS between John and Karen's wedding and Sandy and Ilona's day trip have been eventful. I have begun moving out of my house, my so cherished little house, which for a purely horrific few weeks Evany and I had conspired to share. I have found, too, quite by accident, that in those times when I have not been resident there Evany's new lover *has* been. A long-time neighbor and colleague at the college tells me this one very early morning over coffee, as though it were something I must, surely, have known.

The look on her face when she realizes her error stays with me as an image of blank confounded pity.

Later, in a memorable day of hallucinatory ghastliness, Lucy asks me if I'll be at the all-campus picnic. It is the kind of event little places such as the college like to throw for employees and their families, once the students have cleared out and the slower routines of summer have begun to take hold. I go in the hopes of catching up a bit with Lucy, having seen so much less of the girls in the previous months. It baffles my heart, this sudden yawning absence, like an unworkable puzzle: a bewilderment of sorrow. When we talk to one another on the phone, Lucy and Amelia and I, we talk only of ordinary things. "How was school?" I say. "Who did you see today? What did you wear today?" Nothing else seems speakable. But I am all in knots. *What will become of us now?* I think. *What will we be for one another now?* It feels when we talk like we are walking together, very deliberately, along the edges of something terrible.

I'm sorry, I want to say, *girls, I am so sorry.* Again and again and again. I wonder if I will ever reach the end of my impulse to apologize.

"Of course, sweetie," I say. "I'll find you there."

In the blue sea-salted light of a perfect Maine day, I see Lucy. We hug, and we talk a little, and we tell some old jokes—she is so plainly being sweet with me and, in a way that just breaks your fucking heart, *careful*—and then, in the preadolescent style, she is off into the crowd. The fact of the presence of her, her ordinary nearness, buzzes through me for a moment.

I see, too, every man, woman, and child I know at the college, to many though not all of whom news of this affair-cum-breakup has begun to arrive.

I also see Evany.

She is there very much in the company of the assistant preparator—he is also an employee! and has as much right to be there as anybody!—and is comporting herself on the day, among all the people we have lived with and entertained and grown older beside, with an edge of combativeness that in some other context I might find admirable, if only for its steely audacity.

Fuck each and every one of you provincial busybodies, her affect seems to say. *Fuck you if you want me cringing and ashamed.*

Alas I don't have much heart for admiration.

Two friends flank me shoulder to shoulder as I stand there in exposed imbecile paralysis—thank you, Aaron, thank you, Allen—and one of them leans over to me and says, "Hey. Hey. Hey. Everything's gonna be okay."

Later, once it feels safe to move and I am walking through the dispersing crowds, a woman whose face is familiar in a vague way (I will subsequently realize she works in HR) approaches me.

"Listen, we don't know each other," she says. "But that was *bullshit*." Sheepish, I say thank you, and tell her I am sorry.

AND YET I FIND I AM NOT, as you'd think I'd have the good sense to be, *humiliated*. Though I am learning what it is to be a central player in that dismalest of human genres, the small-town scandal, and though my role there is the Dupe, the Fool, the Man Who Was Replaced, still as it turns out I don't have much room in me to fear the leering gaze of this small public world or to feel undone by anyone's knowledge, however detailed, of what has happened. I am sufficiently undone already. Though the transparency of my undoing isn't the best thing about it, as pains go, that one feels small indeed. Next to the dumb incomprehensibility of what has happened, and of what is *yet* to happen, humiliation hardly registers.

My friend Meredith has taken me to see a lawyer, and the first words out of his mouth were these: "There is nothing I can do for you with respect to those girls."

Humiliation, inside this astonishing new world of facts to be faced, is barely a thing you'd notice.

And anyway I must be walking about with an aspect especially pathetic because everyone is being gracious, decorous, kind. One desultory day I find a card under my office door. It is from my friend and sometimes coteacher Elizabeth, one of the true stars of our at-home dance parties, who in her daylit guise (gifted scholar, unflappable colleague, patient mother of three) might not strike you as the guest likeliest to stay till three a.m. outdancing the junior faculty boys to Prince jams of the mid-'80s. Without quite being confessionally intimate, we are good friends, dear to each other, I would say, and I admire her so much. "Dear Pete," it says. "I don't know that I've ever known a husband more obviously in love with his wife than you. I do not know what to say. I'm so sorry. Call me if you need anything."

It breaks me up.

I keep the card. I do not call.

SO I AM NOT HUMILIATED, not exactly. What I am, however, is spectacularly ashamed. These, I learn, are different.

At the oddest intervals, day into day, these onsets of malign feeling would come tornadoing through me. School was over, and when not at home I stayed with friends whom I did not wish to burden any more excessively with my miserablism than I already was. And so I'd leave the back bedroom my friends had so kindly made up for me and embark on tremendous afternoon-long walks, under these great vaulted coastal skies. Step, step, brood, brood. Even the open spaces, the buzzing meadows sliding down toward a rocky coast and out to the sea, came to feel claustrophobic. It got so bad that I could no longer listen to my beloved iPod on these walks, or no longer do so safely. This was *terrible*, like losing a cherished interlocutor. Over the years of my marriage I had come to love with special force the archival qualities of pop songs, the ways they held within them bright visions of places and scenes, old loves, former selves. But increasingly I could not bear being in company with my former self.

I can remember standing at the edge of an enormous yellow field, edged on all sides by arrow-straight pines, an osprey riding updrafts in long circles, a Sade song from *Lovers Rock* cycling into my headphones. And there I stood, thinking of my lost self, thinking of his stupidity, his unknowing.

The thought returned and returned: *No one else is married to you.*

I had believed, I had truly believed, that I was a person

especially well suited for the making of these joyous, love-bound little worlds, capacious and full of noisy delight. But this was not true. Evany knew it. Evany was *certain*. And soon, I felt sure, everyone else would too. They'd all figure it out.

ONE LATE MAY MORNING I run into Evany on campus, at the little coffee stand in the student union. She is, mercifully, alone. I have been sitting there semicatatonic, a tall cup of tea going cold in front of me, and mainly just staring at the crook of my left arm. There is a little white patch of gauze taped there. When Evany approaches I am sunk so deep in fixated reverie I scarcely notice her. But there she is, and her presence, like her absence, delivers a fantastic quantity of hurt.

We stare at each other dumbly for a moment. With nothing else occurring to me to say, I begin explaining to her that I've been to the doctor this morning.

The doctor had asked me to tell her a bit about why I was looking so terrible, so gaunt and ill—kindly, she didn't put it quite like this—and so I told her. The whole dreary tale, out it came. And then, after a series of procedural questions, a string of have-yous, and did-yous, and when-did-you-lasts, she regarded me evenly. In a neutral voice she said she was going to have to ask me to do something I might find difficult. She was going to need to take some blood and run some tests. She wanted to do this, she said, because we had no way of knowing whether my wife had been using protection.

That was the phrase: *using protection*.

Mentally, I stumbled over it and this caused me to gaze back at her for a moment, and to note, with an interest almost abstract, that here it was again: another moment of unbidden confrontation with this, the New Real, that I was in no human way prepared for.

But then something broke, and my abstracted distance failed, and I was weeping in semipublic once again. My doctor allowed me then to compose myself, took my blood, affixed a little square of sterile gauze to my arm. When she knew more, she said, she would call.

And so, I say to Evany, my little tale complete, I've just been here staring at it. Thinking about how nearly a decade ago, just exactly at this time of year, we got together, fell in love, and then got married and invented a way of being together, of loving the girls, oh, God, *the girls*. And now here I am with this tape on my arm, wondering if I have been made sick or not.

"And honestly," I say, "I'm not trying to be unkind, it's just . . . I am not making much sense of it. You know? I cannot make it make sense."

A few silent seconds pulse between us.

"The girls and I are fine, Pete," she says.

For the life of me I cannot tell if her gaze is exasperated, pitying, annoyed.

"We're all going to be fine."

The days get blacker and blacker.

IT IS INTO THIS CHEERFUL environment, by then tinted a few shades darker still, that Sandy and Ilona have made their pilgrimage. It is a pure mercy. I was supposed to have gone down to Providence to stay with *them* for the upcoming Fourth of July weekend. But no. After another night of sleeplessness at my friends', devoted hour by hour to recrimination and elaborate self-torment, and then a morning, *another fucking morning*, of rolling panic attacks, I came to the unhappy conclusion that I wasn't going anywhere. I looked at my shaking hands, and some spasm of self-preservative instinct spoke through me. It said, *You should not drive a car.*

And so they drove up. Despite the fact that they can't stay the night—that they are driving three hours one way, and three hours straight back—they have come to find me.

Even through the awful myopia of my sorrow I know they have done this for me, disrupted the flow of their own clamoring lives, in the same spirit of care—and, perhaps, semifrightened concern—that would motivate you to make a mix that lasts better than ten hours. They arrive and I feel such a surge of hapless, grateful love for them that I recommence doing exactly what I've been doing all morning already, which is crying. But now it's crossed with sputtering laughter. Even my untiring tearfulness seems for a moment not without its comic dimensions.

We park the car and walk about, and as we stroll around the holiday-empty campus I can feel an unclenching in me.

And yet behind the relief and the gratitude there is, I know, something else, ugly and craven. I am a little scared of them. I have a sense of the person they know me to be. And I have the sense that that person, who we all of us liked pretty well, is gone.

The past weeks have been eventful. There are things that have happened, broken turns of mind that have found me, things I have thought to do—have almost done—that I still do not quite comprehend, for which I have no words, and will not, in fact, for years.

It all puts an edge of nervousness in my throat.

That this is pure manic insanity—that there is not the least thing to be disquieted by in the company of these people—matters considerably less than you'd hope it would. With a longing that pierces me, I wish only to sink into the old steadying familiarities. Of these, we have so many.

Between Sandy and me, for instance, the primary mode of attachment has long been a kind of genial combat—an unceasing disputatiousness, vehement and mostly unserious except when, contrarily, *entirely fucking serious*. One particular fight has been crackling between us for decades, a nourishing little passage of often-returned-to inanity. Sandy, who had grown up in and around the legendary punk and hard-core scene of mid-'80s Washington, D.C., loved—LOVED—Fugazi. And, my God, were they not my thing. That, really, was the whole of it: *I like this band. Yes, but I do not!* The purest imaginable form, really, of stupid fighting about useless things. But if it had given us a way to calibrate, to the last decimal, our microdifferences of tuning, it had also, this dumb fighting, become for us one of the wellsprings of a closeness that had outlasted adolescence and was now charting its way through the heavier weather of adulthood.

As I had waited for them to arrive, all the shaking morning, I'd been thinking of that closeness, playing all up and down the scales of memory. Years and years before, somewhere in the postgraduate mid-'90s, Sandy and I had ventured across the country together—Chicago to San Francisco, in his shitty sputtering Honda hatchback—and it was there that the rituals of this, our ever-renewed dispute, attained what was probably their most ludicrous extended form. It carried on, more or less uninterruptedly, for *days.* (*Astringently militant!* he would say. *Beautiful agit-prop noise!* To which I'd respond, *Tunelessness!* Or, *Anhedonic boys with rules!*) When in later years I would think of the landscapes of the West—the dissolving sight lines of Nebraska, the brick reds of Arizona, the lunar barrenness of Death Valley, through which Sandy *insisted* we drive in the high-sun afternoon of a day in late fucking *August*—the sound of some long-ago Fugazi track would come chainsawing into consciousness.

"When they find our whited bones beside the scuttled car," I said, "who will know to blame motherfucking Fugazi?"

All through our days on the road, rattling along in his little silver Honda, taking any occasion to fall back to fighting—road directions, motel choices, lunch, whatever—one record had formed a kind of demilitarized zone between us. We listened more times than I can count to *24 Hour Revenge Therapy*, a new-ish release by a San Francisco band called Jawbreaker, which I will tell you is a great, if also in retrospect truly hilarious, artifact of the early-middle 1990s. Oh, the emo-kid anguish! So serious! So emosh! It is a record you could aptly describe as a Portrait of the Young Punk Discovering Breakups Are Terrible.

Somewhere out in the wilds of Clintonian America you could surely have found a carful of boys capable of resisting the charm of a record alternating between anthemic scene-critiques and tracks with names like "Do You Still Hate Me?" (These featured the purely unironic delivery of lines like *"I LOVE YOU MORE / THAN I'VE EVER LOVED / ANYONE BEFORE / OR ANY-ONE TO COME."*) Sandy's overheating hatchback did not con-tain those boys.

We'd listen again and again, laugh a little at the airlessness of the singer's stunned heartbreak. "Jesus," I remember Sandy say-ing at some point, "Blake"—the singer—"is for real *hating it*."

After which interval we would return to fighting about Fugazi.

As revelatory as it is to love something in common with someone—a book, a song, a child—to love a person with whom you differ, passionately and on matters of real consequence to you both, can be its own kind of edifying, and its own kind of joyful. I knew bands had given Sandy something richer to him than an aesthetic, the memory of some good shows. They had given him a *stance toward life*, one marked by stridency and op-positional devotion. Whereas I found in myself an instinct to insist on *pleasure*, on the force and breadth of its revelations, which certain kinds of *dudes*—and there was never any shortage of such dudes—tended to dismiss as cheap and frivolous. He was a kind of conscience to me, and I had probably been one for him.

Boys, you will have noticed, will create rituals of fantastic intricacy to say quite simple things. Things like, *You are my friend*, and, *It appears that I have come to love you*.

Or, as the case may be, *I can't do this*. Or, *Please, please help me*.

"TELL ME WHAT'S HAPPENING," Ilona is saying. "Tell me all the things."

We are sitting on a bench in front of a building of stately red brick, ivy curling up its sides, the whole thing. A gold-green quad, bisected by walking paths that a few months earlier would've been dense with fleeced-up college kids, lies before us as still and tranquil as an alumni magazine photograph. Whatever fears I'm dragging around with me and out into this New England collegiate idyll, Ilona has taken in hand and, with her especially fierce style of care, sought to neutralize them.

She is, Ilona, a neuroscientist by training, and her mind is a razored and agile thing. She does not have a lot of patience for indirection or cant. I do not have sisters, but her presence makes me wish I did. Her anger on my behalf, though it is not something I find I can much participate in, is nevertheless comforting to be near. It is incandescent, a Roman candle lit and burning.

She is standing now, pacing back and forth in front of the bench where Sandy sits beside me. "*Dude*," she is saying. "The *fuck*?"

Two unlikely things are about to transpire.

Out of the stillness of the scene-set landscape a figure emerges from one of the buildings to our left. This is the art museum, gloriously renovated, the plinth, which Sandy and Ilona will remember as the scene of my wedding reception, today appearing denuded of the clusters of students usually to be found draping themselves over its railings and across its stone steps. The figure, not quite a hundred yards away and cutting a perfect line left to right across our field of vision, has foppishly lank hair, jeans cuffed up high, a messenger bag on his shoulder. He may or may not notice us. He is walking deliberately but without hurry.

It's him, of course.

"It's him," I say rigidly, and the talk goes dry. We are frozen for a moment, the three of us, into a blank tableau. And somehow his presence there, as if conjured by evil magic, becomes for me something weirdly monumental. Sandy and Ilona are seeing this, too, which means he cannot be mere hallucination . . . and so, suddenly, somehow, the *reality* of him blazes into furious clarity.

Here is this person, and whatever his absurdity—and he is, I'm sorry, a high piece of human ridiculousness—he is real, he is real, he will speak to Evany shortly. He will be in the house I made with her, as will the girls, *as will the girls*, and it will be for all the world as though I was never there.

He walks along, becoming a truth less conjectural second by second, and as he does I feel my own substantiality, the once comprehensive fact of myself, pouring itself out of me. I am vanishing, I feel it.

When he has passed far enough along to have his back to us I start to sob again, but this time in deadly earnest, and I do not know that I will ever stop.

And then the second thing happens.

Ilona has her arms around me; she's holding me and rocking me and talking to me. "Hey," she is saying. "Hey there. Hey. Fuck that guy. *That* guy? Fuck that guy." And it's Sandy who is pacing in front of us.

When he turns back to us his face is fixed and his eyes are burning. It is a look I recognize, mostly from the more colliding moments of our years of dumb fighting, though it is drained now of any trace of unseriousness. He plants himself directly in front of me.

"I need you to stop," he says.

I look at him. God, Sandy—I really do love him. But I can't stop.

He says, "I need you to stop this."

And again. "You need to *stop*."

I do not stop.

He's right up close now. And then, "This is not you."

I am staring at him.

"This is not you. Listen. I know who you are. I've known you twenty fucking years. She does not—*listen*—she does not get to say who you are."

He straightens up, then leans back toward me.

"Listen to me. Stop. Listen to me. I know who you are. Ilona knows who you are. This is not you."

I sit there, transfixed. In the weeks and months ahead I will replay this scene in memory dozens, hundreds of times.

"Listen to me, man. This is *not you*. Do you hear me? This is not you."

I can't say just what it is that happens. But something small in me clicks. I do not stop crying, not just then. But eventually I do. We continue walking and later go out to an early dinner. Ilona holds my hand for most of it. And Sandy says it again, this time in a lobster shack beside a Maine cove, with early-bird diners crowded around us. "No more crying every day. Enough. This isn't you. We know who you are."

A strange fact but a true fact: this is the last day that finds me crying morning, noon, and night.

THE FOLLOWING MORNING is Independence Day. Perhaps because I seem some modicum of refreshed, here in the aftermath of Sandy and Ilona's visit, a friend insists that I accompany him to a semilegal party being thrown on a little island in Casco Bay. These are the kinds of parties he knows about.

This friend—he is called Bisbee, and he's a sculptor, a man with a great Walt Whitman beard and wild eyes and something of the manner of a street preacher given to bouts of public profanity—has been caring for me assiduously in these awful in-between days. When for instance I told him I'm scared everyone is going to discover, any day, that I am not the person they thought I was—that I am not loving, that I am not deserving of anyone's love—he fixed me, paused a moment, then spoke.

"That's true," he said, a little blaze behind his eyes. "Ever since Evany started fucking that dude I've realized what a *dick* you are."

He is, Bisbee, ungentle. But loving.

"No one on the earth needs to get fucked up more than you," he says. "Let's go."

So we go.

Together we take a ferry out of a teensy picturesque cove and arrive at the island to find a ravelike chaos of revelry well under way. And there, amid the energetic young people and home-made explosives and an astonishingly robust arsenal of recreational drugs, I encounter the next passage of unaccountable strangeness.

I meet, and talk to, and then sleep with a young woman up from Portsmouth with some girlfriends.

Even as it's happening, I am mostly certain it is not happening. But it is. It does.

ON THE FERRY back to the mainland in the pale trembling light, Bisbee, who is similarly unslept because of the mushrooms he spent much of the previous day ingesting unto near psychosis, cannot stop *laughing*. Above deck, leaning on the top rail with his head thrown back and his eyes like big shiny buttons, he is in high manic glory, the largest, loudest thing in nature. Because of me, or because of the night, or because of the drugs, or because of the unlikeliness of all of it, he is laughing himself semi-deranged. The sound of it comes Dopplering back and forth over the water, up into the reaches of the curving bleached-out sky, and fills up the sleepy, toy-boat harbor.

ON SANDY'S EPIC MIX, I will later discover, there are virtually no songs from our shared past, no Nation of Ulysses deep cuts or Slant 6 B sides. There is no Fugazi.

There's one track, though, that catches me on first listen—it's a winning power-ballady number, featuring some scratchy-throated dude singing about being in love, being, like, *really* in love—and sure enough, through the swift magic of the Internet I come to find that the band is called Jets to Brazil and the singer is none other than Blake, Blake from Jawbreaker, whose bygone punk-rock heartbreak had evidently resolved itself into something a good deal cheerier.

I can't quite figure the valence of its inclusion here. A suggestion that my life, like Blake's, will arc toward love? Or a funny little suggestion—there are fucking *strings* in this song—that, Jesus, we are now well and truly middle-aged?

Mostly I just love that it's there. Like most everything else that ripples through the hours and hours of sound, it speaks in the voice of an improbable, undefeated optimism.

Sandy and Ilona, I think, know from gifts: unable to restore to me the things I have understood myself to have lost irrevocably— my marriage, my stepdaughters, romance, sex, a whole habitable future—they have started with something smaller and nearer. They have started with songs.

This is fortunate for me because things soon turn curiouser.

7

The Drinks
We Drank Last Night

AND SO, WITH THE INTERLUDE on the island, begins a long strange season of uprootedness, whose chief characteristics are to be borrowed bedrooms, unfamiliar cityscapes, and what my friend Beth and I soon take to calling low-consequence bad decisions. From Maine to New York, and then eventually out into the promising capitals of Europe, these I pursue with a headlong devotion.

You couldn't call it a *strategy*. It's just that between sorrowfulness and stupidity, there isn't much of a choice. I'd choose stupidity. Repeatedly.

THINGS WITH THE WOMAN on the island did not, it will surprise you to know, work out, though we did have one pleasant date a few nights later, a sushi dinner in Portland, after which, having heard just some fraction of the story of my last months, she smiled at me warmly and said it seemed like I maybe needed some time to, mmm, *get myself together?*

Who could argue?

If there was for me a sting in this—and there must have been—greater by several powers was the odd species of relief. It wasn't that I did not want to go on more dates, particularly with Evany stepping seemingly without pause into a whole articulated life, cohabitation and everything, before the ink on the divorce papers had time to dry, before in fact there was any ink at all. It certainly wasn't that I did not want to have more sex. Only much, much later, after some bruising experience, would I learn to mistrust even marginally my often piercing hunger for a body to wrap myself around, as a substitute perhaps too ready-made for the unsleeping grief I'd otherwise lay myself down with night after night. A defining problem of these days of plunging insomniac heartsickness was just how to go about wanting to be in the world *at all*, in the absence of any especially compelling inducement to keep doing so. Though I was broken open and dangerously rudderless, a shambling panic attack wearing hipster sneakers and a dumb grin, still I had enough battered sense to recognize in sex, or its possibility, one pretty fucking compelling reason for being alive.

But, Jesus, was it *unnerving*. I remember reading a passage in a novel in which the protagonist, staggering around lower Manhattan as dazed by the abrupt dissolution of his marriage as by September 11th, finds himself to his great shock falling into bed with a beautiful woman he meets at a party. Back at her apartment, in an unfamiliar room beyond which are the lights of the damaged city, he feels exhilarated, and pleased, and also a disorientation so huge he almost vanishes into it. His world, including the self whose coherence he now understands to have been forged in a slow accumulation of years, comes shelving vertiginously away from him. He is there, with her, feverishly so, but even that intensity of presence cannot eradicate the eerie sensation that whoever this is happening to, this weird and tumultuous human thing, it cannot be him. A passion of bewilderment envelops him.

This, at least, is how I remember the scene, though I won't vouch for my memory. I know I read it with a flash of belated recognition.

Not long after my sushi dinner, out at a bar for the birthday of some Portland friend, I meet a lawyer in town, a friend of friends, and we begin, I suppose you'd say, dating. That is, we go out to dinner, we go to parties, we go dancing. She introduces me to places in Portland, this lovely little city all of twenty miles down the road from the college, that I have somehow never truly seen. She is, Cecily, kind and sharp-witted, a winning kind of caustic. I find I have a surprisingly great deal to say to her, as little of which as possible—which, still, is undoubtedly too much—is about Evany, infidelity, divorce, the girls. And I find, too, a great deal of curiosity about what she'll say back, how she'll take up a question, in what directions her humor turns, and when.

We talk a lot, at high velocity, about whatever is near to hand to speak of: labor law, the new era of indie-rock dance bands, baseball. The key of it is often good-spirited disagreement. I pronounce myself to be a Yankees fan, born and bred; she begins wearing her Red Sox hat when we go out to bars.

I tell my California confidante Beth after the first date that I very badly want to kiss her, but cannot begin to imagine how to do so, since for all I know she does not want to kiss me, and the last, the fucking *last* thing I want to turn into is a guy who presumes his own attractiveness, to anybody.

"If you're worried," Beth says, "why don't you say something like, 'You know, I'd really like to kiss you'?"

Wait. What?

"Dude, say, 'I'd like to kiss you.' And then, you know, see what she says."

To this day I think this may be the single greatest piece of practicable sex advice I have ever been given.

And so, that night, on a walk beside the ocean in the clichéd moonlight, I say something like this, and there we are, Cecily and me, making out in the wet salt air.

It is exhilarating, surprising, and almost limitlessly strange.

A COUPLE OF WEEKS go by. We do an awful lot of sleeping together.

LET ME SAY: when I describe this as the dawning of the era of low-consequence bad decisions what I mostly mean is the bad decision I am making to pretend that I am capable of sustaining even the most basic level of functional intimacy. Cecily has greater purchase on this fact than I. In the middle of one of our first nights she looks over at me and says, more sweetly than you'd imagine, "Listen, I like you—but." A direct gaze. "You're going to need to go away and get yourself mixed up with, like, half a dozen people at least before you'll be any real good to anybody."

I report this to Beth, and she says, "I *like* this girl."

So do I. But producing a sensible account of exactly *why* I do proves trickier by far than, say, making another date. She is very lovely and very smart—wordy and a little combative, like me— and very delightful. In her regard for me I notice that there is an unsurrendered wariness—I am nothing if not a good occasion for wariness—but this she wears as something so much nearer to curiosity, bemusement even, that what I find in her company is mostly a beguiling quantity of warmth. The hours passed in her company trip along and when I am inside them the air comes in and out of my lungs without much in the way of struggle. That in itself marks these hours off as *very different* from most of the rest of my days. But is that a reason to like somebody? She texts me, sends joke-heavy e-mails, even makes me a few mixes for my drives up and down the coast, and all of this, in the speed of only a couple of weeks, I find I enjoy very much.

But I have room to wonder if what I most like is the way her attention, the pleasure she seems to take in my frayed company, arrives to me as a kind of antidote, a crack in the solidifying conviction that I have been exposed to the world as unlovable.

Evidently for the first time, I consider the possibility that you do not do a person the greatest of kindnesses by making her into a cure, your own personal antivenom.

WHATEVER THE SEX I am suddenly inclined to have, or to commence imagining I might have, I find that, as the last days of my time in Maine come upon me, I am alas no nearer to cogency or coherence. The fogs of unreality that surround me seem rather to be growing less and less navigable, for reasons that are, glumly, non-sex-related. There are facts to be faced—departure, the mechanics of *divorce*, a life requiring ongoing maintenance—and these blossom daily into fresh occasions for incredulity.

There is for me, however, a strange cushioning set of circumstances, and these I should explain.

As a condition of staying at the college, and of not taking that other fancy job, I had been granted an extended sabbatical leave: three consecutive semesters. This meant, practically speaking, that I was staring down the barrel of nearly twenty months without teaching, with no place I am required to show up, with nothing to do but collect my pay wherever I may be and research and write my next book. In normal circumstances, this is a *dream*, an outrageous once-in-a-career gift of time.

Of course, nothing about my circumstances feels to me normal in the least.

My friends, in Maine and elsewhere, speak in one voice: Get out, they say. Go far. See the world! Meet some new people and, maybe, while you're there, have sex with some subset of them. *Pursue some restorative derangements of spirit,* they tell me. And then come home.

I hear this so often, from far as well as near—I hear it refracted through Cecily's insistence that many strange bedrooms stand between me and recovery—that I begin to give myself over to it. I talk, I scheme. I make what we all decide to call "plans," though they feel to me like gossamer fancies. A few weeks in New York. Some months in Europe—ah, that old story: Old World cures for American malaise.

"Be the ingénue you never were!" Beth tells me.

Okay, I think. Sure. That could be me.

Even the girls take part. "Oh!" Lucy says on the phone to me. "You *always* talk about how much you wanna go to Italy!" The speed with which she enters into this fragile theater of optimism, of hopes for an unsorrowing future for my life, about undoes me.

A loose itinerary presently comes into focus. I will spend the summer in New York. In the fall I will visit with family in Italy and then travel about a bit. In the winter I'll make my way to the familiar faces, the old haunts, of Chicago. Okay, I think. Sure.

I say the names of the places, one by one, like a little novena, trying to make them spark with good feeling. Nothing lights up.

OF COURSE THE PROBLEM here is not really these places, or the prospect of travel, and even less is it Cecily herself, from whom I am soon to part for, as we take to saying, the Open Road. On one of the mixes she puts a song I've never heard, and I listen to it driving down along the coast to see her, the ocean to my left in summertime tranquility, the islands forest-green, the car still carrying inside it a sweet smell, though now more an undercurrent, of whatever sticky candy the girls spilled or stuck to the upholstery on some ordinary afternoon now irretrievably past.

Two whispery voices, young women in unison then in chiming harmony, sing to me:

> *If you see these tears filling my eyes*
> *It's just the wind that makes me cry*
> *If you could feel this pain inside . . .*

It goes on heavy rotation, this ballad of misrecognition, tranced-out heartache, narcotized sorrow. I come to love it—genuinely to *love* it—and this proves to be its own kind of affirming. I decide to take it, my heart-filled susceptibility to this song with an unimprovable title (it's called "The Drinks We Drank Last Night"), as the smallest of signs that the mechanism of attachment to life is not, in fact, smashed beyond all functioning.

But it seems, too, this little pop song tracing out the drifts of spirit toward oblivion, to give voice to a tangle of problems only now presenting themselves. Here, with Cecily, had been my first encounter with the question that was to bedevil me much further into the future than I could have guessed, that would fill so much of the open space of my rootless year.

What *were* other people, anyway?

What were they for? What did I want from them? How had I learned to want those things?

What, actually, had happened to me?

8

All the Wine

AND SO, JUST like that, I am excised from the life of Maine, its daily mixing of misery and fragile optimism, and catapulted into the heat and tumult of the New York City summer. It does, the city, exactly what you'd hope it would.

One afternoon only a few weeks into my stay, I find that I am not brooding about the divorce to come, its awful legalities, the unraveling absence of the girls, any of the malign invitations to obsessiveness. I am not moony in the least, or sad! I am happy rather to be possessed by one thought, crystalline and bright, and one thought only.

I am thinking: *The drugs are not wearing off.*

A YOUNGER ME, I know, would've long before sunk into panicky paranoiac dread. Back in my later teenage years I'd somehow been persuaded to attend a Grateful Dead show, at motherfucking *Giants Stadium*, and it was in that snug, stress-free environment that I first decided to drop acid, resulting predictably in what was about nine, though it felt nearer to seventy, hours of garish high-density nightmare. Ever since, I had been a committed drinker.

But here and now, at a high summer Afro-pop show in Brooklyn, in the far chiller atmosphere of lovely Prospect Park, with the sun shining and my brilliant young friend Joseph glazed and grinning beside me, nothing at all seems especially amiss. These are far less lively drugs, it's true—Ecstasy and Adderall, producing in combination a mostly euphoric haze of vision, sharpening at its edges toward clarity—and in any case it must be that the prospect of being mired interminably in just this chemically italicized state of consciousness, as opposed to any other I might inhabit, troubles me at the moment very little indeed.

"You good?" Joseph semi-shouts, over the undulating sound of the band, as Brooklynites mill about us in varied states of summery undress.

I smile back into his smile, glassy and content. I nod.

NEW YORK IN THE SUMMER, as you may know, is its own sort of sensory derangement. The furnace room swelter, the swamp of smells, the incalculable variety of human irritation. A rich terrain for the pursuit of decisions moderately to more substantially bad.

I am staying with Joseph and he is for me an odd sort of benefactor, though he seems to experience our reversal of roles without perceptible uneasiness. Not that I had ever been his benefactor, exactly, though I had understood myself, at least for a little while, to be the one looking after *him*. He had been among my first-ever students at the college, and one of a handful of young friends I knew from their collegiate years, now embarked upon city lives of an astonishing variety and vibrancy. Together, with Joseph taking the lead, they have been caring for me in these, the first days of my long seasons of postdivorce drifting. And they have been doing so with such deliberateness and patience—a delicacy of touch, a wariness of harm—that I feel a wondering kind of gratitude toward them. It is, I know, nothing I would have been able to accomplish at their age.

Somewhere, hidden among keepsakes resigned now to the dark of a storage space, is a picture of the group of these kids at our wedding reception—Joseph, Chad, Molly, Abby, Willing, the lot of them—cleaned up and snazzy, standing drunk and entwined and listing over with laughter as the party, a background blur of smudged color, goes dancing on around them.

It is, in these days of reeling summer enjoyment, hard to think about.

Here in the city, though, Joseph especially has been laboring to convince me that there is a galaxy of things to feel that are *not* shame. Mostly this has meant that we spend the days a sunlit and bar-hopping kind of drunk, though we have made ventures into more distant precincts of insobriety. I tell him about Evany, the preparator, the girls. I tell him, in halting little fragments, about Cecily.

Meanwhile, though, through all these turns, Joseph has been his own adjacent kind of intoxicated.

Joseph is newly, brand-newly, in love.

He has reencountered an old friend and has fallen into bed with her and, with a swift sense of rushing downstream, into some new territory of radiance quite apart from any he's known before. He is so in love he shines, with or without chemical enhancement.

He told me over late-night eggs at some Midtown diner, excited—you could see—just to be saying the words. "Hey," I said, "I'm really proud of you."

And it's such an incongruous, such an unearned thing to feel! Joseph only grinned back at me, holding his sense of amazed good fortune close to him, a little shyly.

But the truth is I'm proud of *all* of them, this whole gang of young people navigating their twenties with a grace, a want of fumbling ineptitude, that had been no part of my own. Their care is so winning, and not only in its drunker dimensions. On the weekend I arrived—a weekend that portended only disaster, tears, a reckless indulgence in high-style misery—they'd conjured tickets for us to see a big show on the SummerStage in Central Park.

"You have to come out with us," Joseph had said.

It was the weekend, God spare me, the very fucking day, of my wedding anniversary.

They'd all known this.

"It'll be great," Joseph assured me. "You should come."

Inevitably, the band in question was the National.

AND SO, ON A BREEZY and warm August evening, we trundle into the park together and sprawl on blankets spread across the overcrowded artificial turf. We drink beer and, with halfhearted efforts at furtiveness, get high. The scene is alive for us with ambient hilarity. There are the hipster stylings. The spazzy high school kids. The reprieved parents, metering out babysitter time. In ways less aggravating than it ought to be, everything seems an overrealized version of itself, the people, the scene, the city itself coming into its evening glow around us.

At some point somebody hears a rumor, which proves to be true, that Jay-Z and Beyoncé are somewhere in the crowd, and this somehow invests us with the sudden sense of having been blessed, touched and anointed, as by beneficent royalty.

And, then, the show.

The band stalks through their set and even through the twilit summer pleasantness, the mild haze of drugs and drink, you can tell they are *amped*, coiled and electric. The set kilters this way and that, gathers tension, accelerates. They close out with "Mr. November"—*"I won't fuck us over / I'm Mr. November / I won't fuck us over"*—and behind them the iconic Shepard Fairey print of Obama pulses and glows. Everyone goes wild.

And I confess: the wretchedness I keep waiting for, the bile and the breathlessness and the bent-over grief, does not arrive. I go astoundingly long passages without remembering that it is my anniversary, or following that thought down any of the predictably day-ruining paths. I am happy to be among just these people, an element in lives so vibrant. Something about the company, and the knit-together atmosphere of unrushed pleasure we've made for one another, makes it possible for me actually to *enjoy* them, these so freighted songs. The simple fact that I am hearing them more with delight than lucid misery fairly astonishes me. In the middle of "All the Wine," just after the singer says, *"I'm so sorry but the motorcade'll have to go around me this time,"* Joseph turns back to me, his look suspended for a second, quizzical. And then you see it click. He has, as if for the first time, heard the line. He beams and beams at me, and I beam right back.

It's possible for these long moments to let the low-grade magic of the loud live show do its work, to surrender to the warming fantasy that this is my scene, these are my people. It's possible to feel for a bewitched instant or so that I *belong* here, among these strangers edging toward a shared euphoria, and perhaps even in this city, which I cannot help but experience, in a moment-to-moment way, as a monument to the sheer inexhaustibility of human desire. (Need an emblem of the towering immensity of worldly striving? GO TO NEW YORK.) I know it won't last, this song-induced contortion of thought away from broken pasts and inconceivable futures, and it doesn't. But the elation is real enough for me. I ride it like a long breaking wave.

≈

AND SO, JUST ABOUT A WEEK later, here are Joseph and I: playing once more the role of concertgoers, working up an imitation delirium, a euphoria by other means.

A fun fact about the drug combination we are now pursuing: it ramps up, rather than chastens, the impulse to *talk*. Drinking, I explain to Joseph, in an unpunctuated torrent, has always appealed to me not least for its heralded tongue-loosening propensities. Whereas drugs have tended to work on me more like, say, a stupefacient. I tell him the college story of watching John, deep in some club-drug paroxysm, crouch for long minutes in front of a gigantic dance hall speaker and, with a dilated blankness of gaze, stare wonderstruck into the terrible throbbing heart of its subwoofer. "He was like a cat staring at a wall," I say. "If that cat had just gotten super fucking high." Like many other children of the '90s, I could recall, in visions not nearly as clouded as you'd wish, the epic grinding laboriousness of trying, as we were all evidently obliged to do, to have sex on Ecstasy. An experience not especially joyful, for anybody, as I remember it. But this, I burble along, is so much better!

"The Adderall," Joseph says, loops of melodic guitar swirling around his words. "It really helps."

"It does."

"Yeah, it does."

"No, it does."

"Adderall's great. It's like Willing says. It makes you feel like you can do anything . . . *except eat*."

Haaaa-ha-ha-ha. Etc.

We walk about. We talk in percussive bursts. We leave the show and mill around the park and drift in the tides of pedestrians. We are angling back through Brooklyn.

But then, with no particular prompting, Joseph turns to me.

He is shiny eyed. His face is lit up with kindness, though I suppose it might just be the drugs. All the same, I take him in like a snapshot: here is a young man so transparently in love, so blindsided and amazed, that you can see it radiating off him in waves. It settles around him, I swear to you, like a cloak of brilliant light.

"You taught me a lot about loving things," he says.

I don't begin to know what to say to him.

I know—high as I am, still, I know—that I have been trying to perform an inverted kind of magic. I have come to New York, and have been trying and trying to make myself vanish, to disappear into a place exactly vast enough to make any grief brought to it seem only a trick of perception after all, a misapprehension of scale. But my grief is no such thing. It is not a trick. I have, I know, lost *everything*. And there appears to be no delirium large enough—not even the delirium called New York City—to hide me away from the desolation of it.

I look back at Joseph, all my talk gone dry.

"You don't think it matters," he says. "But it does."

MAYBE HE'S RIGHT. The city summer, at any rate, has a few more intoxicants reserved for me before I depart for my next adventures, which are to take me across the ocean, to Italy, to family, to the enduring monuments of Europe.

In a Carroll Gardens bar one afternoon I fall to talking with a bartender who recognizes me from the crowd at the National show. I find this disarming and delighting. After maybe an hour of what is, on my end at least, pitifully unpracticed flirtatiousness, I give her my number. Later she texts and just like that we have made a date for the next night, at a bar just across the street. This actually happens: I am in such a state of nerve-jangled astonishment about it that I demand Joseph accompany me to the appointed bar, early.

"Okay. Why, though?"

"Could you just make sure nothing's, like, *weird*?"

What sort of intervention would be preferred, if needed, we never manage to say. He agrees, stipulating only that I buy, and that he is my first postdate call.

My date arrives. We talk as we did the day before. No disaster ensues. At some moment I don't notice, Joseph departs. She and I make our cheerful conversational way.

We go back, a few bars and many hours later, to the place where I'm apartment-sitting. A happy night transpires, a tiny blinking node in the vast circuitry of the city's carnal life. The next afternoon she texts to ask if I've left yet, and if not do I want to come by her place for a few hours while her roommate goes out on a date? And this is how I find myself in a windowless Boerum Hill garden apartment, sober as a judge this time, trying nevertheless to make consciousness click back into some more accustomed state.

"Hey," she says, looking down at me, her hands pressing on my shoulders. She's petite, has a pale round face, these laughing dark eyes, her hair a great controlled chaos of ringlets. "You're lovely."

And you want to know from pathetic? I'll tell you. She says this, and I take it in like a long indrawn breath. I have to *concentrate* on not dissolving into the stupid amazement of it. Instead I let my mind fold it up and tuck it safely away.

A few hours later I am walking up Court Street, which at the moment I am having trouble making seem anything but a gauzy fantasia. The lights, the flowing crowds, the beckoning restaurants and bars. Everything is wrapped, once again, in a pleasing unreality that will take some time to dissipate.

We are not boys much given to locker-room explicitness,

Joseph and I. (My best, most photo-realist sex talk was to be reserved for Dana, for Beth, for the politburo of queer ladies looking after the errant trajectories of my postdivorce intimate life.) Discreetly, Joseph asks instead what I think I'll most remember from my first-ever New York one-night stand, extended into two. I cannot bring myself to tell him the truth, to say out loud to him what she said in that one instantly archived moment. So I tell Joseph about how, on our first long blurred night, she started nudging me over on my side at one point, lifting my arms, turning my wrists over in her hands.

"Hey—what're you doing?" I asked.

"Looking for secret tattoos."

Joseph *loves* this. "Oh, man," he says. "Welcome to your twenties, I guess."

9

On the Mouth

WHAT ARE OTHER PEOPLE? What are they for?

The question finds me in a café in East Berlin. It is a bright October morning, all high clouds and brisk radiance—the previous day, at a bustling flea market of improvised stalls assembled on the grounds of a soccer arena, I made the next of what would be several European scarf purchases—and I am scribbling in a notebook, a pack of cigarettes angled invitingly toward me on the table. I am trying to finesse into coherence the last weeks of travel, which in time I will come to think of as my European journeys of failed recovery.

They have seen so much: train stations and hostels, meals to be dreamed of later on underfed nights, a truly massive download of beauty. With these, too, an almost schizophrenic toggling of spirits. One day, amid a crowd of cousins in Naples, drinking watery beer in a roadside bar halfway up the sloping side of Mt. Vesuvius, my mood had been running near on to jubilant. Two days later and I was zombied, glassy-eyed and desolate, following every thought through to its most self-harming extension and pleading with no one in particular to please, somehow, make it *stop*. The ease with which a violence of dejection returns to me, the startling variability of my moods, is a kind of mystery to me, a sentence I cannot parse. I try to write it into sense.

What I think to write, this morning, is: *I have started smoking*.

And it's true. I'm not sure you'll have been to Berlin before. I had not. East Berlin, where I'm staying, is fascinating. I keep sniffing the air for the residues, the ghostly presences, of decades trapped inside a particularly vivid form of totalitarian absurdity. They are harder to detect than I thought they might be. The neighborhoods I wander in and out of are instead a not unfamiliar subspecies of *cool*: young, leafy, stately, Georgian you'd even say, though, as I'm finding with all things German, a small bit of weird as well. More hippies among the hipsters than I would have expected—the blond-dreadlock and ferret-having demographic, if you know what I mean—and then, too, across all sectors of life in public, there is a bearing, a certain severity of manner, that is so utterly predictable and predicted that it's hard not to delight in it.

Also, every man, woman, and child in Berlin smokes. Without visible exception. As if in obedience to some civic edict or, I don't know, zoning requirement. It is the smokingest place on earth, so far as I can tell, and I have just come from southern Italy, a place not known for its abstemiousness. I go maybe eighteen hours until, with a small inward sigh of *fuck it*, I buy some Marlboros in a barroom vending machine and take my place among the *Volk* and *Kinder*. There's a moment of inebriate rush to it, that comes as much from the illicit thrill of smoking indoors as from the frazzling nicotine buzz, though of course mostly it ends up feeling terrible.

Buzz, nausea, buzz, nausea. It's good, I suppose, to have adopted so perfect an emblem for these unsteadied, semischizoid days.

Stumped, wordless, I stop pretending to write. I light up indulgently. Whereupon I tumble headlong into the other of my growing stupid compulsions.

Somewhere along the route of these allegedly restorative travels I've developed the habit of falling fitfully in love with strangers. Bartenders, subway riders, slender men in beautiful scarves knotted with impossible intricacy. Italians washed in warming bar light, Germans in café morning glow . . . I see all of them through the haloing blur of my lovelorn ill-spiritedness. It is exactly as sad as it sounds and it is, for me, irresistible. A shopgirl's smile blossoms a little more warmly than professional courtesy demands and in an instant the machinery of daydreaming begins its ridiculous hum and whir.

Across from me now, for instance, is a young woman out with someone who is or is not her boyfriend, Germans both, thirtyish, engaged in cross volleys of smiling talk that, because it is incomprehensible to me, seems cheerful and flirtatious. She is not overly tall. She has this great bowlish haircut, dyed a stylish citrusy blond, and lovely flecked brown eyes. She talks and she sips a coffee. Her hands move in a fluttering blur, though she does not touch the young man seated across from her. She's wearing what I can only think of as a *Flashdance* sweater, cut open asymmetrically around the collar and arms, and as it dips periodically off one bare shoulder she shrugs it back into place.

She smiles a lot. Her cheekbones are as high as alps.

All at once, my heart aches.

There I sit, feeling a guilty conspicuousness for having noticed this much in a person not after all on display for my delectation, or anybody's. But the radiance of her smile, the brightness of her gaze across the table, the pleasure she exudes . . .

I am a knotted tangle of unclarified wishes.

I can't look, and I can't not look.

They continue their amiable animated chatter. I smoke. In a few moments all my interior discordances at last resolve themselves into coherence.

I give way to an immense and voracious loneliness.

That is all it is, not a thing else. It is like a sea I keep pitching myself into.

What has happened to me? What's going to happen?

ITALY HAD BEEN A MARVEL. You might reasonably suppose this was because of the inarguable marvelousness of Italy—the climate, the food, the people, the offhand ravishingness of everything—but you'd be only partially right.

I spent all of my time in Naples, among extended family there. I had been before, as a child on a once-ever family trip, from which my strongest memory was the fear that the mountain looming out all the windows, the *volcano*, would come to sudden murderous life. Despite the fact that I'd seen these people, these cousins many times removed and second-nieces and great-aunts, only a very few times, and that years ago, they welcomed me like some kind of deposed prince regent, at last restored. I was never to be hungry. I was never to be alone. Cousins rallied around me, introduced me to their friends, and though my Italian was pitiable, a halting morass of misremembered phrases and unconjugated verbs, we soon worked our way into revelry, and then something better.

On my first full-family evening, I show everybody pictures of the girls, to whom I am writing a stream of brief touristy letters and sending the occasional especially scenic picture.

One cousin, Rosaria, tells me Lucy looks like me, and I discover I can't properly explain, because I don't know the word for *stepparent*. When through a variety of patchwork lexical fixes I manage to convey I am neither Lucy's nor Amelia's father as such, Rosaria gives me a puzzled look and shakes her head. Of course she knows that. That's not what she means.

Whether it is coordinated or not, I can't say, but I soon come to see that theirs is a campaign of consolation through absorption.

In talk, in food, in the intricacies of a language not my own. Above all there is Naples itself, chaotic, criminal, hot, foul, carnal, gorgeous, Naples. I walk in the downtown precincts with my cousins and the streets are convulsed by these huge flows of people and machinery, all acting in accord with some internal principle of order that is, to me, wholly inscrutable. The dichotomies are unreal. No matter where you are, the landscape pulls you toward one or another variety of exaltation: the sea, Capri, the glittering lights of the city hugging the harbor, Vesuvius presiding massively behind it all. Your thoughts are forever vaulted skyward. At the same time, everything about *life* in Naples pulls you militantly down, toward the heat and tumult of carnal existence, the desiring life of the flesh. The ugly housing blocks, the trash, the casually furious arguments in the street, the selling and the buying, the meats and the fish and the caffeine. The unfettered lawlessness of the Vespas. You're pulled violently up and down at once, and the mix is intoxicating. Florence may be lovely, and Venice is a jewel. I'd take Naples.

My family fits here and so, they have been suggesting to me, do I. I give way, for a while, to the impulse to believe them.

One day my cousin Gennaro—the husband of my blood cousin, a little younger than I, movie-star handsome, and in possession of almost no English whatsoever—takes a day off working as a customs agent in the port, and just like that we're on a ferry skimming across the Bay of Naples to Capri, where we spend the day among vistas of Mediterranean beauty so postcard bright and gaspingly extreme I keep stopping to laugh. I feel like a misplaced extra in a Fellini film. We have spent virtually no time alone in one another's company before today, and we speak, Genni and I, at what must be no better than a third-grade level. No matter. By the end of the trip out to the island he's catching me up on family gossip, asking me about my marriage, suggesting what would be for me a better shade of scarf.

I say what I can.

I have not yet learned how to tell the story of my disaster in the key of downbeat domestic comedy. So, pretending a little less than I usually try to, I tell him mostly I'm afraid. I tell him I'm afraid sometimes I'll never stop being sad. I tell him I'm afraid that, maybe, I've spoiled being alive. I tell him that, despite everything, I still miss Evany terribly, all the time.

But then I go on.

"Genni," I say, and haven't the least idea if he can understand me. "I had these little girls. And now I've lost them."

The Mediterranean is a dreamy expanse of twinkling blue. I keep talking.

I say, "And now . . . I'm not sure I loved them enough. When I had the chance."

Immediately after I utter this, this thought I had not known I had, the truth of it comes collapsing in upon me. My heart feels heavy.

I say, "I'm really afraid."

He does not try to dissuade me, only makes a shrugging half-frowning nod—a paradigmatically Neapolitan gesture—and says he recognizes the feeling. His father died, suddenly, three years ago.

He tells me the next time I come to Naples it will be because I am in love.

ON MY LAST NIGHT Roberto takes me to the Vomero, in the center of the city, to watch Napoli play someone . . . Juventus, maybe? Torino? Some team they are not supposed to beat. We sit, a dozen of us, in a basement bar. Before the match starts they present me with a team scarf, dusty blue and white and inscribed NAPOLI, and this I wear throughout the night, in a knot that, once back in America, will impress everyone with its Laocoönian complexity. I am embraced, I am kissed, drinks appear before me in unbroken succession. (There is wine, then beer, and then, later, some ghastly hazelnut liqueur, the effects of which will prove to be impressively malign.) *"Lui è mio fratello Americano!"* Roberto hollers to all the strangers in our orbit. Through some extra-time heroics I no longer recall, Napoli wins, and the jubilation expands and intensifies and finally overflows. We spill into the streets, which are madness, and I follow along, arms hooked in arms, as everybody sings club songs I don't understand.

Later, six or so of us confined to a car of about the dimensions of a washing machine, the singing continues. We try out American staples. I lead us through AC/DC, Madonna, an unexpected burst of Hall and Oates. *"Pri-i-vate eyes! They're watching you!"* We are a traffic-stopped karaoke bar. And then Roberto hushes everyone. He puts a track on the car stereo that, within seconds, I can tell is dear to them all, important in ways both private and shared. It's an Italian pop-rock song and I will confess to being surprised that, despite this, there is in it none of the clumsy amateurishness I tend to identify, maybe a bit too readily, with Euro pop. It has a perfectly serviceable rock-radio production, layered and clean, and is sung by a man with a lowish resonant hum of a voice, stagy and a bit self-regarding. I swear he sounds like no one so much as an Italian Neil Diamond, the notion of which causes me to think, *Jesus, imagine the pants*.

The man is called Ligabue—the cry goes up in the car, *"Ah, Ligabue!"*—and the song is "Il Mio Pensiero," which of course I don't know at the time, or even after it is played through three or four times on repeat as we climb back toward Ercolano. I learn this only when Roberto gives me back my iPod the next morning, to which he has somehow managed to add the song, so that it might accompany me on my subsequent travels. I play it enough to memorize some lines in the chorus, and puzzle them out:

E adesso che sei dovunque sei
Chissà se ti arriva il mio pensiero ...

Now, wherever you are, I wonder if my thoughts arrive to you ...
It's a good way to remember the Italian you've learned, Roberto
tells me, and then, with a half-frowning nod, kisses me good-bye.

IT SHOCKS ME, honestly, how quickly a sense of being attached
to the world can disintegrate. Long before I arrive in Berlin, long
before I decide to improve my impulse toward desolation through
the addition of nicotine-fueled jitteriness, I find myself slipping
from my own grasp.

An afternoon spent in a Florentine square about undoes me.
I'm trying as ever to write in my little notebook of sorrows, to
nudge into syntax the flaring desolation that memory, that
thought itself, seems continually to occasion. Scratch, scratch,
scratch. It's a warm Italian early fall, which is to say the square
does not want for travelers, tourists, students, diners, passersby
in infinite conjugations. All at once I am besieged by the inescapable fact of *couples*. They seem, suddenly, the element of
which the world is made. These vacationing English sightseers
canoodling over their map, these slitheringly entwined young
Italians, these well-fed American pairs. I look at them, on relent-
less parade, and as they pass one by one all I can think is, *How did
that happen?* How, in the gargantuan and chaotic world, did you
manage to effect so improbable a connection? How did it happen
to you and how is it possible that it's happened so often and to,
evidently, everybody?

Look at the life of this square. All those held hands, all
those palms sunk in the back pockets of somebody else's jeans—
all those tables shared, those meals enjoyed in idle chat, the

infinitesimally small gestures of affection exchanged and registered and registered and forgotten. People! I want to shout. This is *it*! This is the whole deal. You are in the realm of the blessed! You are enjoying more or less as much of grace as the world can give! Stop, slow down, savor, *notice*!

It would appear that I have become lonely as through a kind of terrible metamorphosis, some cruel enchantment. I have become lonely with the certainty that loneliness—this unrelieved separateness from the world—has become for me not a state but a *condition*, an unalterable fact of being.

Nothing about this bodes well.

I VISIT FAR-FLUNG FRIENDS. I haunt the cities of Europe— from Italy to Berlin, from Berlin to Paris—a spectre of bourgeois indolence, sorrow, and self-pity. I arrive in Paris only to realize that this, going to Paris, is a *grave error*. If you want to curtail your habit of falling in love with passing strangers, allow me to suggest you avoid Paris. The effortlessness with which Parisians carry off any imaginable stitch of clothing is, in itself, enough to undo me. The men, the women, everyone. The gathered fall of a scarf, piled in impossible elegance around someone's shoulders, propels me into these stupid little frenzies of unreciprocated ardor. It is a city of detailed majesty and somber exhilarations— the fog-swept squares, the cold soaring stone—and everywhere I go, in this most romantic cityscape on the face of the fucking planet, the air fairly crackles with the sound of all the sex I'm not having.

Onward. I ride on trains, write letters longer than they are truthful, and begin my reacquaintance with the delicate art of sitting alone at a bar and not seeming creepy as fuck. In the long hours of bar sitting, strolling through cities, inexpertly navigating every variety of transit, I think about everyone I've slept with or kissed or otherwise conjured up some reciprocal and at least moderately erotic attachment to. I write down their names, listwise, a sad little Whitmanian poem. All my thwarted little devotions, I pour out hour by hour into the "shuffle" function of the iPod, for which I develop an outsized gratitude. I sink for a while into the ill-advised habit of writing letters to Evany, though these I find the sense not to send. I speak to fewer and fewer people, go at last days on end without exchanging words with anyone not involved in a commercial transaction, and smoke with what I hope appears to strangers to be philosophic intensity.

I kiss no one and no one kisses me.

FINALLY, FINALLY, on a night in Madrid, something shifts.

I go to see a band called the Wedding Present, who by blind luck are playing a show just after I arrive. The evening proves to be a joy much grander than anticipated, a sustained immersion in something very much not misery. This is relieving, of course, and exhilarating and, if only by force of contrast, restorative. But it dawns on me later, as in the morning glare I prowl around the streets of a neighborhood called Chueca in search of caffeine and salted meats to apply medicinally to my hangover, that I have encountered a new possibility.

For the first time in months I have been alone and also, for an impressive stretch of minutes, undemolished. I have been, in fact, alone and ecstatic. And while it's true that standing in a pressed mass of concertgoers singing along to the indie rock hits of your youth stretches to fineness any definition of *alone*, still I am willing to mark this evening on the calendar of my heart.

Something about that night starts murmuring to me. I cannot quite make out what it's trying to say, but I'm paying enough attention to note that, whenever it speaks, it does not speak in the voice of harm.

In the immediate aftermath of this two things happen.

In walks that grow more unmapped and elaborate as the impulse to sit moonily in cafés gradually recedes, I begin to discover in the recesses of the iPod a novel sensation. One morning I make myself go to the Prado—museums remain a kind of toxic space to me—and afterward, as I walk around the city in expanding concentric circles, there is a blip in the algorithm, one of those unlooked-for microrevelations. By pure accident, I find myself listening to an uninterrupted succession of these high-tempo rockers, all screams and shredding guitars. It's as if someone's set the program to SPEEDY POSTPUNK FREAKOUTS. Here's another, then another, then another.

And what begins to glow within me then, and eventually to catch fire, is different from the live-show exhilaration that had visited me at the Wedding Present gig.

There's this Superchunk B side called "On the Mouth" for which I long treasured up a great deal of affection. It's a breakup song, but one that I'd always figured was just too rancorous to make it onto any record. It is velocity, noise, and bile. There is not much else.

But this, it proves, is *plenty*. Because there in Spain, in the long sunlight of an autumn afternoon, it seizes me, this song. (*"Five minutes on the phone and I'm completely sick,"* is how it begins . . .) It lifts me up. It rattles and it blares and it wraps me in an embrace so voluptuous that it feels, I swear, absolutely as exhilarating as making out with someone.

I hit repeat and repeat and repeat.

What is this? I wonder. This catapulting violence of sensation? And then I think: Oh. This is *anger*.

It riots its way through me, a pure adrenal rush, and my God does it feel good.

By the fourth listen I'm a junkie. *More,* I think, *now.* How have I gone so long without listening to Bad Brains? To some Archers of Loaf? What the fuck could Hüsker Dü records be for, if not for the nurturing of these propulsive euphorias of rage?

Here, then, is the second great thing that transpires in the warm afterglow of the Wedding Present show: mile upon striding mile, as I give myself over to these bursts of spazzy bilious noise, I find that they are not *just* ecstasies, not just three-minute reprieves from the hard labor of sorrow and self-contempt. All of that would be welcome enough. But they do something else too. My thoughts, which for so long had been traveling the well-worn circuits of recrimination, find themselves battered and contorted, propelled into new configurations.

For instance: that Evany has told me such egregious lies, one after another, begins to seem something I did not *cause* her to do. For instance: that she has moved this man, this ridiculous cow-eyed *stranger*, into the house she and the girls and I had dreamed up together, and built, and lived in, begins to form itself before me not only as an exquisite fucking torment—it is that, still— but, also, an outrage. For instance: that my life with the girls should be voided in exactly this way begins to appear a kind of travesty, as well as a heartbreak.

One by one, as if pulled in from some outer orbit, they come to me like flashing visitations.

For a long exhilarating moment, anger is entirely as real as grief.

And then, from inside it, coaxed out by songs made entirely of velocity and bile, some occulted possibilities begin to find a voice for themselves. They start speaking and speaking and what they say fairly astonishes me.

Perhaps, they say, you did not fail *quite so utterly* to love Evany.

Perhaps, they say, you did not fail *quite so utterly* to love the girls.

Perhaps, they say, these were parts of somebody else's story—parts of a fiction someone else needed to tell herself—that have tangled themselves around you, like rope.

There is nothing I need more, I know, than some other way of telling the story of the last year. Over these dour troubadouring days, that need has set in me like gnawing hunger, like an unmet yearning to be touched. So these possibilities, as they flare into consciousness, arrive as a kind of blurry elation, positively sex-like in its absorptions.

None of this stops me smoking or writing unmailable loss-blinded letters to Evany or falling in love with bartenders. But I look around me in Madrid—at the loud cafés, the twisting thoroughfares, the overspilling bars—and the light seems to have changed.

MY EURO-ADVENTURING at last complete, I travel to Maine to see the girls, which, after some tight-lipped negotiation with their mom, I am allowed to do. We plan a little night together, dinner out on this, our wee coastal town. It is now December, season of holidays and, additionally, of both of their birthdays, and we have not gone this long without being in each other's company since almost before they can remember. (It is now, I think balefully, just a little more than a year since Evany declared to me, *I've been unfaithful.*) Our reunion, though the source of swamping anxiety for me, proves to be as untroubled and as full of ordinary happiness as I could hope. I am carrying bagfuls of little presents and souvenirs, two birthday mixes, and a commitment to telling all the tales of my travels as small funny anecdotes, stories of missed trains and botched translations and silly happenstance. I tell them I missed them, which I have, and they are so themselves with me—delighted and offhand and jokey—that I spend the evening after they've gone home not sad but weeping all the same, filled with a stunned gratitude. *They are happy to see me*, I think, and it's a thought so radiant I can neither hold nor release it. I cry and cry.

We take about a million pictures. I show them some of me in Europe.

"Dude," Lucy says, observing one of me in front of some cathedral, "that color is, like, *really* good on you."

"Yeah," Amelia says. "You should maybe wear more green."

They talk a lot about my scarves, and as they do my heart is a paper lantern, filling with light.

To my friends, I say I think going to Europe was a good thing to *have done*, even if the signature experience of those weeks was of an incapacitating loneliness. A colleague at the college throws a big party on a snowy December night for my return, and dozens of our friends are there. We drink and we dance and there is an unestranged familiarity to it that's as warming as the bourbon. Someone takes a picture of me. I'm out on the porch, despite the cold, where I have come to smoke, wearing only a sports coat and, beneath it, the ass-kicking Wedding Present concert tee I procured for myself in Spain. In a halo of lamplight behind me there is a blur of angling snow. A cigarette dangles precariously from my mouth, because I'm about to laugh, and my hands are held together palm to palm, prayerlike, in a fully Neapolitan gesture of explanatory emphasis I seem to have acquired.

I'll spend a lot of time looking at it in the weeks ahead. Were you a stranger, you could easily look at this person—his gestures, his bearded grin, his expression of lit-up hilarity—and think, *He seems happy*.

10

The Boom on Mizar-5

BIRTHDAYS ARE FUNNY—until, of course, they're not. Now, thirty-eight: it is hardly the kind of traumatizing passage that requires ritual and high ceremony. For this I could only be grateful. What it mostly meant, I had taken to saying, was that I had come through thirty-seven and it hadn't, finally, killed me.

So, thirty-eight—twice nineteen! we kept saying—was a good occasion, a mark of the end of all that. Living had, in its dumb dogged way, gone on without me for a while, and waited for me to catch up. But now, here at my neighborhood North Side bar, John is insisting, I *had*. The paperwork, as the lawyers called it, had come through. With the turn of the new year, and still on sabbatical from teaching duties at the college, I had moved myself to Chicago and had been sinking deeper week by week into the pleasures of urban life in this, what I kept describing as America's Greatest City of Bars. I was writing, reading, and returning by small degrees to a life of scholarly diligence. I had appointments, assignments, deadlines.

I was also just then at juncture points in several affairs—dissolution, combustion, attenuation—and the days had acquired an intricacy that set them at some distance from the arid solitude of previous months of European misadventure.

And it was about to be my birthday.

"You know what this is?" John is saying, a stein of frothing kolsch in hand. "This is the season of triumph. This is the season of motherfucking *victory lapping*."

AND REALLY, who better than John to be riding out this milestone with? He had been the roommate assigned to me, by randomized computer lottery, back in freshman year of college, in one of those miraculous turns of machine-generated fate that caused me to pronounce, as often I did, that the algorithm was as much of God's grace as we were ever given to know in this broken mortal world. He had conjured me to Chicago. He had found an apartment for me on the North Side, right across the park from him and Karen, and most nights that winter had found me trekking there, a bottle in hand, to spend the hours around the table or getting their little boy into bed or just listening to records until exhaustion caught up with us. To have this much time with John and Karen, to be able to luxuriate in their company so greedily—it feels nearer to rescue than I like to admit.

But that was John: a rescuer. I would tell people that John was the friend that, in a just world, everyone would have, without exception. He is the person about whom you know there is nothing you can do, no version of yourself you might become, that would derail the unerring stridency of his love. And it is, that love, full of an easy grace. We do what are, on paper, the dullest things. We eat takeout. We take the kid to the playground, out to the bar for an early dinner. (Only one of the joys of Chicago: *kids in bars*.) We sit on barstools in taprooms up and down Lincoln Avenue and, when there is no place else to be, we listen to records.

When I'd showed up to college nearly twenty years before, eager but also twitchy with fear, John wasn't there. He'd arrived a few days before, set himself up, and hit the road to follow a touring band. (I *swear* it was the Jerry Garcia Band, though John would later dispute this.) He left a bed neatly made, a friendly note, a turntable, a minifridge containing eighty tabs of acid, and three crates of vinyl.

The acid did not outlast the semester. But the crates, the records, the whole atmosphere of brimming conviviality: these had survived, even if bruised a bit by estrangements and divorces—his, I'm sorry to say, had been no less a shock than mine—all the sadder transactions of grown-up life.

One slow March afternoon when the kid is home sick, John and I decide to play for him, in reverse chronological order, the complete discography of those greatest of '70s yacht rockers, Steely Dan. It's hard to say what prompts us to do this, but soon enough we fall into the project of *ranking* those records, and this, over what becomes days of deliberation and dispute, leads us down long winding paths of esoterica and hyperbole. We talk and talk, and it's all velocity and volume, cheerful counterfactuality, an easy shuttling between a style of largely absurdist speculation and swift descents into pockets of *very important assertion*.

"Do not fuck with me about *The Royal Scam*," he is saying. "I'm not even talking about 'Kid Charlemagne,' alright? I am talking about '*the boom on Mizar-5*.' Do *not* fuck with me on this."

Even as it's happening I am filled with the pleased sense that this is, in a phrase I learned in college from reading Faulkner, "the best of all talking." We are not as unselfconscious about it as once we were; we are staging these fights for one another, in some ways, certainly. But why would we not? It is how we build these little thoroughfares between our long past together and this, our middle-aged present. And, John keeps saying, our ample, open futures.

If the days in Chicago find me slightly less manic in bewildered sorrow, and more sensible of the possibility of a future consisting of something that is not grief, John is why.

Or most of why.

THEN, TOO, there are the affairs.

I am not yet able to rid myself of the vivifying delight that comes with the discovery that someone wants, actually, to fuck me. It happens and I feel lit up, filled with a pop-song-like radiance of heart. That delightedness makes me, in turn, ardent, intemperate, full of a gushy enthusiasm. I am, as dates go, *fun*. I spend a lot of nights dancing in bars. I talk and talk, with the unguardedness of rushed intimacy. Given my demographic and the general inarticulacy of dudes—given the habitual emotional unforthcomingness passed off as masculine stolidity—this makes me, I know, not the worst kind of object for an affair.

It does not, however, make me into a good boyfriend. Not by miles and miles.

I spend several steadying months in the company of a woman who lives in a nearby Midwestern city to the snowy north of my own, and our time together is all high points: passion and talk, extravagance and indulgence, pleasure first, last, and foremost. These are luminous weeks, a champagne winter. But I cannot sustain it. It all falls apart, or begins to, when I accompany her to a dinner party in her town. We are one of a few couples. There is pleasantry and wine, very little of the gossipy professional snark that can make such occasions so dour, and finally a good deal of amusement and warmth, all of it exchanged over hours around this table in a house far, far away from what had been my life. You'd have called it a lovely evening—I did, to our hosts, when we left, and I meant it.

But on the walk home, and then through the rest of the night and into the morning, my breath comes short and tight. Something like dread keeps fluttering past me, inexplicably, and the persistence of it sends me nearer to panic than I've been in some time. I can feel myself sinking into my own thoughts and these, in a bad little feedback loop, grow tangled. If my friend is exasperated—and I am at this point nothing if not steeply fucking exasperating—she doesn't show it. She is calming, and smart, and fantastically gentle. She reminds me that we had been behaving, that night, much like Evany and I must have behaved, at hundreds of dinner parties, over years of married life.

"There's no reason that wouldn't feel unsettling," she tells me. "Or at least very, very strange."

That she is right, and that she has read my enclosing fear back to me in the kindest and least shaming of ways, doesn't make it go away. Things soon begin to feel untenable to me. Gracelessly, hurtfully, I back away.

Later in the season I meet a woman in Chicago and something in me starts to uncoil. Here, too, is less a "relationship" than a series of elations, though they are different in tone and texture. It is she, Theo, who takes me home one night, to my blank astonishment—she is the bartender at a Bridgeport taproom to which John had introduced me, and where we would sometimes convene—and not many nights after this she looks at me and declares, "I need a springtime boyfriend."

Finally! A task for which I am perfectly qualified.

What this entails, almost exclusively, is being in bed together.

I find myself suddenly in the throes of something that is as much like my first summer with Evany as anything since then has been, a long dizzying blur of nights and unhurrying days. I walk around half-drunk with it, my thoughts tracing out a tight circuit between disbelief and vivid recollection. *Holy shit,* my mind says, *this is happening.* Every sensation soon resolves into renewed carnal impatience. The days feel cyclonic and, mostly, very, very good. Theo in turn becomes a type for the women I will, in subsequent years, keep falling hard for. She has blunt-cut bangs, a laugh that's barroom loud, an exquisite tattoo curling up one arm, elbow to shoulder, and another, a trellised vine rendered in greens and fractured blacks, winding down the opposite forearm and past her wrist. Trailing in her wake are a string of ex-girlfriends and ex-boyfriends. There is a lot of swagger in her manner—you can watch dudes coming into the bar and, with this kind of body-long double take, noticing her—but there is also, running through it all, a steeliness you would not be likely to miss. Even the sweetest of her affects, her smiles or her solicitous glances, have a hard glinting edge to them.

Why me? I think to ask one morning. Of all the men in that bar, unshy in their affections, why this professorial guy with the tweedy coat and the heartbreak story in his pocket? Across a little mountain of pillows she gives me a point-blank stare.

"Are you being serious?" she says. "It's *obvious*."

Astonish me, I say.

A long sigh. "I am the hard femme of your dreams, Peter." (She only ever calls me Peter.) "And you—you, sweet man, are one soft butch."

That hardness, the filthy laugh, the avariciousness—at first I think these are just things I've happened to discover I like, a lot. *How about that! Who knew?* Such a *departure*, I tell myself. Someone more rock 'n' roll than arty, younger rather than older, extroverted more than inward . . . I go on, congratulating myself on having put such distance between myself and the well-worn paths of desire.

But no. In the long charmed hours in her bedroom, across which her bed stands diagonally to all the walls, other congruencies begin to appear.

An inescapable fact about Theo is that she has had to fight a lot, and to kick a lot of ass, to become the person she is. Hers was not the easiest of lives to have emerged out of, let alone as a person so sturdy and self-collected. She'd had to stand up through the ordinary fires of familial tumult and disapproval but much else, too, even beyond the measure delivered to young women everywhere, as an ugly matter of course. That coming-through she wore in every part of herself, her laugh, the set of her shoulders, her voice. *None of you fuckers ruined me.* She carried it with her everywhere. She carried it with her, inevitably, into her bedroom. It is there we pass the better part of our hours together and these, for me, are edifying passages.

There's a sentence I would read in a novel years later: "every prohibition lost substance in her presence." That was Theo for me, precisely, and if I'm walking around half-drunk all the time, this is the intoxicant.

When we were splitting up Evany had said, in a phrase calculated to haunt my sleepless hours, that our sex life was, and I quote, "the least pathological part of our marriage." Which of course left me wondering dumbly why she'd gone and fucked someone else. It haunted me and haunted me, a roaring—half shame and half grief—always in my ears. Would sex, too, be a ruined thing?

With Theo, over the nights that turn into mornings that turn into afternoons, in the bedroom we conspire not to leave, one long-belabored sorrow begins to lose its voice.

LONG AFTER THE AFFAIR ends—and it ends just as it's meant to, with the season—the vision of it stays with me. I convince myself maybe I've fallen in love with Theo, though it is observed to me that maybe I have fallen in love with going to bed with Theo. Or, perhaps, with feeling desired by her just in the ways she makes vivid. There is a lot to this. We've listened to a great deal of Neko Case in her bedroom—she has a new record out—and what could be more apt? Neko is the great singer of desire in its most volcanic iterations. What she calls "that teenage feeling"? I am fucking awash in it. Because, truly, it *is* curative to be desired by Theo. "I wish I could go to Maine with you," she had said, "just so that woman can see me look at you." The feeling of being wanted, the delirium of it, the way it is all at once consolidating and undoing—it all comes back to me in an addling rush. I tell John I know the name for this feeling. I decide to call it *survival*.

But even as I'm disappearing myself into Theo's bed, even as Neko is singing of desire like a rampage, a tornado, a force that devours and destroys—even then, there are familiarities I can't push aside. I won't say Theo reminds me of Evany. *They are so different!* I observe to myself, as though this were an accomplishment. But she does recall to me that Evany, too, carried herself like a person who had survived something awful. Her circumstances were much, much easier—more propped up by upper-middle-class security, for instance—but she, too, had lived inside a difficult family, a larger world brimming with casual misogyny, a punishing adolescence. When I met her she might have said she had survived a grindingly bad marriage, as well as a storm of postpartum depressiveness, itself a bad echo of the miseries of her youth, which had been harrowing and scarring and full of a corroding shame. She had, she might have said, survived her own cruelest instincts toward herself.

I had found that heroic. I had found in the determined ferocity of that wish to be, finally, *happy* a sort of moral triumph that filled me with an admiration closer, on many days, to awe.

But as I carry on sleeping with Theo, feeling drunk on her desire, I begin to wonder if saying I "admired" this in Evany isn't, at the very least, distorting. I am after all *reveling* in my gig as Theo's springtime boyfriend. I am loving especially what I take to be the incongruousness of it. (Tell me, oh, please tell me again: *why me?*) Without anyone's permission I offer myself the role of "exception," the man not like other men, and walking through the early Chicago spring, visiting parks and bars and dance floors, I fucking delight in playing it.

Who does not want to play that role?

Neko is singing through all the days—*"My love, I am the speed of sound,"* she says—and in a slow and seeping way it begins to occur to me that if I'd loved that bravery in Evany, that drive toward a brighter self, I must have loved at least as much the role I'd scripted for myself in that beautiful drama. Who does not want to be the bringer of a happiness long desired? What could be more satisfying than the story that says, All that this battered pain-riddled person needs to break loose from her deep histories of shame and self-contempt is *me, my* love, *my* care, *my* body, *my* words?

Satisfying, I mean, for me.

Theo has nothing but articulate contempt for Evany. "After you're thirty," she says, "it's up to you to mind your fucking damage." She says this with such cold conviction that I cannot but take it seriously.

But I think, too, in terms a little less exonerating, that maybe my greatest mistake wasn't falling in love with Evany in the first place, which is the story that the voices of anger have been shouting at me for a restorative few months now. The engines of my indignation have of course continued to rev. But something else begins to press its case.

In my less frantic downtime, in contemplative moments between visits with Theo or nights out with John—on walks through the parks of the North Side, edging themselves toward spring—I allow myself to dwell for a bit with the pride, the preening vain delight, I took in Evany's loving me, and in having brought her, at last, to some steadied richness of feeling that together we would have called—that we *did* call—happiness.

Oh, the narcotic joy of it, to think of yourself as the exception to the rule of unhappiness! I turn it round and round.

And then, like a comet trail streaking across the face of these reveries, another thought glows into dim visibility.

I wonder: Did I really need Evany *never* to hate herself?

Was that the bargain we had somehow wordlessly struck, the inner logic of our besotted togetherness? Had I made every day murmur to Evany in a kind of implicit interrogation: *Are you happier now, my love, than you've ever been?* And when the old shaming impulses once again rose up in her, the unextinguished griefs—did this make her feel so trapped and lonely, so optionless, that she could imagine no way out of it, this secret story of our lives, that wasn't destruction?

I wonder: Was I really *that* fucking bewitched by my own confected heroism?

Something about how I am sleeping with Theo, the headlong and escalating wildness of it, suggests to me an answer to these questions. It isn't the one I want.

"I THOUGHT I WAS DOING OKAY, you know?"

"C'mon, man. You are."

John is beside me at the bar, and I am unspooling. Each day that's not overcrammed with pleasures, I am saying, is now a mad toggling between this new form of shame and, somehow, with it, a revivified and—I can't help but feel—pointless churning *anger*. When will it end? I want to know. This mad cycling between fury and new-dawning shame? The back-and-forth of these riptides of regret and spitefulness and grief?

John, John: when will it fucking *end* already?

In the window behind him spring is coming like a traveling carnival into Lincoln Square, which at the moment is all brightness, blossoms, flashes of bared skin. He is listening, though the quiet neutrality with which he now regards his beer suggests to me he is underconvinced by my recriminations.

He exhales. He takes a thoughtful pull.

After a bit he says, "Dude. Listen."

And he wonders, then, in respect to this new vector of shame, if I've got matters in the proper proportion. He wonders if we've not come upon another spoke in the ever-turning wheel of my own great and lasting grief. He wonders—and he asks me to take this very seriously—if I haven't *contracted* a habit of self-contempt from Evany, like some malignant virus.

"I'm not saying you're wrong," he says, both hands up. "But."

I think about the woman I'd spent all those delighted days with in the winter. I think about my abrupt retreat from what had been scenes of joy, how I'd broken something that indeed had been nourishing to me. I wonder, in a queasy little wave of conjecture, if I'm not grieving Evany by *becoming* her.

Jesus, I think. Jesus.

But John is here. There is time ahead, a whole world of it, he says, to think all this through. My birthday is coming and this we will celebrate, with vehemence and style. (This is how much he loves me: on the day itself he will surprise me with tickets to see the Mountain Goats.) Meanwhile we commence our favorite idling bar conversation. What, we quiz each other, is the greatest *career* track one? The greatest first song on a first record? "'Summer Babe,'" I say. "Don't sleep on 'Do It Again,'" he replies. We talk and talk, and a small steadying rightness flows back into the world.

Time opens and expands around us.

"Anyway, man," he says. It's later now, a few drinks in. "You were asking when it all, like, ends?"

Blearily, not quite sober, I take him in: a divorced father, remarried and happy, a life rebuilt around him. The very image of sorrow's short shelf life.

He leans toward me, a woozy little tilt. He rests his head against my shoulder, in companionable sweetness.

"It doesn't," he says.

He straightens up and looks back at me, wearing his own furrowed sort of grin. "Sorry, man," he says. "It does not."

11

I Kissed a Girl

THE VERY WORST thing that happens in this whole year of fumbling recuperation transpires on an iconically beautiful New England afternoon in the ripening month of May, where only one year before I had wandered desolate through that all-campus picnic. One year! It hardly seems possible.

Spring meanwhile comes slowly to Maine, typically after an interval known locally as "mud season," so its dawning is always a bit momentous. Like the diva arriving hours late to the stage and then basking in your grateful applause, Spring in Maine says: *I am well worth your minor inconvenience.*

I have left Chicago, left John and Karen, left Theo, left my North Side apartment, and for a few in-between weeks have returned to Maine. I'm here to catch up a bit on my life, gather some needed books, see friends. Most of all I am here to be with the girls.

It has been, once more, longer than I would have wished. A few months before, they had visited me in the glorious and frigid Midwest, and this had been a four-day burst of the intensest Chicago-proud joy, though it was followed in turn by some long black days of bereavement. They'd never before traveled as "unaccompanied minors," as the phrase goes—I got a special pass and met them at the gate—and something of the thrill of it buoyed them through all the days. My own buoyancy of spirit was different.

We went to parks and museums. We ate ice cream in quantities recommended by no pediatrician or stern nutritionist. At their request we twice took ourselves bowling, at the venerable Lincoln Square Lanes, with its vintage WPA mural arching above the dozen or so alleys. One cold and blustering afternoon, along with John and Karen, I took them shopping at hipster boutiques, in one of which we acquired for them their first pair of Fluevog shoes—moderately chunky heels with ankle straps and leather in a fetching robin's-egg blue—and these they would go on to share and fight over for the remainder of their teenage years. The highlight without question was the afternoon we "took tea" in the majestic tearoom at the Drake Hotel, in a ceremony of porcelain and flowers and tiny sandwiches that sent both Lucy and Amelia into deliriums of overcaffeinated joy.

I have this one picture of the day. Lucy is caught in a moment of wide-eyed gesticulating explanation. She had been describing to me, in tones of astonished discovery, the décor of the ladies' room.

"No, *listen*," she was saying. "There are *couches*."

When they were with me in Chicago there were of course the obligatory passages of protoadolescent boredom and irritation, though these seemed to me even as they were unfolding more like gifts than anything else, little fragments of grace. For a few bracketed days it was as if I were, once again, just their stepdad, nothing more or less fraught than that. At one point, in an offhand way, telling me the story of one of her days, Amelia said the name of the assistant preparator and I watched Lucy flash her a warning look. It did not happen again.

When they'd gone I reached back into my archive of accumulated sorrows and decided to dwell there among them a while.

Theo, after they left, had said there was going to be a lot of this in the future. A lot of what?

"Happy things that remind you of how much you've lost."

Returned to Maine these few months later, I am dialing in on the happiness, or trying to. On my first afternoon the three of us celebrate our reunion, as well as the full-flower gorgeousness of the season, by taking a walk down to a field at the end of a peninsula jutting out into the ocean. In the warm gusty wind, a vista of sea and inlets and islands all around us, we catch ourselves up with one another. We talk and titter and joke. If there are sorrows and estrangements afflicting their days, they do not say. In just the same way, I leave out from my Chicago stories whatever of incurable grief I encountered there.

But we are not, I don't think, treating each other dishonestly. There can be no doubt that much in the way of confusion, anger, and fear had found them. I know this without being told. They have in some real way lost me, or at least the dailiness of me, though I don't kid myself that this much ranks among their griefs. Far more frightfully, they have watched their mother come apart piece by piece—"like a plane falling out of the sky," as one friend puts it. (Evany has detonated her Maine life with impressive comprehensiveness: she has been fired, has alienated most of her friends, has moved in a man who was even more a stranger to the girls than I had been, all those years before.) What kind of scary this has been and is for them, I can scarcely imagine. I watch them as they walk and talk and squabble, and I know, with a familiar seizing of heart, that they are exactly the kids who will convert that fear into a watchful tenderness toward their mother, a determination to care for her.

It's anguishing to think about, the already grown-up compassion that they, these kids, will have learned how to extend.

Accordingly I speak only lightly of myself. I say to them I

have missed them, which of course is true, but that I am un-harmed, that I am thriving, that I am eager for what's to come. None of this is untruthful, exactly. I am filled rather with the sense that to say anything else would be to make them fretful, worried *for me*, in ways even beyond what I know they already are. This I do not want.

Behind and beneath this all, there is a pulse of thought that begins keeping time with my heart. *How, how, how had I not prevented all this?* I was the steady one, the competent one, the keeper of rules, the policeman of tone. If their beautiful mom was sad, shouldn't I have done more to make her better? Wasn't that why I was there? Who else could've helped her? How would they ever forgive me? *How, how, how?*

But as we go scrambling over the rocks and sea grass, as they chatter away in untiring loops of recurring phrases ("Your mom!" "*Your* mom!"), that small inner flinching in me begins to recede a bit. If there is the shadow of a lot of sorrow lying upon us, we are not for that standing together in a place without light. We are in fact making for each other, in this gradual and accreting way, a good deal of easiness. What's between us now, I remind myself, is nothing false or unforthcoming. We are caring for each other, just that. We are learning how to do it.

Today, for instance, being their ex-semistepdad—divorced from their mom now, really and officially, and so in no legal relation to them whatsoever—mostly means entering into the elaborate theater of their sisterhood, where my role is to be instigator and audience. This I can do, with great gladness. As we stroll we begin speaking of the mixes I've made them over the year—I have made them a handful of mixes, obviously—and I am informed that I have underappreciated, *grievously*, Katy Perry.

"Dudes," I say. "I dunno. 'I Kissed a Girl' is pretty pleased with itself."

In one voice, and with the exasperated vehemence of young people explaining the obvious, they tell me that "I Kissed a Girl" is not, is *not*, the issue.

"Unless you're talking to me right now about 'Hot N Cold,' maybe you shouldn't talk so much," Lucy says.

"*Seriously,*" Amelia says, mock-serious.

And then they're off, a two-person floor show under the tall Maine skies.

The prized picture from this day is of two sisters, a blur of tween exuberance, striking dance-floor-superstar poses as they belt out the chorus of "Hot N Cold" for my edification, Lucy with eyes closed in mock transport, Amelia smiling, her eyes fast on her big sister, my green scarf stacked at her shoulders and flowing out behind her.

For all that stands unspoken between us, it is a splendid day. I think later that here, in glimpses, are the outlines of a future we all three might live in. The sky above us is a huge dome of chalky ocean-blue, large enough to hold it.

AND THEN IT all comes apart.

A few days after my walk by the sea with the girls, on an afternoon so beautiful and warm that the winter-battered citizens of coastal Maine are flooding the streets, I am driving into the little town where the college is. I am coming not from the city but from the country, where I've been staying with my friends Franklin and Susan, who are once more acting toward me with in loco parentis charity. It's been lovely to be with them after so long away. I spent so much of the previous spring imposing upon them, turning their gracious invitations to eat out there with them, and stay the night, into occasions for filling their tranquil home in the woods with the sounds of my jagged collapse. They have three grown daughters of about my age. Clearly, they did *not* need to be visited by this much sobbing wretchedness. And yet they kept inviting me back. Frank had said something to me in the midst of it that had been like a planted seed. I'd been saying, with the stunted inconsolability of all my utterances back then, that it seemed like I'd lost my chance. I had gotten to love Evany, and the girls, and that was incalculably lucky, but she had left me, it was all gone, and so I would never get to be happy again.

I wasn't trying to be dramatic or self-assaulting. It just felt like *logic*. Frank assured me then that, despite the force of this feeling, it was a misapprehension, a trick that sorrow was playing on sense.

"Character is a kind of destiny, Peter," he said. "We believe in your character in this house."

So to have returned, to have tales of John and Karen to tell, of a city-life indulged in, of concerts and dates and work accomplished and visits with the girls, feels like a small-bore triumph. *Look! I am so much less in ruins!* I take a long walk around Merrymeeting Bay with Frank and we talk in the way we've learned to with one another, largely about books, and then, woven through this, about the puzzling and often painful untidinesses of what Frank calls "just living your goddamned life."

He asks me what I've made of the weeks and months, the travels, the being away and the coming back. So I try to put it together, with as much confessional concision as seems appropriate to a springtime walk. I tell him that I'm coming to believe Evany was not right about me after all: that I was not, in fact, unloving or unlovable. I can almost believe that, I say to Frank, and that seems a worthwhile transformation.

But I'm wondering, too, I say, about the ways that she was *not* wrong. I'm wondering if I did not love her with my own confinements. I'm wondering if, in wishing so for her to find in me a long-sought happiness, I did not leave too little room for whatever in her was broken, unhealing.

"Nobody made me love Evany like that," I say. "All that crazed passion—all the *need* that came with it—I made that up all by myself."

If only because he retains much of his outrage from the previous season's more egregious deceptions and unkindnesses, for which he had been a near spectator, Frank resists this a bit, though not too sternly. We stride on.

And then, when I tell him about my afternoon at the ocean with the girls, he tells me he is proud of me.

I keep my eyes on the muddy path, a little amazed at how much it means to me to hear just these words.

There is, on the main drag back in town, crawling traffic. I have the town green to my left, complete with picturesque gazebo, and to my right a sequence of shops rolling by in slow motion. One of these, the ice cream shack that remains a boarded-up monument all off-season, a reminder of all the New England winter demands you do without, is open now and doing the business you'd expect. A line snakes up the block.

I crest the hill, pass the church where Evany and I were married, and as I pull around the corner and out of traffic, there they are.

Evany and the assistant preparator are walking up the street, there on the sidewalk just to my right. They have come from downtown. They are carrying ice cream cones. They are surely heading back home, to the home where I lived. Between them, ice cream in hand, is Amelia.

They are the most unexceptional trio imaginable, middle-class white people in a New England college town. A town's advertisement for itself. A family, out for a stroll.

The sight of them is scalding.

Nothing I can do gets it further from me. It proves more indelible than any cityscape, any tourist vista, any bar-lit dance floor or stranger's bed. For a few days it fills up consciousness the way a siren fills an empty street.

I leave Maine, go to New York, eventually Chicago, even at one point back to Italy. There, amid a crowd of family convened for my return, I have a full-scale breakdown. One afternoon, on a jetty curling out into the Bay of Naples, under the long shadow of Vesuvius, with only my uncle for witness, bright-hearted Zio Mario, I start to tremble and sob. It comes upon me like a saturating rain.

I lose a handful of months, torn right off the calendar.

12

We Are Beautiful,
We Are Doomed

I RECOVER FROM THESE MIASMATIC sorrows, to the degree that I do, with a New York summer and another season out in Chicago. I am allowed to say "recover" if only because the floors of the rooms I'm sleeping in never yawn open and devour me, though I spend a great deal of time imagining they might, and some hard bright mornings wishing they had. But no. If it has done nothing else, the year or so of vagabonding through the outer suburbs of my actual life has taught me how to stage a plausible enough performance of unwrecked personhood—and has taught me, too, how much of the work of recuperation can be done by performance alone. The days have actually taught me more even than this. Despite Maine, despite Naples, despite these throwback collapses, I discover some new resources.

There is, for instance, work to do, and I find at last a real measure of comfort in this. I have been nominally writing a scholarly book all this time, though with mortifyingly little forward progress. (It is about sex and nineteenth-century American literature—both things, I grow fond of saying, of which I am strongly in favor.) But one day at my workstation in the coffee shop I notice the thing is, in fact, well under way. I tell people writing a book is like getting your car out of the snow. It rocks and rocks and rocks, a lot of effort and very little movement . . . and then something catches, and you're off.

Besides scholarship and its weak absorptions, there are all the intoxications of urban life. I am not quite so frenzied as when last I was in New York, which means in practice a decreased commitment to fucking myself up one untried drug combination at a time. In the many hours freed up by these experiments in moderation, other pleasures emerge, and they are different degrees of steadying. Foremost among them is talk, and what it foments. New York, as everyone knows, is one of the planet's great crossing points, and I find that, as my sojourns there have grown in number and in duration, a happy little tangle of intimates and acquaintances has taken shape for me—a *world*, you might even say, small and increasingly coherent, in which I feel myself beginning to establish a place.

Dana and her partner, now with a blond-ringleted one-year-old in tow—my godson—make occasional treks up from D.C., and we push his stroller through the dense summer crowds, pause for pizza and gelato, run him around the green spaces out on the piers. Here's an experiment. Do you want to up your attractiveness quotient to heights previously unattained, and perhaps unsustainable? Try being a dude walking around the city with a wide-eyed and extroverted and irresistibly beautiful baby on your hip. When you are approached by shockingly beautiful strangers, who look upon you with kindliness and indulgent warmth, presumably because you are showing yourself capable of carrying this child without dropping or scratching or otherwise bringing him to visible harm, you will be asked if he is yours. Have this line prepared: "Oh, no, no, I'm his *godfather*. Isn't he gorgeous?"

It is, as Dana observes, a potent magic. "We can't come up here too often," she says. "You wouldn't use it wisely."

But Jasbir is here, too, in Chelsea. And Sarah is in Park Slope, and the kids long graduated from the college are in Fort Greene and Carroll Gardens, and Katherine and Katherine are in West Harlem, and Glenn is in the Bronx, and José is downtown . . . These worlds intersect and overlap and, sometimes, in bars or apartments, come into glancing contact. I ride the subway with an unsurrendered visitor's delight, the sense of a titanic city being transformed, assignation by assignation, into a series of navigable private maps. Each landmark is a scene of overspilling talk.

Jordan is in Midtown with his boyfriend, here for the summer like me, and the days of café writing throw us together more often than not. We read a little, and write a little, and give ourselves over to growing increments of chat. Soon enough we are walking along the river and deciding the day's work has earned us, surely, an early evening martini. It is Jordan who gets me talking, in the gloaming of a West Side rooftop bar, about the replenishing pleasure of all this wordy sociability. He knows it well, because he shares it. (He is a Jew with a job in Colorado, as I'm an Italian with a job in Maine. "We come back here," he says of our New York summers, "to be reminded that talking fast and loud is not, in itself, an affront to propriety.") But he presses, too, gently but insistently, on the *relation* between all this pleasure, all this restorative immersion in discourse and dispute, and my ongoing and—he's sorry—obvious desolation. For a person who loves crowded and expansive intimate worlds as much as I plainly do, I seem to be grieving for *couplehood* awfully hard.

I am drinking a Hendrick's and tonic, because it is summertime, and I am watching the high-rises stacked along the West Side Highway turn a metallic pink. I don't quite know what to say.

"It's curious," he says, as our glasses sweat and night comes on. "It's like you *believe* in all these looser, unformalized kinds of love. Wherever you go, that's what you try to make, to live in."

He turns to me. "Isn't that what you're doing with the girls? I mean, what you've always been doing with them?"

Before I can take this in, he goes on. "But it's like without Evany nothing—not even all this"—he fans a hand out, cityward—"can be nourishing to you."

We are getting on toward drunk. The evening will soon tilt back toward book talk, sex gossip, and the happy blur of a sequence of bars in Hell's Kitchen. But we're not there quite yet. Jordan drains his glass, puts it down, once again looks across at me.

"You were saying before you've been trying to work out what other people are for—for, like, a *year*." He grins. "Look around, sweetie. I think you know."

I DO AND I DO NOT. Or so it seems. One thing I am certain people are for: *going to rock shows*. On a close muggy night in August I take Heather and Steve to see a band called Los Campesinos! at a downtown venue crowded with NYU students, venturesome suburbanites, and hipster kids in glorious array. Heather and Steve are down from Maine for a few stolen days, their young kids are with relations, and I am determined to plunge them back into the high seas, if not of youth, then of youthfulness. This show is just the thing. I'd first heard Los Campesinos!, this band of Brit kids playing hyperkinetic heartbreak rock, only a month before, when in the midst of a wedding trip to California I'd detoured north to see Mark and we passed the obligatory hour in the record store. He'd said I'd like them and, sweet Jesus, was he right. Each song on the record ran a kind of footrace, with twentysomething mopery forever chasing behind the jubilation, the bounding postpunk bliss, that comes of turning it all into frazzling chaotic noise. They are touring on a record whose showstopping number is called, splendidly, "We Are Beautiful, We Are Doomed."

They're like the Smiths, if you can imagine the Smiths tending at most every instant toward some euphoric spazzy Ritalin high.

From the sweaty swaying morass of the pit I point out to Heather the bass player, who is, like the rest of the band, throwing herself into each of the numbers with jerky abandon, her hair up in a great swirling pile. But she is also, just now, *beaming*. She's wearing a grin almost impossibly open and wide and though there is no mic in front of her, and an avalanche of sound caving in from all directions, she is *singing along*. She mouths all the words and jumps around and smiles and rocks completely the fuck out. Heather shouts in my ear that she's never seen a rock star so charming and so outlandishly sweet. They are fantastic, utterly winning, and they're reminding us what it's like to be sad and overjoyed all at once. *It's like being a fan*.

Later, in the encore, they cover a Pavement song and it occurs to us that the songs of our vibrant indie-rock twenties are, for these beautiful brilliant kids, throwbacks, "influences," *classics*. It doesn't matter. Like the middle-aged vampires we have no choice but to be, we siphon off all the youthful elation and spin back out into the city, which offers plenty of room for it, and us.

There are sorrows still for me to get lost in, I know—if I've learned nothing else it's that it takes one misfiring thought for everything to combust—but they do not find me tonight.

Nor do they find me later that tipsy and exhausted night, back in the dark of my borrowed apartment where, with Heather and Steve in the bedroom, I fidget and turn on the couch in the living room. Instead of sleep, instead of mournful visions of the girls, I find myself making a kind of insomniac litany out of the year, the impossible year, now trailing behind me. In this blurry accounting are bars and bedrooms and couches, concert halls and dance floors. There are bands. There are bands and bands and bands.

With little distinctness at first—it is so late, and I am so jangled—but then with something at least nudging toward clarity, I begin thinking, too, about songs.

What, I wonder, have I *not* asked them to do?

When thought buckled, they wrenched it out of its direst patterns. When the days turned dark, they shook the world out of its sense of airless impossibility. For three or four flashing moments, they somehow made it seem that even a world whose truest, least negotiable facts were bereavement, sorrow, and loss might *also* be something luminous, unfinished, a scene of transformation. When we needed to hold ourselves together, the girls and I, songs—fucking *songs*, of all trivial things—made a place where all that had seemed to be voided between us, all the nameless aspects of our devotion to one another, could find traction, presence, a way to be held to the world.

I am buzzing and drunk and awake and happy to have Heather and Steve with me. I'm happy to be in a city so filled with reckless pleasures and friends I love and I am thinking, again, of songs. I am thinking that whatever I might find myself impelled to say about them, at whatever pitch of vehemence or agitation, all I am saying is that they are a gift, a gift, a gift. A blessing from the fallen world. And here they were again, working their sweet confected magic, filling the days with something awfully close to joy.

SO I DO KNOW WHAT PEOPLE are for. (*Going to shows; fighting about bands.*) Though, also, I do not—or not quite. The New York summer, like the Chicago fall that follows it, consists of more than coffee dates, concerts, brief passages of academic labor, and bar talk. Among these pleasures of the city there are, again, a lot of microromances.

More precisely: I keep falling into bed with people.

I won't say this comes to feel stale or that the thrill of new desire begins to get dulled by repetition. It very much does not. In much the way dissolving into the textures of songs I already know does not cease to deliver these swift, stark replenishments, sex does not lose its radiance. I know it's supposed to. I know the stories about sleeping around, their familiar narrative arc—how blind exhilaration gives way to ennui, and then, with slow inexorability, to self-contempt. I consider these bland morality tales and think, *Wow, is that not my story.* My entanglements follow different outlines.

These dalliances can have a kind of turbulence, it's true, but this I try to minimize with genuine forthrightness. I am not in town long, I say. I am eventually moving back to Maine, I say. I'm newly divorced and so a little fragmented, I say. It's all true, or true enough. Here's a discovery: The number of people to whom the idea of an *un*entangling dalliance directly appeals is, as it turns out, greater by far than you might imagine. It is greater certainly than I'd imagined. Speaking to me from opposite coasts, Jordan and Beth suggest I am entering now into the slutty phase I managed to miss in my more plausible twenties. Be safe and have fun, they tell me. Be prepared to find yourself surprised. Follow these rules: no lying, and no shame.

This is excellent advice, and I take it.

What's striking is not how variation and novelty come to seem, eventually, unvarying, or pleasurelessly predictable. This does not happen. (I think often to myself of that patron saint of midcentury New York modernity, Frank O'Hara, and his motto: "Grace to be born and live as variously as possible.") More startling by far is the way the amazement at *being desired* refuses to diminish. Every time it happens I ride a little cresting wave. It feels, on more or less each occasion, like a rush of pure possibility.

And it's not just fucking, honestly. I realize that if the long postbreakup months have imparted any shiny new skill to me it is nothing so much as the aptitude, as well as the appetite, for *affairs*. More than "dating," more than one-night stands, I have come to love the affair, with its compressed temporality, heightened intensities, upsurging passion. It's like a small-scale staging of all that is most beguiling about couplehood. When it reaches its inevitable termination—like the pop song, the affair is defined largely by its brevity—it leaves me with this odd lit-up sense of *place*. This dive bar, that living room, the bathroom stall just once. This park at dusk, the intersection on the cab ride home with the sun coming up.

On better days I feel an unearned kinship with Walt Whitman—"one of my life's spirit guides," I tell friends, "along with Stevie Nicks and Prince"—as I walk around inside this private carnal map of the city.

Why, then, these bouts of clinging sorrow?

It makes so little sense. Shouldn't all these days of dalliance and discovery, of sex with obliging semistrangers, be making me *better*?

"Oh, *paisan*. Are you being serious?"

This is Dana. On a catch-up call back east, taken up on her side with tales of one-year-old hilarity and exasperation and on mine with detailed narratives of assignations I might've known better than to pursue, she is offering me, along with sympathy and satire, some tonic counsel. I must be hungering for precisely this sort of care, or I wouldn't be talking to Dana. We share, she and I, an East Coast Italianness that expresses itself most frontally in volume and in vehemence, though in her this is wedded to an intelligence as piercing as any you're likely to encounter. She is not caustic, Dana. She is just commandingly smart and, if she loves you, not that interested in aiding you along in your self-misapprehensions. It can be searing. To be loved by her, which I know I am—I have known it since I was twenty-two, as I have known that I love her—is sometimes like a warm embrace and sometimes like a punch in the solar plexus.

This is one of those latter times.

"Why would it make you better?" she wants to know. "That's not a reason not to keep doing it—not even a little—but you seem a little confused."

What does *that* mean?

"Listen, sweetie," she says, and in her pause I can all but hear the phrases gathering strength. And then it comes. "You don't have to *throw* yourself at every person you think might want to fuck you even a little."

Oh.

"I'm happy you're having fun. But it's like—" Another pause. "It's like you're trying to prove something. And whatever it is you're trying to prove to yourself? This isn't going to do it."

Oh. *Oh.*

"It can seem a little desperate."

Desperate for what, she does not say. She does not have to. I catch a sudden glimpse of all I might be said to be desperate for. It's not sex, the thrilling strangeness of new flesh, any of it.

"Oh, *paisan*," I say, crumpling.

She waits me out.

"I want this all never to have happened." And then, "I want it so fucking bad."

"I know, baby," she says. "Me too."

BACK IN CHICAGO, after a month or so of committed New York sluttiness that even I start to feel unsettled by, I spend the better part of the fall allowing myself to fall half in love with a woman I remeet at a huge street fair one deeply drunk September night. She is a friend of Theo's. (In fact, a little mortifyingly, they are *teammates*, on the same local long-distance running squad, which makes me . . . what exactly? "Mascot," Lise helpfully suggests.) We drink a lot and dance a lot and, in her unexpectedly accommodating bathtub, listen to playoff baseball on the radio. On Halloween she makes me a costume—I go as Max from *Where the Wild Things Are*, complete with homemade crown and tail—and we go out dancing. A flashbulb memory: a sterling '80s hip-hop track called "Rump Shaker" cues up and Lise, a little circle of awed delight expanding around her on the dance floor, rocks out *every word* to *every verse*. It is tremendous. Meanwhile, sex is a thing we find we can do together with the sort of vehemence that feeds on itself. Occasionally that Chicago fall I find myself thinking of her until I realize I've dropped a moment or two, that desire has blinked out consciousness for a spell. It feels, a good lot of the time, like being high.

It ends terribly.

From the start I have said that I can't really imagine us continuing together when I return to Maine, if only because being back there fills me with such steep dread. This, too, is true enough. But Lise, after these months in each other's company, is having *none* of it. On a night involving perhaps too much vodka and surely too little regard for neighbors, we have at last the fight that we've been conspiring to hold at bay, not least through the grand conspiracy of sex. There in her kitchen, a blanket around her shoulders against the cold turn of winter, she unlooses a storm of steeped, thwarted anger. It, too, is like a saturating rain.

She wants to know where I get the nerve, exactly, to be so fucking *sad* all the time.

She wants to know if I can think of *anybody*, anywhere in the *world*, whose friends take better care of him. Whose *kids* take better care of him.

"Tell me a story," she says, nearer to shouting, "tell me a story about somebody more fucking *drowning* in love than you are. I will wait right here."

To this I do not have a lot that is useful to say.

"But you're *so sad*," she says.

Her face is outraged, and raw. "Well, how about this—how about *fuck you*? How about fuck you and your fucking sob stories."

We are at her kitchen table, two bottles and four glasses between us. I look at them, and at her.

"I'll tell you what you want." And so she tells me. She tells me I just want somebody to get lost with. She tells me I just want somebody to make me feel so drunk and excited I don't remember my train-wreck marriage.

She tells me, too, that this is a terrible way to treat people. "Even if you like them only *a little*," she says, and when she does I feel a new dimension of shame, malignant and hot, open itself inside me.

"Oh, Lise," I say. "No, no."

"Fuck *you*," she says, "and fuck your bullshit—fucking—*man tears*, fucking all of them."

I spend the whole of the night sitting across from her, holding her hand and not, looking at her and not, saying I'm sorry—"I'm sorry, Lise. I'm sorry. I'm sorry"—though not nearly enough.

I LEAVE CHICAGO at last and, before returning to resume my left-behind life in Maine, spend a bleak and penitential New Year's Eve back east, at my parents' house. It is now, I realize a bit to my amazement, more than a year and a half since I left my little college-town life behind, and the prospect of return is filling me with a deep inarticulate fear. It seems a passage, a juncture, far more momentous than the turning of the year. On the festive night itself my mom and dad decide to retire at about ten p.m., which is late for them, leaving me solitary in the basement, sending periodic texts, but mostly just listening to records and moping, in the teenaged style. I spin through a raft of familiars, waiting for some exhilaration to visit me—turning from Liz

Phair to the Jackson 5, Jackie Wilson back to Van Morrison, even reaching back to some late-period Led Zeppelin. Nothing catches, though.

This happens, I know. Records, like the people we're in love with, can sometimes leave us cold, unexalted. It's hardly their fault. With a certainty beyond argument, I know these songs, or songs exactly like them, have spent the whole of the past chaotic schizoid year *rescuing* me from more or less every variety of harm. That's more than anyone has any right to expect. My gratitude, though running perhaps a little cold tonight, is unshaken.

But then another thought blinks into view.

I wonder for a moment if, along the way to inoculating me with reasons for *being alive*, they haven't also been providing me an obscurer sort of instruction.

I am thinking once more of the year. I am thinking of affairs, and the places they happened, and of rooms filled with happiness. And it comes to me that what I have come to these songs hoping to find tonight is another excursion into pop bliss, some blinding passage of inrushing captivation. I remember what Lise has said—*all you want is to get lost*—and it occurs to me that if I've been letting anyone or anything suggest to me what it is going to be like to fall in love again, finally, savingly, for real, it has not been family or friends or shrinks or even books. It has not been Freud. It has not been Beth or Dana or Jordan or John or Mark. It seems I've been taking my cues instead, all of them, from the things that have saved me. I've been listening to songs.

Has that been a mistake?

Around the world, at hourly intervals, horns are blared, corks popped. Couples kiss, in huge synchronous pantomime, in city squares, apartments, the living rooms of friends.

I am alone in my parents' basement, listening to records. One year becomes the next.

Part Three

SILVER DAGGER

The house is still and bright, full of morning. Boxes, half-packed, stand in corners and in the kitchen is a little chaos of stacked glasses and bowls and plates, rolls of green packing wrap spilling off counters and pooling on the floor. There is a low suburban sound of birds, cars breathing along side streets, someone's dog giving warning to a midmorning jogger, though without much urgency. Nothing hurries.

It is an ordinary early June weekday in a little college town in Maine. This is my house. Or it was. It will cease to be my house in a few weeks, when I am to leave it behind—Evany and I, for some brutal days, having been trading places here—at which point I am to commence an extensive passage of life elsewhere, away. There has been talk of New York, of Chicago, of Europe.

I am not thinking of any of those places at the moment, however. None of it seems likely now to happen.

I am kneeling, sitting upright on my heels with my legs folded beneath me, on the floor in the corner of the dining room. I have taken off my sweatshirt and so, now, am shirtless.

Birds, cars, someone's dog.

I am kneeling, shirtless, in the dining room and on the floor beside me is a kitchen knife, retrieved from the wooden rack of knives I had just that moment been wrapping up to pack in one of the boxes marked KITCHEN. But then a different idea came to me.

It is not a new idea. I have had this tenacious vision, you see. It's been following me everywhere, like a lonely stray. It first appeared to me just a few weeks before at John and Karen's apartment in Chicago, in eerily cinematic completeness, an aftereffect of the series of breakdowns that took hold of me there on the weekend of their wedding. Since then it has stood patiently around every corner of thought, unchanging, awaiting my return. Like a dream, its logic is weird but coherent. I have this idea that grief is filling me up, like black fluid. I have the sense that I am drowning in it, on the inside. I have this idea that I can release it, that I can open a small seam and out it all will come. I have a vision and this is what happens: I make a little narrow opening just below my breastbone—the knife goes in gently, without the least struggle or violence—and all that is poisonous and vile comes pouring out of me, in smooth and soothing relief. I see myself from above, kneeling inside a little black pool.

I see this, exactly this, so often, and with such granular clarity of vision, that it comes to feel like a strangely mislocated piece of objective reality. Thinking about it seems nothing more than the exercise of reason in a time of otherwise deranging sorrow and fear.

And so, today, I am upright and kneeling, and telling myself that all I need to do is lean forward—that's all: a little leaning forward—and the misery of everything that's happened will stop. I can release it, let the whole terrible volume of it spill out of me so that I'm emptied, and done. A little leaning in, there. Whatever is left of my mind flows to exactly that point, and nowhere else.

*In the driveway there's a sound of tires. I look out the win-
dow and there, startlingly, is Bisbee, stepping out of his repurposed white police cruiser. For a moment he makes no sense.
He is radically out of place. Why is he here? I think. And then
the world, the one we share and of which I am evidently yet a
part, heaves back into place around me. I'm sobbing now and
Bisbee is hustling me into his car and we're off. I remember the
centrifugal force of the turn he makes out of the driveway, how
it pushes me hard against the passenger door, and his voice filling up the car, and twisting myself into a shirt. I have no idea
where we go or what happens next.*

≈

Long, long, long after this, when I've learned how to talk about
the day with some equable sense of proportion—as a thing
that happened, not the sum total of my life up till then—a
woman I'm falling for asks me a clarifying question. *Where
were your friends, your family, when you were doing this?* she
wonders. *What were you thinking about them? Where were
the girls?*

She's not being unkind—I know she's trying to understand
something—but as I think about her questions my mind goes
a blank bright white for a second. I don't say, as I know I could,
that I wished only to free them of the burden of my collapsing
self. That would not be less shameful; it would be untrue.

"They weren't there," I say. I suppose that, for a moment,
they'd stopped being real. "Everything had," I say. Everything
that was not Evany, and grief.

"It's terrible to think about," I say. "For a long time, I
didn't. Think about it, I mean."

"I'm glad your friend came by," she says.

"Me too." On many days, this is the truth.

13

My Tears Were Never Enough

IF YOU LIKE FRIGIDITY and isolation, January is an excellent time to return to your life in northern New England.

The day after I arrive, Maine enjoys one of those unforecast squalls of snow that sometimes besiege the coast. Before my bags are unpacked or my refrigerator fortified with anything nonalcoholic, I find myself looking out the front window at a foot and a half of fresh wet snow. It flashes with a dull gleam, like porcelain. Later, when Amelia and I trudge from my car to the door around the side of the house, she suggests I might want to buy a shovel. Which is helpful, because true.

I have made some miscalculations.

I have not come bearing a shovel. I have not acquired snow tires for the little green Mazda I've been driving since the summer I arrived at the college, now more than a decade ago. I have left myself only five days before the beginning of the new semester in which to unpack and prepare and settle myself in, however I might, to this new domestic scene.

Above all, I have miscalculated—maybe, I am realizing, somewhat grievously—the matter of home.

Amelia meanwhile is walking around the house, and reminding me how well she knows it already. I have picked her up from downtown in the dutiful Mazda and slalomed back through the narrow corridors of piled snow. I've wanted to show her the place, to introduce her to it, my new rented home. But of course she's been in it, she's seen it, she remembers it. She spent a number of grade school afternoons here. A colleague at the college, with girls exactly Lucy's and Amelia's ages, has been kind enough to rent me this, his *entire house*, for about as much as I would pay for a one-bedroom apartment down in Portland. It is an act of tremendous generosity, and also reassurance, and humane care. He and his family have since relocated to Paris but, loving Maine as they do, wished to keep hold of the house if they could manage it. I could help them in this—looking after it, paying a rent truly nominal—and they could help me kick-start a new life back in the place where I had once been, it's true, pretty convincingly happy.

This, then, had been the plan. But if I have come to learn much at all in my postdivorce meanderings, those mopey and fitfully radiant travels, it is that trusting the flimsy promises of *plans* is an invitation to grief. Haven't I gone out in the world these many aimless months in search of unconsoling truths, bitter recognitions of just the sort to keep me better grounded to the spinning world? I have, and here, I have apparently decided, is one such truth: "Plans" are an affront to the chaotic arbitrariness of which the world is made. They are a kind of misrecognition, a category error, prosecuted on the scale of life.

Armed with this feather-light conviction, telling myself it is world-weary knowledge, I have returned to Maine. But even this little theater of self-deception proves unballasting. I have returned to Maine and suddenly every least thing I determine to do, virtually the instant after that decision becomes irrevocable, seems to me overbrimming with the likelihood of having been a great and humiliating mistake—of having been, in fact, *astound-*

ingly stupid. Signing up for this phone service, belonging to this bank, teaching on these days and not those. There is nothing I can't look back on and say, *Jesus, that was foolish*. This is so much the case that the more or less life-traversing paralysis of will that follows starts to feel like a bit of thoughtful cautiousness, an expression of mature levelheadedness, rather than an obvious malignancy of spirit.

I wonder in idle moments: Is this lunacy? The nearest-to-hand occasion for an unexpended self-contempt? The newest symptom of a postmarital commitment to obscure self-sabotage? It is not easy to say.

It is easy to say, however, that moving back to the town where, not long before, your life caught fire and burned down around you—this, we can agree, is a mistake. But it's not the worst one. Amelia is walking room to room, saying that she remembers playing in this bedroom, reading books in this study. I have to trail behind her to keep up. This is because—have I mentioned this?—I have rented for myself a five-bedroom house.

I have made some miscalculations.

Amelia is showing me the feature she most vividly remembers "from childhood"—it is wonderful to hear a brand-new teenager speak of the misty distant precincts of *childhood*—which is a laundry chute, leading from the upstairs hallway down a straight drop into a basket in the basement. Amazing! She narrates the house to me, chamber by chamber, and I busy myself with the effort to recall how exactly this has come about. I remind myself that I had, in some bleak Chicago moment of missing the girls terribly, imagined the need for a house large enough to hold all of us.

Me *and* the girls.

I can recall the trajectory of thought, the air of plausibility with which it arrived to me. I had imagined they would stay over sometimes, as they had in Chicago, or maybe that they'd want another space for themselves, besides the ones they had with their dad and his girlfriend and with their mom and the man with whom she has continued to live.

No one encouraged me in this plan, I don't think. I suspect I made it up, cold, and then followed it through.

Of course, this will not happen. No one will forbid it. No one needs to. The girls have homes, rooms of their own—they have in strict fact an excess of them—and I am not their father and I am not living with their mother.

Me, making plans.

If it occurs to Amelia that there is something, oh, *weird and unhappy* about me taking up residence in an echoing and largely empty house, around a few corners from where we all used to be together, she shows no sign of it. She is instead all reminiscence and narration, cheery nostalgia for the adventures of early grade school. "You're going to need a shovel, though," she says. "Like, soon." And then, looking at the glinting snow, "Do you wanna go get gelato?"

WHEN I COME BACK TO MAINE TO STAY, I surrender to the grip of two preoccupations, which alternate in intensity and pre-eminence, according to no pattern I can discern.

The first, the one that waits for me in the corners of each of the many unpeopled rooms of my new residence, is with the shape of the life the girls and I are going to make with one another. They are here, Lucy and Amelia, shuttling in a way long familiar to them between two houses, and I am here, belonging to neither. If stepparenthood had been a moment-to-moment invention, a fabulation we undertook in daily conspiracy with one another, then what would it mean to be an *ex*-stepparent? How would we make a place for each other? How, in the midst of lives already uncommonly complex and emotionally demanding, would they make a place for me?

Would they want to?

Like every parent, though at an angle very much my own, I ask myself and ask myself: *What will become of all that love?*

THE SECOND PREOCCUPATION is plainer, more ignoble, a different variety of feverish, and visits me most commonly in the quiet of the small hours.

Think of the world. Think of the vastness, the empty spaces, the breadth of all that was unlikely.

Who is going to fall in love with me? I think. *Who am I going to love?*

A FRIEND OF MINE likes to say that the terrible thing about departures—from places, jobs, friends, lovers—is not, actually, the inundation of loss that comes with them. You think so, but that's wrong. The terrible thing is not the rupture or the dislocation but the hard fact that, no matter the force of any of these, you take with you, inevitably, your own obdurate self. There is, sadly, no departure so estranging that you slip free of the deepest facts of yourself—though there are few fantasies quite as enchanting as the one that says there is, and that you do.

To come back to a place after long separation is to en-counter—in something of the way a moving car might be said to "encounter" a telephone pole—the intransigent truth of this. It is also, I discover, to remember much that you had done well to forget.

I unpack. I retrieve boxes from my storage space, the air of which has been undisturbed since John and I closed the door behind us many, many months previous. The crates dislodge their contents and every now and again I am blindsided: that framed photo, that trinket, that crayon drawing.

And so, having carried my self away and brought it back, I beguile the hours of drifting, directionless anxiety exactly the way you'd expect.

I fill the house with the sound of power chords, anthemic shouting, cleansing little frenzies.

Here, some unconverted part of me thinks, one song cycling into the next, *these will save you.*

I am, to appearances, quite stubbornly myself.

I fall, I remember, into a peculiar sustained fascination with Elvis Costello, late early period, and not just for the brilliant romantic nihilism you find there, in tracks running strong to the cruel and the bitter. There is solace in this, certainly, but mostly I hear in them the presence of my friend, an American transplanted to England, who when we talk music speaks with such stinging eloquence about Elvis, Dylan, the Stones, her long-nurtured aesthetic fatality for, as she says, "smart, mouthy misogynists." The phrase crackles in my memory, and I hold it to me. Years and years before, back in a memorable passage of grad school, I had offered her inexpert barroom consolation at the end of a bad affair, insisting that she could take heart in the fact that the world would always be overfilled, beyond any reckoning, with songs and books and bands for us to love . . . more, I remember saying, than any one life could contain. "They're bigger than grief," I had said, with the assurance of a half-drunk twentysomething.

I think of it now, of having said such a thing to a person stricken with sorrow, with a small flash of shame. Was I ever that young?

But it's comforting too.

Elvis snarls out pithy put-downs and one after another I rewrap the household items too freighted for me to want to see them every day—*"My tears were never enough to keep that girl alive"*—and it's as if Pam's there with me, even here, and I feel steadied.

I can use the steadying.

"Do you think you're *better*?" people have been asking me.

"Totally," I've said. "Yes. A lot."

But the truth is a bit afield of this. My mind keeps murmuring something else.

What will happen to me here?

It occurs to me, as I stand amid crates and cartons and boxes opened and quickly resealed, that what I have wanted is a way of missing Evany, and the whole of our life, that doesn't make me feel so stupid. Or so all-the-time afraid.

I cannot seem to find it.

BETH IS ON CALIFORNIA time and so, sleepless, I call her often in the middle of the soundless night. When things are bad, for either of us, we call one another, we say, to have a witness. "I don't need you to do anything," one of us will say, "just be with me in this." Despite being thousands and thousands of miles away, she has been every kind of with me in this.

And she is asking me, just now, a good question: "What *are* you so afraid of?" she says. "Like, can you name it? Would it help to try?"

It would, I think, it would, though as it turns out it's a bit like asking me to pick a favorite Dickinson poem, a best Helium song from 1995. Who could choose?

I do not say that I'm afraid I'll never find a way of doing without a life with Evany that doesn't make me feel smaller, a bad imitation of my former self. I do not say that I'm afraid Amelia and Lucy and I will be set adrift from one another, that there will be no good human way to knit our three lives back into something vibrant and durable. I do not say I'm afraid of what's happened to me here, what I almost did, and how I might encounter it. None of this yet has words, the disentangled simplicity of the declarative sentence.

So I take a simpler tack. I say I am most consumingly afraid of running into Evany or—God help me—the man she lives with, in some unsteeled moment.

"I'm adjusting to this," I say, "by walking around steeled all the time." We agree this is a strategy with some limitations.

And, of course, running into him is exactly what happens.

Henry, my most beloved Englishman, my colleague of foul mouth and indefatigable good cheer, takes me out midweek to one of the little bistros that have opened downtown since last I lived here, with the intention of drinking me into a renewed sense of confident belonging. It is a fine idea, and I don't need much persuading to enter into the spirit of it. He catches me up on collegiate inanities. I narrate back to him the story of the bar I ambled into when my travels took me at last to London. A loose riff on the gastropub concept just then sweeping through the High Streets of southern Britannia, this bar in Notting Hill had to have been, I am telling Henry, the single smuggest room in the whole of England, a cataclysm of banking-class arrogance wedded to Oxbridge noxiousness, all of it brewed up inside a space tricked out in a décor you'd have to call yuppie-Edwardian. It was, in the comprehensiveness and immediacy of its vileness, an *amazement*.

Henry, a former Hong Kong banker who attended Oxford at the exact moment when Rob Lowe was there to film the deathless early-'80s classic *Oxford Blues*—in which Henry, as he would not be slow to tell you, *actually appears*—Henry is loving the shit out of every word. It feels warming, remembering how to make him laugh like this. By the third pint it occurs to me that we're instructing each other in how it is we are going to carry on, he and I, here inside what is for me a life both old and scarily new. We are finding out what we can talk about and laugh about, what we oughtn't to, what we might and might not hazard. Word by word—also drink by drink—we're piecing together a language for one another. It feels a winning kind of easily done.

I tell him the story of Amelia's recent visit to the house. I offer it more in the key of my own hapless miscalculation than, say, of a fear of what awful passages of loneliness I may have set myself up for. Henry, I suspect, can hear the one through the other. We talk about the kids, when they were tinier. Henry reminds me of the day he had been charged with watching Amelia and his daughter for the afternoon, back when they were . . . in kindergarten, maybe? They'd vanished together into the playroom in the basement, and from the noiselessness, the companionable silence he understood the girls to have dropped sweetly into, he assumed all was well. Time passed. When we arrived to retrieve Amelia and called her up from the basement, two girls appeared before us, transformed. They were doused, *plastered*, in a quantity of multi-colored glitter Henry had not known his house to contain. The girls capered and giggled and shook and when they did handfuls of glitter dropped from them like sparkling snow. We found it in their hair, their clothes, their *food*, for weeks after.

"Henry!" Evany had said. "They were quiet? Dude, silence is the *worst* sign."

Exactly as we had then, we laugh about this now, retrieving one small quadrant of the past from the realm of the unmentionable.

And then, there he is.

He comes in, joined by a man I don't know, and takes a seat at the bar. We are at a table in the window and as I look over Henry's shoulder I take him in with a jolt, which then becomes a transfixed gaping stare. I am drinking in the details, which are acquiring the hyperreality of dreams: the rolled-up cuffs of his jeans, the awful lank '90s-boyfriend haircut, the blankish pin-eyed look. He is a richness of information. And so greedily am I given over to downloading it, to feasting on the suddenly non-imaginary sight of him, that I forget for a long moment that I am with my friend, that I am nakedly glaring, that a look of pure murder has set itself in my face.

A seizing coiled tension starts to sing through me and I am all at once feeling as dangerous, as actually *violent*, as I have in forever. There is no soundtrack this time. There is only me, and this person, and a tremendous visitation of boomeranging rage, stewed in for months, finding at last an object on which to spend itself.

Later, I will remember fantasizing about the infinitely satisfying crunch of broken teeth against a balled-up fist, the resistance and the give, which is strange as sensory hallucinations go, since I've never punched anyone square in the face. The impulse to do so burns the drunk right out of me—that, or, with unbelievable velocity, enhances it.

Henry meanwhile has gone a bit furrowed but then sees. And with a smooth defusing cheerfulness that somehow finesses my attention back toward him, he says, "You know what? Let's go, chief. Let's us go." He drops a few twenties on the table and we're out in the rushing cold and walking back up the hill toward the college, toward his home, toward my house. But not before I catch sight of the guy turning sideways at the bar and—I am *sure*—catching sight of me. His look is blank, unreadable.

In bed later, in shaking postadrenal sleeplessness, I think, *Well, that was terrible.* I wonder what being back in Maine is going to be like. Like an evening with Henry, stitching together old loves seam by seam? A remaking of worlds, like the world the girls and I *may* have lost, but, perhaps, have not, not entirely?

Or will it be a series of awful confrontations that leave me in a scattered unavailing fury?

I have my suspicions.

THE SEMESTER COMMENCES. I return to the classroom, and to campus. I am reunited with much-missed colleagues and encounter, too, a number of colleagues I realize I had had no difficulty doing without. The dearer ones, the veterans of parties past, say they've heard of my travels, from Franklin, from Meredith, and are glad I'm back. Some hazard a question or two about the girls, and I say they are, in the greatest of ways, still very much themselves, only taller. *When's the next Prince party?* they want to know. I am by this point well stocked with disarming anecdotes, stories of travel, ways of setting at a manageable distance both the past and the humiliations everyone knows it to have contained. The performance of unbrokenness is, by now, one I accomplish with a convincing fluency. But it is a fragile little masquerade.

One day, talking on the phone to Lucy to make a date to meet in town with her sister, I hear in the background a colloquy of voices, a woman's and a man's, and realize with a start that one of them is Evany's. The ordinariness of it lights a kind of fuse in me. A scene flashes up, of domestic mundanity, schedules being arranged, lunches packed, dishes to be done. What I am listening in on, it occurs to me, are the inner workings of a *life*, crowded and intricate, from which I have been neatly excised.

The rooms of the house where I am standing do not, in the moment, feel any less airy or unoccupied. A wave of queasiness passes over me. It persists.

Meantime, as might have been predicted, jostled fragments of memory keep toppling upon me. I soon discover that it requires a focused concentration *not* to be swept downstream by them. This is what it is to live, once more, in a place that had been a scene of happiness and, then, abruptly, ruin. In a big house, in the absence of lovers or drugs, with only songs to fill the space between me and the thoughts I do not invite, concentration falters and flags.

Walking to school one morning in the piercing January sunlight, I cross a small quad and run hard into a recollection of the morning after our wedding, when Evany and I had arrived back in town after a honeymoon night in Portland and found here, exactly here, our friends Marc and Suzanne, indefatigable late-night wedding guests, making their struggling way through the day after with their toddler, who of course had had them awake since dawn. We talked to Suzanne, recapping the day and the night and comparing moments to savor, as behind her Marc was to be seen executing these rolling little somersaults in the grass, to his son's squealing delight. A little remembered tableau, called *Happiness*.

But then I drive downtown and remember the day, back in the wretched in-between time of Evany's paralytic indecision, I bumbled upon her and the assistant preparator having an after-work drink together at a little-frequented German restaurant. Oh, God, the dismal conventionality of *that* scene. He had seen me approaching, the miserable shit, and fled. But he'd forgotten his bag, which had been left in Evany's car—in *our* car—and that was in the parking lot, locked. *So he came back.* In a halting voice, eyes on the floor, he approached the table where Evany and I now sat, and said he needed his bag. And so I watched, in a trance of unreality, as Evany walked with him out to our car, saying to him along the way I can only imagine what.

The sensation that trails along after this vision, as it bounds back and forth across my optic nerve, is not one of achieved tranquility, no.

When I retreat back to my snow-lined cul-de-sac, I see to it that the house echoes and shudders. The winter quiet without will be matched by an unceasing silencelessness within. It is a campaign of many hours, and I am prepared. I have for instance a little speaker for my iPod and this, like a sensible person, I keep beside the bed. I may be without spouse or lover, a stepparent solely by the lights of memory and straining wishes. But I am not uncompanioned.

I am, to appearances, intractably and ongoingly myself.

If there is something misbegotten in seeking restoration in

four-minute doses of noise, it speaks to me in a quiet voice. It does, however, speak. I put it to Beth, when we talk, like this. I had once lived in this place, I tell her, on these streets and among these people, and I had believed myself *so fucking lucky*: exempted, loved, stealing happiness from the teeth of the world. Rounding the corner of twenty-nine into thirty, at precisely the moment the news of the chaotic arbitrariness of the world *might* have reached me, that news that is not news, I had found Evany, and grappled her to my heart, and made her over into the anchor of all things.

The world is violent and uncontrollable, my heart had said, *but this,* this *will be certainty itself.*

So to listen to the Pogues romp through "Body of an American," or to dial up Prince singing, *"You walked in, I woke up"*—as in these long cold nights I am evidently much inclined to do—is not only to plunge back into a scene of a busy happiness, now lost. It is to be returned, too, to the whole hypnotic theater of that belief.

Evany herself remains an undoing sort of mystery, a blur at the edge of the thinkable. How a life she seemed to love became so abruptly unlivable to her—this continues to be a puzzle of mostly missing pieces, a sum that will not figure.

But in the quiet of an upstairs master bedroom, with snow-sculpted pines arrayed beyond the light of the windows and a little speaker buzzing beside me, a new kind of mystery has begun to present itself. I tell Beth that I'm coming to wonder if dwelling here, in these jolts of elation that pass so readily for certainty, for belief—for the feeling if not the fact of restoration—isn't its own failing strategy, another kind of miscalculation.

What she says then stays with me, in part because I cannot, in the moment, quite take it in, or wrestle it into sense.

"I hear what you're saying, love," she says, whispering, because her baby is asleep in the next room. "Not everything that saves you is going to make you *better*."

≈

DEEP WINTER IN MAINE is an extended experiment in cabin fever, whose chief variables are snow, wind, and cold, coming in combinations that range from the light to the life endangering. It is a great grace of Lucy and Amelia, these hardy children of New England, that the violent extremities of climate unsettle them not in the least. The sky-dumps of snow, the cold beyond endurance: none of it alters their determined sense that, after dinner, there must and shall be gelato.

We eat together and talk about their days, toward which I feel a straining, truncated familiarity. (The names of some friends I recognize, though not all, and the names of teachers I confuse a lot. *Just like a real parent!* Henry, with great sweetness, will say.) I tell them stories, and they tell me stories back. We speak lightly, sparingly, of Evany, and virtually never of the man with whom she lives, and they do as well. We start to build a little edifice of jokes and phrases, references traded and honed. And we go to gelato.

For hours before we meet, I feel excited, eager, but also braced up, flinching with preemptive disquiet. Am I being too unforthcoming with them? Or is it obvious, too much so, that I'm uneasy and afraid in this life? Is coming out to be with me bringing a complication to their emotional lives that, God knows, they could do without? Is our being together harder for them than it is quietly joyous to me?

"You're keeping the flag raised," is what Henry tells me. "You're letting them know you're there. That you're not going away. That's *plenty.*"

And then he adds, "With kids, you're never playing the short game, you know? It's always the long play."

It's always the long play, I think to myself. *Remember that.*

The girls no longer live in town (their mother has by this time sold our house and moved out), which means that I drive them back up the coast afterward and kiss them good-bye there, in the driveways of their parents' houses, where I try to notice as little beyond their faces as I can. My heart clutches, though not as much in bitterness as you'd think. The long driveways, these far-away houses, their repeopled lives: I hate that their days are made of these things. I hate, with a familiar flush of shame, that I could not prevent it.

What it means, also, is that they are not as much in town as they used to be. Out in the world together, we see people who remember them. We see their friends.

One night of knifing cold we trundle once more down the main street to convene ourselves around our gelato. The tables fill up, on weeknights like these, mostly with local teenagers, a bit older than the girls for the most part, fighting off suburban ennui with little riots of hypercaffeinated talk. As we stand in line a kid that I don't recognize notices Lucy and starts talking with her and Amelia, welcoming them into her knot of high schoolers for a moment. I know my role here. I back away and become as unobtrusive a presence as I can manage. I check my phone, send a text, attempt to fade invisibly into the texture of things. When at last we gather up to go, Lucy straightens a bit and, returning herself for a moment to the world of grown-ups and its mannerly codes, introduces her friend to me, and me to her friend. "This is Pete," she says, and we shake hands.

The friend, though, is less interested in placating the adults and, from inside the freer world of kids, says to Lucy, "Who is he again?"

"Oh, yeah," she replies, unpausing and unembarrassed. "He's my stepdad."

I drive them back up the coast, kiss them good-bye, drop them off. They make it inside—I watch them vanish into these rooms that I don't know—and I back out and am off.

I spend the whole ride home, through glittery swaying pines, crying. A steady, even stream of tears.

This will happen again and again. Dinner, gelato, drop-off, a carful of tears. What's riding with me isn't sadness, exactly. Our hours together mostly produce in me a kind of baffled happiness, this sweet little bubble of elation.

And yet they keep returning: tears and tears and tears.

I have no idea what to make of it.

14

Something Like Distinctness

ONE FROM THE archives:

In a suburban landscape rendered almost featurelessly gray and white, two figures strike poses. They stand together like triumphant mountaineers at the ridged peak of a great wall of packed and piling snow, and to one side of them, *beneath* them, peeking up through the drifts, are the jagged wooden slats of a fence top. They gaze down at the camera from on high, a fixed beaming look, mock-proud, about to break back into laughter. She is wearing an elaborate fuzzy hat, cartoonishly tall and wide, made of some synthetic fabric dyed a raccoon-dark. Through the fraying holes at the knees of his jeans, you can see his flannel long johns. She has a shovel balanced over one shoulder, a gladiatorial cock to her hips. He holds his planted in front of him, like a territorial flag, his other arm around her waist.

A number of plausible captions or titles suggest themselves. *The Winter Palace,* maybe. Or *Spring Comes to New England.* I'd likely settle upon something simpler and more historical: *January 2001.*

When I say this is from the archive I mean I find it one winter day pressed between the pages of a Dickens novel. How it has gotten there is not, in the moment I discover it, immediately obvious. I am too caught short even to wonder. Coming upon it like this, so without expectation, is like blundering into an overlit room. I squint at it. And then the moments, the scenes, come rushing back.

This was our first winter together. I still lived in an apartment a few blocks nearer to town, on the other side of campus, and I had spent the summer and the fall taking these little walks back and forth, full of the dreaminess and exultation proper to a young man in his later twenties who, in the deepest ways possible, cannot believe his luck. Everything wore the brightness of romance, of sex, of falling in love. When it was possible, while the weather allowed, I'd steal these handfuls of wildflowers from somewhere along the route—often from the beds of the public gardens tucked into some intersection, which Evany kept insisting was *illegal*, though I did not care—and present them to her in a ragged bunch. And then winter came and it was a different adventure. I'd march into darkness and blowing snow to arrive frosted white, my peacoat stiff with ice.

"I'm like the Pa Ingalls of coastal Maine," I'd say, and Evany would undress me layer by layer. And then, if things broke right, we'd be snowbound.

This had been one of those lucky lost days. I remember the picture being taken by a neighbor of Evany's. She'd come over to see if Evany, now single, needed extra help. "Oh, I got a boyfriend," she said, deadpan. "He can do it."

And there was the image of it, smudged at the edges from handling, marking out a climactic passage in *Bleak House*.

The little delirium of recollection subsides. I come back to another winter day, brighter and less snowy, in the same small town, and I've got a book open in my lap and an old color photograph staring up at me. And then, in another buckling onset of memory, I remember how it got there.

⁓

I'VE MADE IT seem like I never see her, like Evany is some kind of spectral presence, vivid in consciousness but unseen in the flesh. That's not right. We see each other.

Sometimes she is there when I drop off the girls. Sometimes she drops them off, or meets them, downtown. Sometimes we share space at concerts, recitals, games. She is mostly, mercifully, by herself. Most of these encounters are scheduled, so I can see them coming, like dangerous clouds over the horizon. I arrive nerved up and braced: friendly, distant, rigorously uninquisi-tive. I am in fact so wholly devoted to the work of self-composure that afterward, though I remember her in small exposures—the set of her glasses, a familiar dress—I find it hard to describe back to myself what Evany was *like*, how she seemed. Keeping vigilant guard against any toppling irruption of feeling, I mostly fail to take Evany in.

In the ringing hours after an encounter, the unfunny irony of this—*there is Evany, and again you do not see her!*—does not es-cape my notice.

In time it comes clear that she's not well. She looks glassier and drawn, though still a kind of beautiful that pierces me. In-voluntarily, I find myself remembering what I wrote in that last letter, the one I sent her the day we found out she wasn't preg-nant, right before everything broke. *You're the most beautiful woman in every room you walk into,* I'd said. I wish I'd stopped believing this.

But something is off. There is a brittle nervousness in her manner toward me, a subtle sad flinching, and this melts me a little.

And it is *so strange.* I'd spent so much useless time dreaming the contours of some shattering encounter between Evany and her long-forestalled remorse. This sounds exactly as wishful and inane as it was, though it was an exercise not easily forsworn. I had poisoned myself, very nearly to death, with the thought of how little mourned I was, how little the loss of me had meant to Evany. The ease with which I was made to vanish from her life, I thought, told a story, livid and terrible, about how cumulatively inconsequential I had been to her.

When alone my mouth had filled with recriminations, which I'd then rehearsed into maximally shattering pithiness, a wounding precision.

But these killing phrases, I begin to realize, I will never, ever speak.

I can't say if what I'm seeing now is Evany grieving. I can't say if this is the horror of regret that everyone said—or, said *to me*, in a weird effort at consolation—would catch up to her one day, no matter how she tried to bury it, hide it in the face of her new lover, push it far away. I suspect it is not. My battered heart tells me that having a lover to wake up with every day, and little girls to devote yourself to, keeps the tide of regret from rising too high. But I can see Evany is unhappy. Very little in the way of joy lights up around her, at least that I can perceive. She has lost her job and her house and many of her friends.

And, somewhere among these less chosen losses, she has lost me.

I may be involved in this unhappiness very little, or not at all. I do not incline to ask. I know only that seeing it, the shadow of a sorrow that is or is not regret, there in her eyes and in her mouth and in her carriage, is awful. It satisfies no recriminatory wish. It restores to me absolutely nothing.

"I'm sorry," John tells me on the phone. "It doesn't." He knows much of this, from his own bitter experience. And then he says something stranger. "Her unhappiness isn't *food*, you know? There's nothing there that's ever going to nourish you."

≈

IN THE DIREST period of our dissolution, when Evany had promised to stop "seeing" the assistant preparator (as we said in delicate euphemism) but did not, when she responded to being exposed over and over in some papery lie or other by sinking into a recessed unspeaking blankness, each retraction pure terror to me, I stopped sleeping. My mind was all combustion, a brush fire feeding on any least thing. I stopped eating and, anyway, found myself throwing up all the time, so what was the point? I thought in self-devouring little circles and tried to do something, anything, with the desire that sang through the days without cessation—the desire, I mean, to hold Evany, to press her to me, and to be held.

But you cannot ask the people who are leaving you for solace. Which is part of what gives to being left its particular inflection of horror.

I had stopped sleeping and so, with the hours stretching out in desperate immensity around me, I did what I imagine many of us would do. I read books. I read and read and read. I read, first, through whole collections of poetry, less because I thought to find steadying wisdom for the heartbroken there than because they were short, and the compass of my consciousness was not wide. (To Robert Lowell, wherever you are in the world of unhappy ghosts, I say now: thank you—thank you and thank you and thank you—for your care. I read one exquisitely despairing passage from a poem called "Skunk Hour"—"I hear / my ill-spirit sob in each blood cell, / as if my hand were at its throat . . ."—and thought, *Oh, now I know what this means.*) But my hunger for sustained transport from the scene of my own mind only increased, and so, between the hours of one and five in the morning, I began devouring novels.

I read old comforting favorites first—James, Pynchon, Baldwin, Eliot. I read *Vanity Fair* for the first time, that mordant reflection on disaster. And then, setting aside a distaste that I'd incubated since a bad high school encounter, I read Dickens. I read *a lot* of Dickens. I think I read around eight novels over the course of six miserable winter weeks. I read Dickens like you'd fall down a lightless well.

A true confession for an English professor: I had, honestly, *no idea* these novels were so good. With what slender and eroded quantity of mind was left to me, I hurtled myself at, and into, the clamoring world of Dickensian Englishness. And I'll tell you what held me fast. It was not the sweeping panoramas of life, the frenzied glut of picturesque characters, the overstuffed excess of Dickens's imagination, which was so well suited to the squabbling urban tumult of midcentury London. It was not the humor, the overworked plotting, the weepy melodrama. No. Somewhere along the way of this amateurish plunge, something else had occurred to me.

For all his avuncular geniality, Dickens was a writer of seething and gargantuan rage.

Did you know this? If I did, I'd managed to forget.

It flashes out everywhere, this rage, in captivating moments of horror and accusation. I knew something had happened to Dickens as a child, in the blacking factory. He had been sent away from his indebted family, abandoned to industrial work, and the terror and the pity of it never left him. To be abandoned and alone, in Dickens, is a fate of almost inconceivable horror. (Abandoned, alone, I drank this voraciously down.) But it had made him, too, an incendiary kind of *angry*, that a world so prosperous and miraculous in its accomplishments could be arranged in such a way that tolerated these scenes of orphaned grief, that in fact produced them as a matter of course.

And yet what was *truly* amazing in Dickens wasn't just this fury, unfolded in novel after escalatingly raging novel. Rather, he took the harm that had been visited upon him, which a part of him must have known he would never outdistance, and by some incredible magic transformed it into an overspilling *love* for the damaged creatures of the world. This can seem treacly, at moments, and sententious. I had long felt him to be so. But not on these late-night binges, oh no. There, he is a revelation. There, I find a writer laboring to imagine a kind of affection for life that does not forswear rage, but is not exhausted by it. I find a writer who imagines he might amend the broken world by pouring out upon it an impossible quantity of love.

I'm really just telling you that I read *Bleak House*.

One passage in particular struck me, when I first read it, as a kind of pure astonishment, of the sort that by then I maybe ought to have professionalized myself out of. It was like a song that wouldn't release me: I reread it and reread it and reread it.

It features a man who, throughout the book, has been an object of fun for Dickens, a stuffy and bloviating representative of the reactionary aristocracy whose name—Sir Leicester Dedlock—tells you most of what you need to know about his position in the novel as the voice of a smug, blustering, witless traditionalism, one that glories in forms, is scandalized by nonsense, and is limitlessly self-regarding.

But then, near the end of a novel throughout which this man has made himself obliging ridiculous, Sir Dedlock must confront the fact that his wife, whom he cherishes with everything that is genuine in him, has had a youthful life not at all what he had supposed. It is around her that the whole elaborate plot turns: she has had an illegitimate child—it is a Dickens novel after all—and here at the brink of exposure has fled the Dedlock estate, likely to do herself harm. The news breaks him; he has, in fact, a stroke. But he has, as he is collapsing into this stroke, a final full vision. And Dickens, his caustic regard for Sir Dedlock dissolving into a tenderness so sudden and expansive it about unravels you, tells us what it is he sees:

> It is she, in association with whom, saving that she has been for years a main fibre of the root of his dignity and pride, he has never had a selfish thought. It is she whom he has loved, admired, honoured, and set up for the world to respect. It is she, who, at the core of all the constrained formalities and conventionalities of his life, has been a stock of living tenderness and love, susceptible as nothing else is of being struck with the agony he feels. He sees her, almost to the exclusion of himself; and cannot bear to look upon her cast down from the high place she has graced so well.
>
> And, even to the point of his sinking on the ground, oblivious of his suffering, he can yet pronounce her name with something like distinctness in the midst of those intrusive sounds, and in a tone of mourning and compassion rather than reproach.

He can yet pronounce her name with something like distinctness—a beautiful, beautiful sentence, for sure. That unsleeping and arctic February, in the midst of my own night terrors and clinging desperation, it struck me, I'm afraid, as a good deal more than merely beautiful.

This is precisely how sick of mind I was: I read these dusty Victorian sentences and decided that I was being taught something invaluable.

He sees her, Dickens had written, *almost to the exclusion of himself.*

Compassion, Dickens had written, *rather than reproach.*

Like a hypnotic melody, these words adhered to me. I could not stop hearing them.

I decided that, however broken open and terrified I was,

Evany was surely suffering something more grievous. I decided that holding this revelation near to me, refusing to let it be dislodged by my terror, was the very best I could do at that moment by way of being married to Evany, and being devoted to her, and loving her.

And so, in that winter of unrelieved wretchedness, I made of my determined private vow a little talismanic gesture. I marked the passage with a photograph of the two of us, from some winters before, in which the wondering surprise at having found each other, and having fallen in this kind of love, seemed a brightness in the air all around us.

And then, as you know, everything collapsed.

And this little totemic act? I had forgotten it.

As I say, to return to the scene of old grief is to discover just how much you have managed not to retain.

WHEN IN THE DIFFERENTLY apportioned loneliness of this new winter I find the picture of Evany and me, I tend to the Dickens passage it marks with different eyes. It is still, I find, fairly staggering. The sympathy, the precision, the inner tracking of an exercise of stricken devotion, in a character so marked by narrowness and uncharity. The distilled fucking heartbreak of it.

I have now, of course, a specific recalled sorrow to go with it—the memory of that great resolve, that improvised devotion, and of how useless it was. A part of me wants to take hold of the self that put the picture there, to shake him. *She does not want your love,* I'd tell him. *That is exactly what she is struggling to get away from.* Books are not manuals for living, no more than a pop song is a guidebook, and you do a kind of harm to them if you treat them like they are. I say this to students all the time. How could I have allowed myself to believe otherwise?

But, like songs, books do have the virtue of not sitting still.

Leave them alone for a while—a few errant meandering years, say—and they grow, in secret, into different creatures. They hold on to you, they steady you as you pour yourself into them, but sometimes, also, they talk back. Sometimes they start fires.

You would not think that, after months now gone to years of gnawing obsessiveness, there were new thoughts for me to have about Evany, Evany who flinches in my company, Evany who opens the door to the girls when I drop them off, ushers them in to spaces where I have no place, Evany whom I have made into a great and abiding mystery. You'd think I would have run right through the imaginable lot of them. But no. I turn it around. I pick up old fragments. Other voices start talking to one another, and other objects, and the memory of other scenes.

I teach my classes. I do my bits of work. I see friends and sometimes the girls and very occasionally the person I suppose I have to start referring to as my "ex-wife." I enter less and less fitfully into the wintertime life of a small college town in New England.

I start to think about Evany in an unaccustomed way.

15

Katy Dear

I USED TO SAY that the greatest show Evany and I ever saw together was back in about the year 2000, at an irreplaceable Chicago venue called the Hideout.

We had flown out from Maine on one of our first-ever treks together, as I remember it mostly to see John, who I was eager for Evany to meet. And who should we discover was playing there, at the Hideout—and on Halloween itself!—but Neko Case, not yet as famous as she would become but plainly on the ascent. John and I had first seen her performing on stage in the slashing rain at a street fair in Lakeview, back when she was just another upstart talent in the insurgent country scene that Chicago did a lot to nurture—punk-rock kids returning to the radical leanings of generations of country music—and whose center was, in a lot of ways, the Hideout. (I would have a good deal of life pass at the Hideout: it was there that Lise and I, years later, would go dancing.)

A Halloween show with Neko and Kelly Hogan and the Sadies! At the Hideout! Days of plenty, without question.

So we went out to the gig that night only to find that it was, inevitably, sold out. The bouncer told me and John, and that was that. An apologetic shrug. This was before any of us had cell phones. Being sold out of a show: it happened. It happened to me more times than I could name in the '90s. (I believe I hold a kind of record, having been sold out of not one but *three* Pavement shows between 1994 and 1998.) We were disappointed, of course, but not shattered. We ambled our way back to the patio outside where Evany was waiting for us, broke the news, and turned to go find the car.

Not Evany.

Evany insisted that we were going to see this show. Um, but it's sold out? "Oh, it's not *really* sold out." This—"*really* sold out"—was a new designation to us. It made Evany incredulous. "Jesus, you guys are *children*." And off she went. John looked at me, but I didn't know what was happening any more than he did. We followed her. And there, and then, standing before the bouncer, she commenced delivering to the poor man a speech of unrehearsed intricacy and, as it would prove, strangely entrancing persuasive power, by turns sweet and cajoling, a shade flirtatious, somehow insistent as well, filled with lapses and leaps, pleas that became admonitions—in all, a great woven spell of words that concluded with the guy, now fallen into some kind of hypnagogic enchantment, selling us three tickets and wishing us the enjoyment of the great city of Chicago.

John and I looked at one another, in frozen stupefaction. Evany glanced back over her shoulder, a crooked cocky grin on her face. In we all went.

And the show! The show was a fucking triumph, a delight in just the way it is when acts on the rise come back for an intimate gig with a hometown crowd. You feel at such times like the sea of strangers pressing in around you is in fact a body of old friends and acquaintances, with whom you've shared in some small collective labor that's coming, just now, to sweet fruition. You recognize a gratified devotion in each other, and there's a reciprocal joy that travels back and forth between audience and performer. It is intensely winning. It certainly was that October night.

And then there was this: After disappearing from the stage for a few puzzling moments, leaving the Sadies to vamp and jam, Kelly and Neko returned in full Halloween splendor, a blur of wigs, shawls, scarves, and glistening spandex. Wait. Are they . . . ? Is that . . . ? Oh, sweet Jesus. *They had reappeared dressed as Heart.* They took the stage dressed as the Wilson sisters, Ann and Nancy, whereupon the band kicked into a thundering rendition of "Magic Man," followed immediately by "Crazy on You," those fantastic '70s hard-rock anthems, more Evany's era than mine or John's but recognized immediately from years of replays on classic-rock radio. The crowd greeted it all with ecstasies, distributed chiefly between the gawping and head-clutching varieties.

And then, because these two numbers were the Heart songs the band had learned how to play, and no others, they played them through *again*.

I used to say this was the greatest show we ever saw together. And John was there, in a moment that saw my Chicago youth come stumbling directly into my Maine maturity, with a sweetness hardly to be improved. And there was Evany, in the midst of it, cajoling, dancing, joining John in shouting out for "Dog & Butterfly," a vision of '70s-kid swagger and dauntlessness. It was a good night.

But the woman who was radiant and tough, who talked her way into shows and told stories about dancing with college boys to the terriblest of '70s ballads, was Evany in only one of her guises. It was one I loved, one that the sound of a key change in a stadium-rock jam could call back to me in glowing comprehensiveness.

But there were others.

I loved those too. But differently.

≈

ONE NIGHT A few years into our marriage we went to see another singer working the edges of the country tradition, where it
blurred a little with postpunk and indie rock and the like. We
went to see a singer called Gillian Welch, which is to say that we
went to see Gillian Welch and David Rawlings perform at a mid-
size space down in Portland. The two of them, together, make up
"Gillian Welch," and they play unamplified songs that have the
starkness, the burned-away elementality, of the kind that typically gets called "traditional." That's not wrong—their spare
songs do indeed have a way of sounding *found*, like something
borrowed from the Carter Family or maybe the Louvin Broth-
ers, or from the old-time folk ballads. But you hear so much else,
too, a gathering and condensing of influences much more messy
and promiscuous—much more impure—than is usually embraced in committedly roots-Americana songwriting. You catch
errant snatches of Neil Young and Gram Parsons and Emmylou
Harris, of the Dylan who drawls out dreamy ten-minute epics,
even some faint afterimage of the Grateful Dead.

"I love this," I remember saying to Evany. "It gives me everything I might want from the Grateful Dead, while relieving me
of the burden of having to listen to the Grateful Dead."

We go, Evany and I, and there are no dance floor ecstasies,
no bursts of hilarity. Mostly there is this kind of tranced captivation. For a few hours, we settle into the hushed intensity of
two voices tracing lines around each other, finding harmo-
nies that chime along dissonant lines of melody, wander, and return. It is beautiful and eerie and, in the stretched-out time
of the songs themselves, weirdly tranquilizing. They do a few
covers—"Pocahontas" from Neil Young is one of them, if I remember right—and these come across as old familiars lovingly

estranged from themselves, de-tuned, made over into novel idioms. There is something almost druggy about the night: the warping elongations of time, the hypnotizing rhythms, the feeling of music assembling itself around you as a kind of *space*, into which you are invited to move and drift.

Like everyone else in the place, we are, for the hours we stand there, spellbound.

We don't talk a lot during the show—the atmosphere is, pointedly, *quiet*—but afterward we do. We are driving back from the city to our little house up the coast and, in the lulled low talking of our concert afterglow, we're listening again to a pretty Welch-Rawlings number called "Dear Someone."

"I want to go all over the world," the singer says, *"and start living free..."*

I can see myself going on, full of gushy enthusiasm. *I liked this, I loved this, did you see this?* I can see myself talking and talking.

Evany does not disagree, not exactly. She loved the show as well. But something about her tells me she is still partly inhabiting the hazed space of the concert, that dimension adjacent, crosswise, to our own. She's saying something else.

"Those songs," she says, and I look over at her.

She's watching the road, the night accumulating beyond us, above the sea.

"She knows something," she says then, "about unhappiness."

We are listening to "Dear Someone," and did I mention that this was our first-dance song, on the day of our wedding, those few years before?

We drive. We play some songs. We talk, in the way of long-coupled people. And if we are talking about the show we've just seen, and about the songs we've just heard, we are also, in the way of long-coupled people, making a little idiom, the language of our being together.

Like all critics and all lovers, we are telling each other stories. Evany is telling me a story about herself.

It was a story I knew. But she was asking me, really, to listen.

EVANY HAD HAD, as I've mentioned, an adolescence of real, if not uncommon, difficulty. A bland accounting would say: It was the '70s, she was adventurous, she was young, she was more inclined to wildness than temperance. She loved beauty—this much, she always knew—in ways not easily squared with the kinds of life anticipated for her, and this gave her a halting rebelliousness.

She got into trouble. She felt ashamed but also, because she was smart and by temperament unplacating, angry about being made to feel ashamed.

All of this is true, without being especially illuminating.

By the time we met, Evany had launched herself, with an edge of defiance, into a youthful marriage, had thought of leaving it, had stayed, had had two beautiful babies. And then had broken herself free.

She suffered, I knew, in these later years, from an unresting fear, which was that the placeless grief that ate at her, and could sometimes wrap her in an incapacitating darkness, might be an affliction she would somehow pass on to her girls, like some heritable malady of soul.

She suffered, I knew, a dim conviction that had come to her from nothing in particular, or from everything. This was the conviction that, no matter what she might tell herself and even on occasion believe, she was not a person who deserved, actually, to be loved.

It was a fear as real and as changeable as weather, as persuasive as gravity, and it pulled at her. She invented a range of ways to fight against it, and these worked or they did not.

Loving me was, for a while, one of these strategies.

≈

LET ME TELL you about another song, one that, in the accumulating hours of the long Maine winter—alongside the reencountered Dickens novel, alongside the spectacle of Evany's seeming unhappiness—starts speaking to me in a new voice.

This song is called "Silver Dagger" and it's a country ballad, a reworked traditional that in other iterations goes by the name "Katy Dear" or "Drowsy Sleeper," though in Gillian Welch's spare and simple updating it resists the shape of those previous songs of dangerous lovers eluded or embraced. Her song is weirder even than these old-timey murder ballads, and also—if this is possible—bleaker, more dire.

There is a singer at its center, and the song finds her in a state of arid despair. There is no story offered, only the evocation of what the song calls a "mood," and it is one of a cold shattered vacancy: a sickness of heart that has slipped free of the singer's solitary person and come, somehow, to cover the whole of the world that surrounds her. Nothing solaces. The singer says, *"I'm through with Bibles,"* and then, as though the connection between these notions were plain, she adds, *"I'm through with food."* It's a flat declaration, the breadth of which takes a moment to land. The world around her is only unnourishing.

But if this is anguish, a wrenching devastation in the singer, it speaks in a matter-of-fact voice, as though the period of struggling against it has long since passed. Now, for her, there is only this stilled sorrow, and the afterimage of a joy most present to her in its negation. The time of possibility, for a feeling that is not one of malign fatedness, is gone.

All this makes the culmination of the song terrible. We have dwelled so closely with the singer's desolation, have been so tuned to its devouring power, that when in the final verse we arrive at what seems like the preacherly brimstone moral of the song—about the terrible destructiveness residing in any grief-battered heart—we have reason, in the pause that follows, to fear for her. We wonder what awfulness of purpose sleeps inside *her*, what she might visit upon herself.

But then, in the next phrase, the song pivots, hard. We are returned to the territory of the murder ballad.

A man appears: the demonic lover, the bringer of doom.

Something is strange here, though. With a chilling solicitude, almost *voluptuously*, the singer announces him.

And then there he is before us.

"*With that silver dagger*"—long suspended pause—"*in his hand.*"

It is awful, this ending, with an awfulness that rings and rings and rings through the song's last wordless moments.

It is awful because if the song has adapted itself to the old form of the murder ballad, it has also, in that fixed attentiveness to what illnesses of spirit lie *within* the singer, made it say something else. It is awful because whatever the violence set to break upon the singer, she regards it less with dread or even impassivity than with something nearer to *desire*, a lover's hunger. It is a murder ballad whose heroine is at once victim and, in her stricken grief, half-willing perpetrator.

It is a song, "Silver Dagger," about a special kind of illness of spirit. The kind that makes you a conspirator in your own destruction.

SONGS ARE NOT GUIDEBOOKS, any more than novels. They do not offer instruction in how to live a life—unless your life is impressively more dramatic than my own. But they are for many of us where we encounter possibilities, inferences, angles of blossoming thought, that for whatever reason come to be accessible to us in no other human way.

When I come to "Silver Dagger" again in Maine something about it, and about the sadness I can't pretend not to see in Evany, folds itself over into *Bleak House*, which of course makes no sense, except that, as it happens, it makes a swift and inarguable kind of sense. They speak together to me somehow, in the jumbled way of things bound into coherence by nothing so much as private sorrow, the esoteric logics of grief.

I had pleased myself, over the years of my marriage, with the belief that I knew the griefs that held themselves fast to Evany, that I had taken their measure. I knew the malign impulses that crept over her, the descents into cold darkness, the corresponding tendencies to self-sabotage. I had in real ways made myself in a kind of unresting relation to them. Here was Evany, with her susceptibilities to desolation, and here was I, determined to love her away from any and all of them. We would go to shows, and we would travel, and we would raise children, and we would have all the sex and throw all the parties and do all the dancing. I would pour out all my love upon whatever was broken in her and, together, if we couldn't undo it, we could make it smaller, quieter, unscary, less.

I am in Maine and it is the winter and I am alone. No one shovels the driveway with me. No one goes to bed with me and no one—I think of this all the time—knows that I've woken up in the morning, made it through another night. But I listen to "Silver Dagger," I let consciousness snag on it and drift toward it and dwell in it, and it's here that the strangest alchemy commences.

In damning little visions, hallucinatory and bright, it comes to me how little I had known—how piteously fucking little—about anything like adult sorrow.

Two of these awful visions, a conjoined pair, rise up before me.

In one, we are driving, Evany and I. It is a long trip, without the girls—I seem to remember we are crossing the cheerless stretches of upstate New York—and Evany is crying. *She* is crying, not me. There is a song filling the space between us, and it has shaken something loose in her, made a quick little tear in the textured ordinariness of the day. There are tears on her face, and what I'm noticing is an awful, frightened look. And she says—I remember, she says *exactly* this—"I think we should have a baby."

And she turns to me, her great eyes pooling and gray.

And in the other vision? In the other, I am alone. I see myself, kneeling, shirtless, leaning forward, on a bright morning in the corner of our house.

What arrives to me then, in the wake of this song-induced conjunction of scenes long suppressed, hidden away from myself, made over into mysteries—what arrives to me is the strangest sorrow I have yet encountered in all these glutted months, a thing so filled with pity and confusion and guilt I hardly know what to call it.

I know this, though: Evany had to have struggled against every malevolent thing inside her when we were married, a pain whose gravity I did not begin to comprehend. That struggle was, in real ways, the condition of her being married to me. She had to have said to herself, over and over, with and without words, *I can be happy; I do deserve this adoration, this love.*

I think of it, that daily, determined willing herself open.

What could induce a person to take up such lacerating work, to turn herself toward the grinding scary toil of it? What could possibly hold a person to it, in it, despite the flaring recurrences of shame, of sorrow, the old combustible griefs?

Even I can't get this wrong.

We should have a baby. She had said exactly that.

She had to have loved me.

She had to have loved me a very great deal.

Until something awful happened. Until something broke. Until she couldn't.

IF YOU ASKED me about Evany in the back end of the winter of my return, I'd have told you she was not, whatever you may have heard, a villain. I would have told you that she was not an insoluble mystery, a black box, the demon lover.

I'd have told you Evany was right.

Nothing is clearer to me, in the still, blue light of the hard-frozen Maine winter, in my echoing and empty house, than that Evany was right. She was right, she was right, she was right. I *had* conspired to make up a story about us, a story of our togetherness. It was a story in which our love was larger than any grief, in which no sorrow was as real as our being together. It was a story in which she got to be happy, and I got to be heroic, and, my God, had I wanted it to be true. I had done that.

But I had not been alone.

Evany had made it up with me.

Evany told it too. Evany *wanted* it to be true. And this, when it comes to me, I take to be about the saddest fucking thought the world has ever known.

16

If Magic Made It

WE ARE, MY YOUNGEST stepdaughter and I, at the bar.

It is a school night.

It's true there are not many other thirteen-year-olds here, poised on stools and leaning, as if expertly, toward the beer spigots and ranks of bottles, but nobody seems to mind. Amelia certainly does not. She swivels this way and that, bends to her straw, checks the scene. The clamor carries on around us in an ordinary weeknight way. There are dudes twirling their big-bellied glasses of wine in scholarly scrutiny. There are clutches of ladies laughing over neon cocktails. There are couples angling toward one another. And there is, additionally, a lank-haired and, for this little city on the coast of Maine, impressively beautiful young man working the bar, who attends to each and all with an able smooth-flowing flirtatiousness.

"Yeah," Amelia is saying to me, "but he's just so . . . so *arrogant*."

"Sweetie, of course he is!" I say. "Wouldn't you be? If you were him?"

In fairness to myself I should say that I have not taken my newly teenaged stepdaughter out to a bar, or at least not intentionally. We are not at some speakeasy or portside dive. We've gone in fact to a restaurant—a fancyish French restaurant in Portland, of *her* impromptu choosing!—which proved to be overcrowded with diners looking for a winter night's escape, and so we have been sat here, at this elegant curving bar. And anyway, I tell myself as I fidget just a bit nervously in my seat, what's the harm? We haven't ordered a pair of double bourbons (we haven't even ordered one!) and Amelia, to appearances, is as deep in the enjoyment of this slight alteration of context as I am in the fact of her company.

I'm noticing that she has grown over the past year into a kind of poise I, at least, do not much identify with the early teenage years. She holds herself so unanxiously. She still can be a touch overawed by her big sister, but you can see her working not to be, not to be baited out of her self-composure. She knows somehow how to look around her, to measure and assess, without seeming to gawp. She is watchful, observant, cool.

I notice, too, that she has not stopped tracking this bartender, whose striped black-and-white shirt (in campy "French" style) does not quite manage to descend to the belted top of his skinny jeans. Tousled, bearded, lithe—you look at him and want to guess the name of his inevitable band—he is the very type of new-millennial hipster handsomeness. He's also, in a funny way, *terrible*. Preening, a bit leering, so wildly overdelighted in his small-market beauty you can't help but relish him, if a little meanly. He cajoles and chats, tells stale little jokes, receives from his patrons indulgent grins. He hands off drinks and, with the cocktail-drinking ladies, grazes their forearms with a discreet touch as he passes.

"I guess," Amelia says. "But nobody should get to be that conceited. It's *annoying*."

"Dude, it is so *not* annoying. It's awesome! It's, like, the awesomest part of him."

We are speaking, as sometimes we do, of Kanye.

≈

ONE SLOW-DAWNING HEARTBREAK of losing the girls—if that's what's happened—comes with the realization that for a long time I had been looking forward to their teenage years, not at all with dread, but with an impatient excitement.

People are filled with horror stories about adolescent girls, I know—about the volatility, the meanness, the volcanic emotionality, but of course these are things I have always tended to *like* in people. These are just the things I've tended to treasure up in myself, perhaps a bit indefensibly—as if in the fear that when these vivid impulses have receded, they'll have taken with them all the most vital parts of being a person. You could call it an unoutgrown immaturity, I suppose, this harkening to the call of emotions at fever pitch, but I'm not sure I'd believe you. When caught suddenly in one or other of the swoony brief blisses of a new record, I'm pretty sure I'd say it's something a lot better, a childish thing you really oughtn't to put away. (As Adam Phillips writes, in a sentence that always meant a lot to me: "As only adults can know, maturity often involves putting away the wrong childish things.") When the girls were little, their toddler rages and gusty sorrows could undo me, in part because they were so unmappable to me, so unpredictable, so out of touch with any sense of proportion I was able to bring to the scene of, say, a five-year-old's crying jag. I was impatient, shamefully so. But the proportions of adolescence, the special turbulence of its emotional weather, had never felt far from me. Of course they hadn't. *I had headphones and an iPod.* I looked forward to Lucy and Amelia's arrival at teenagedom with something of the eager expectancy of new parents waiting for their infants to learn to talk.

But then, just as they were poised on the precipice of this arrival, we were jolted apart from one another.

And yet here we are—apart in some ways, certainly, but in others we have yet to figure out . . . unsundered? Maybe? Yes, maybe. I go out as often as I can with Amelia, with Lucy; this is once, maybe twice a week. They are busy people, and they live a bit farther away. But whenever I manage to be in their company I find that I am for long moments released from the encroaching little panics that otherwise take such free hold of me, often in the long hours without them. I watch them, and they talk, and I listen, and talk back—it is all so unexceptional—and the sheer *ordinariness* they are able to stake out around us, that we find a way to make together, strikes me afterward as a small bit of earthbound miraculousness.

Girls, I think to say when I kiss them good-bye, *you are miracles of awesomeness.* But I don't. I hear, or imagine I hear—or imagine *they* might hear—the neediness tremoring through it. So I keep it to myself, unsaid, another private little novena.

Meantime, once they've gone, the unhappier formulations arrive. I have been thinking a lot these days of my other reason to regret being a presence somewhat more distant from their lives in this, the first turbulent passages of adolescence: *this was my time to shine.* The teenage years, I mean, had always seemed an especially good time to be a stepdad. The job of the adolescent after all is to separate herself from her parents, and in this way become a new and necessary kind of autonomous. She does this, typically, by hating, with unsparing precision and detail, the person of her mom and the person of her dad. But I was neither of these! Another joy of adolescence for the stepparent: with so much articulate despising of Mom and Dad happening, there just isn't much traction in hating *you.* Being a stepparent means in lots of ways being second-string, and this could be its own small heartbreak. In adolescence, when one of the foremost things exchanged between children and their parents is a laser-sighted loathing, it is a gift.

We have a good deal to exchange between us these days. It takes the form of in-jokes, stories, songs and vehement opinions about them. It is surely not loathing. What it is, like so much else between us, remains hard to name.

AMELIA'S SISTER AND I HAVE had a many-tiered debate about Kanye West circulating between us for a while, as Amelia knows. Like more or less everyone—certainly like my grown-up friends—Lucy cycles between aversion and attraction. The delights of a record like *Graduation*, Kanye's latest, are not much lost on her—the wild lexical dexterity, the sick groove—but his persona, its hyperbole and relentlessness, the self-deification not ever quite rendered ironic . . . it is fair to say Lucy finds these grating. In response I tend to offer defenses spun around genre—"Can you imagine an MC *without* arrogance?" I say; "Can you imagine how dull that would be?"—and the world's ever-renewing uneasiness around black men who refuse to cringe. Of course she knows all this and, in truth, I get what she's saying. Lucy is nearing the end of her first year of high school. Her days are spent in the company of fifteen-year-old boys. She needs no tutorials in male arrogance and self-hyperbolization.

Amelia, here with me and without her sister, is taking up the question and running with it—talking about what she likes better in Jay-Z, which Kanye tracks are the most excellent and why, and what she finds off-putting, exhausting, *annoying*. Is there anything more killing than the inflection given by a thirteen-year-old to the word *annoying*? It straightens your spine. And so we drift, in conversation, among the ever-expanding varieties of teenaged annoyance, as I drink my beer and Amelia attends, with winning vigor, to her steak-frites, and then to mine. All the while, she keeps a watchful eye on the bartender, who minuets among patrons, striking brief poses, basking a bit in the light of all the erotic attention diffusing around him. Our conversation meanders. It shifts and grades. And this is how we begin speaking not of annoyance in its general appearance, but of the pressing and particular annoyance of *boys*, boys both generic and in Amelia's acquaintance. On this topic, she has much to say.

She tells me of this one kid's fair-weather kindness, this other kid's jerkishness, of the modes of "dating" swimming up into sudden possibility for the world of seventh graders. She warms to the topic. She talks and talks, and I follow. We decide together that "adolescent boy" is indeed an unpromising genre of person, though I remind her that boys, too, have many things to be frightened by, even if their way of being afraid is, often, very, very dickish. Her tone is derisive and light but there is, too, tracing through it, some faint urgency. I notice this and find that I feel toward it, and her, a great rush of tenderness. Like the smart kid she is, she's trying to work it all out—girls, boys, their odiousness and attraction—and she's doing it here, now, in real time.

I have some sense that my role here is mostly that of sounding board and I am wary, with the practiced wariness of stepparenthood, of overstepping. But how to calibrate these distances and proximities, here in the more uncertain terrain of this new thing we are together, whatever it is, this *ex*-stepparenthood?

We eat, we talk. We tell familiar jokes. We speak of Kanye, in little arias of disparagement and praise. We take each other's cues.

And so, here at the bar, balancing my wariness against this glancing invitation to ampler talk, I risk a little. I invite Amelia to consider, with me, the many subgenres of straight-dude ridiculousness. I say, in a stage whisper, "Okay, sweetie—check this guy *out*." And together, with commentary running largely to the satiric, we observe our so striking bartender. "Dude, watch these moves," I say. And we do, noting his coy smiles, his calculated touches, the whole wonderful preening theater of him. We try to

locate him within a matrix of Annoying Boy Attributes and decide he is conceited, though in degrees not yet approaching
Kanye levels of self-besottedness, but he is also, without question, a little charming. *Adorbs* is the term we use, and Amelia allows as she finds him so, yes. She further allows, after I suggest as
much, that he is indeed very pretty. Very, very pretty.

"That's the thing," I'm saying. "Boys are annoying in *so many
ways*. But that doesn't mean you don't get to want to, like, smooch
his face."

Amelia gives a quick braying laugh. I have no idea where the
phrase comes from—*smooch his face!*—but, just as soon as it's
been uttered, it sticks. In the weeks and then months ahead, we
will say it back to one another, a shared bit of idiom, an agreed-
upon term of art.

"Sometimes there's a boy and he's whatever he is, he's this or
that, and you just want to smooch his face. And that," I say, "is
totally fine. I mean, don't let anybody be nasty to you, but you
know that. But sometimes, sweetie, you know . . . sometimes you
want to smooch somebody's face."

Amelia's bright-eyed, maybe a shade abashed, but also grinning. "Yeah," she says. "It's true. Sometimes you just wanna
smooch his face."

This is how Amelia and I learn how to talk about sex.

THAT I WOULD PRESUME to offer wise counsel about sex,
boys, or dating, or anything that is not American literature or
indie rock, is of course a high-end piece of ridiculousness. I could
with as much authority be proffering advice about trigonometry
or plant DNA or how to cook a moose. In truth I'd have *more*
authority. With respect to not any one of those was I failed and
floundering.

It's lonely being in a big empty house—have I mentioned

that?—though it is a loneliness that, this time around, is not allowed to become so wild and overgrown as it had in my days of
sorrowful ingénuing through the stony capitals of Europe. Routines ballast me. The recurring patterns of work, of teaching and
writing and living an ordinary academic life, throw me often
enough into contact with people who are dear to me that my solitude never quite degrades back into the manic desolation it had
been. For what's seemed like ages, I've been telling myself that
the work before me is to find some less desperate way to miss
Evany, and the girls, and our life. Do this, I think, and all other
things will follow from it.

In a novel I've returned to this winter for no good purpose,
other than a hunger for a sterner kind of solace, George Eliot
says of a character whose vaulting ambitions for herself have
come to ruin that, after a terrible passage, "she was no longer
wrestling with her grief, but could sit down with it as a lasting
companion." I underline the passage. I write it out by hand and
then type it up. Its cadence becomes something I remember like
a melody.

I have this grief. I am trying to make it a companion.

"YOU ARE, PETER. You are so much better."

My mother tells me this when I'm home for a visit over the
March break from classes. This is what mothers say, or at least
my mother.

We are at the kitchen table, just the two of us, warming cups
of coffee between us. It is morning and she presses food upon
me, which I do not want. She is, I can see, so happy I am here, in
a state of noncollapse.

"Do you remember what it was like two years ago?"

I do, and I do not. She's thinking about the week after Evany
had left me, that cold early April. I'd had to teach but wasn't quite

sure how I was going to manage, oh, my next breath. Evany had vacated the house for a week—to her mother's, I had believed— while the girls were with their father, and so, frightened of what might become of me, my mom had come up to Maine to stay with me. But she had not come alone. She had taken her sisters. *All four sisters* arrived in Maine to look after me. They had each taken off work, and driven up together, and walked me through my mornings, and my afternoons, and my nights. Though I do not in truth much remember what I was like—it's a blur of heaving incredulous terror—I can imagine.

So yes, I say, I'm better than that. In the morning stillness, I try to explain something of the past solitary months, of my brief encounters with Evany, of my widening sense of the sorrows she'd had to wrestle with, all the time, just to be married to me at all. I tell her I'm finding ways to understand my part in this cataclysm, and to understand, too, how much Evany *had* loved me. I'm trying to find ways to experience that love as, let's say, uncanceled, though this is hard. I tell my mom I don't know that it makes sense to call this reckoning "forgiveness"—I'm still so sorrowful, I still so hate doing without Evany, I'm still so frightened for the girls—but I can tell it's made grief something ever so slightly *smaller*, and less frightening, than it had been.

The early sun climbs the walls behind us. I look over my mother's shoulder, out the window. It's too early yet for blossoms, but the snow is gone. And there, with the light shifting gradients from red to yellow, the notion rises in me that I should tell my mother, now, here, about what happened that one day in Maine, on the floor of the dining room. What almost happened. What I almost did. She is smiling across the table at me with such beaming happiness—that I am here, that we are talking, that whatever it is that's had hold of me for so long seems to be loosening its grip. The shame of how much I have put her through, and my dad—the shame of having been loved so well, and then having *failed* to make a love for Evany that was similarly nourishing—is a faint pulsing in my chest.

I watch the thought of confessing it all form as if in the air between us, and dissipate, and dissolve away. I don't say anything.

"I can't think about her, Peter," my mother says, with a sharpness that surprises me. I must look puzzled, because she goes on.

"You don't think it's important, but I'm a Christian. I'm a *Catholic*. It matters to me. If I think of everything that happened, every terrible thing she said . . . I can't find any forgiveness in my heart. So I don't. I just can't think of her."

It occurs to me, in one of those childish moments in which you realize, yet again, that your parents are real, that my mom has struggled with this, with the impiety of her unforgiving anger. I stand up and go to her. I kiss her on the cheek. I say I'm sorry.

She tells me not to be sorry. She is happy, so happy, that I'm *better*. And then, because she is my mother, and this is what mothers evidently do, she looks at me. She holds my face between her hands, just the way my grandmother, her mother, used to do. "Love will find you, Peter."

And just like that, there it is—that slight insinuating claustrophobia that finds you under the parental roof, even in moments as brightly lit by love as this. What is it about parental kindness, this giving grace, that makes it so difficult to receive? Why would any least uneasiness find me here, in a house where I have known so much unstinting care?

I think again about the girls, the poise with which they make room for the love I still want for them, the care I cannot help but offer, however fumblingly. (*Smooch his face!* Amelia and I say to one another.) They seem, in the instant, not a lot less wondrous.

But meantime, in the company of my own mother and her care, I feel myself going unsteady. I sense the tingling beginnings of a transformation into a more petulant, contrary, infantile version of myself. "It's not that easy, *Mom*," I want to say, or something equally asinine and childish.

But I do not.

I say instead that I need to get some work done, so I'm going to drive over to the coffee shop.

"But you've just had your coffee."

What?

"You *had* coffee. That makes no sense."

"Give me a break, Mom."

BACK IN MAINE I deliver to the girls a sweet little care package of gifts from my mother and my aunts, of the sort they have always loved to give: trinkets and baubles, stuffed in matching little purses, each with a card to the girl in question.

Unlike their stepdad, they receive these affections with a pleasure uninflected by impatience or irritation. They write back little notes of thanks.

"Should we call your dad 'Papa'?" Lucy wants to know.

"Um, sure," I say, not having devoted much thought to it.

They scribble on, perturbed in no ways immediately visible to me.

"Lucy," Amelia says, holding up a little bracelet, "wanna trade?"

17

Cruising and Shooting and Fucking

THE STORE CLERK has let us in and we are riffling, one by one, through the racks of dresses, skirts, hipster tops and jean jackets and embossed hoodies, tank tops and tees. I am walking along with Lucy, behind her really, and offering light editorializing on this item and that. I'm doing color commentary, you could say, not play-by-play.

"Sister Amelia would *kill* in this," she says and sets a cute shirt back in the rack.

I am as happy to be here, beside this stylish girl, as I am a pleased and half-puzzled kind of bemused. That I would have anything worthwhile to add to a consideration of *clothes*, to this keen-eyed young person, is the kind of joke that takes years, decades even, to ripen into just this sort of ridiculousness. But it has. I know why I'm here.

I am here because, without really trying to, I have begun to cut a different sort of figure. I am skinnier by a lot since Evany left me, in the drawn and somewhat sallow way of the freshly divorced. But if my clothes sit differently upon me it's not just because I've shed some fraction of the sedentary posttenure paunchiness I'd long been cultivating. (Sex makes us stupid, my friend Jennifer liked to say. To which, in my married years, I used to add: *Love makes us fat.*) As Lucy knows, and Amelia, too, I have been in the world—I have in fact spent those years throwing myself at the world, and trying to stick. In time, at last, this has made an appreciable kind of difference.

And it's true: despite the weird hermit's lair I've established for myself in small-town Maine, I do not retract myself from the circuits of the living. I go out with colleagues there. I travel to visit friends. I take more trips to New York in this season, returning each time with trinkets for the girls, than ever before. I catch some winter shows in Brooklyn, where, a little to everyone's amusement, I have begun, too, to acquire, item by item, a wardrobe in which I appear at least marginally less in the thrall of the unforgotten '90s and its preference for plaid, flannels, XXLs.

"You know what might look good?" Jordan asks, in the midst of one Soho venture. "A *medium.*"

If this is what swimming in the waters of eligible singlehood is to be, I am willing to suit up.

Perhaps most mockably, I've been getting regular haircuts in a Williamsburg establishment beneath the BQE—a *salon*, in fact, though it is also a tattoo parlor—from an excellent woman to whom I was recommended the summer before, with the admonition that, if I was actually planning on being a person who was *dating*, I might as well get a grown-up haircut. But when, with the unerring sartorial attentiveness of teenagers, Lucy and Amelia notice this shirt, that jacket, this rhyming sneakers-and-scarf combination, they are less cutting about it than you'd think. Actually, they're sweetly encouraging. Only recently, Lucy had paid me about the greatest, most improbable compliment I'd ever received. In the midst of a little thrift store excursion not unlike today's, rolling through long racks of shirts and debating among them, she had turned to me.

"You know," she'd said, "you're the only man I'd let help me choose my clothes."

I'd let the breadth of it wash over me, until I was veritably afloat with happiness. I have, to appearances, come a long, long way from 1997.

And so today we are trolling once more through the offerings, with a pleasing idleness. Lucy talks about what she likes, and why, in little bursts of observation, woven back into the fabric of what she'd been saying. Like her sister she holds herself, even here, with a kind of rangy poise I can't imagine in myself at her age. Whereas Amelia is watchful and cool, Lucy is fluent and fast and funny, garrulous, the note of a broad teenage irony never far from her voice—except, that is, when she drops into these sudden passages of brow-furrowed contemplativeness. They can be about anything: her sister's friend circle, her grandmother's childhood, one cousin's struggles with his dad. These, when they come, are quick enough, and offhand, but so wrought around with patient thoughtfulness, and so startlingly in earnest, you have to remind yourself you're keeping company with a teenage girl in her first years of high school.

That grown-up poise is wonderful to see—I won't lie and say it doesn't make me feel proud of her—but it breaks my heart a little too. Here is Lucy, the big sister still, the taker of care, prepared already to be the adult any circumstance requires.

I remember, in one of those errant gusts of recollection, that first of our conversations after it had all happened, after Evany had told her she was leaving me. *Everything's okay, sweetie,* I had said. *Nothing will ever, ever stop me loving you, and being proud of you.* And Lucy had cried and cried and cried, returned for a moment to that little-kid inconsolability that had so rattled me when I was new to her life, and to parenthood.

I'm so sorry, love, I kept saying.

"I know," she said. "I know. I know. I know."

A voice in me can't stop saying it. *I'm so sorry, love. I'm so sorry.*

All of which makes her turns to the silly and the satiric—and these are many—only sweeter to me. Today she is busy imagining Amelia in any number of unlikely fashion combinations, this teensy skirt, that top.

"That girl will light up the seventh grade. She will bring it *down*."

We return the garments of choice. We drift and chat. We note together the things we think we could pull off, the things we suspect we could not. I make a lament of how very, very little, at this late stage in the game of fashion, I can actually hazard for myself.

"Oh, I don't know," Lucy says. "You're a *lot* better than you used to be."

Nothing rises or ripples in her voice when she says this. She offers it casually, in the easy flow of things, in that teenaged tone located unreadably between satire and seriousness. I try not to stumble over it, to derail the day.

"Thanks, man," I think finally to say. "I'm like the Keanu of coastal Maine."

She gives me one of those wonderful adolescent *whatever*s, an eye roll of the entire body.

"Dude," she says.

We make our way out into the day.

I AM AT LEAST PARTLY willing to concede the point about being, in some conjugations of the sentence of my life, *better*. I am even ready to enjoy small indulgences of pride about this fact—to look back at the passages navigated, the places seen, the friendships made more impassioned, rather than less, over the course of what were largely awful years.

"Think of all the sex you've had!" Beth says encouragingly, on one of our late-night coast-to-coast catch-up calls, and we laugh about it, and gossip, and trade secrets. Here, I know, is a love made ampler, and given more breadth, by the new kinds of care we've learned to make for one another. She is close to me, all the time; I carry thoughts of her, and her baby, and her partner, and the knotted intricacy of their lives, around with me through the day.

And there are others. My far-scattered friends, who together make up what feels daily to me like a *world*, coherent and holding, have not loved me less because of how broken I have been. I tell Beth that I remain opposed, with something near to militancy, to the idea that grief is educative, *improving*. There is nothing improving in being broken, despite what many narrative genres want to convince you: loss, I keep saying, is the thing that nothing redeems. It is awfulness and only that.

And yet I confess that this discovery, that I might be broken *and* loved . . . ? It has been a slow-release revelation.

"And if you stayed broken," Beth tells me, "I'd keep loving you."

In these moments between us, I am as held fast to the world as I have been since Evany left me.

So why doesn't being better feel, actually, like much at all? For all my shy pride and low-watt fulsomeness, I can't quite make this downscaling of misery feel like a fact of large consequence. Maybe this is what it means to recover? Walking through the days less besieged, less faltering and frantic and full of a sense of being close to the knives. That's not nothing, but I find it does not mean, either, that I am any less tangled up.

All my habits of self-confoundment remain remarkably intact.

THIS MAKES ITSELF EVERY KIND of clear to me on another small springtime trip I take down to New York, not long after my little shopping junket with Lucy. I've come to the city over break to get, yes, my hair cut. ("Middle-aged vanity is expensive vanity,"

Mark texts me from California.) But immediately following my salon appointment I go meet a friend at a bar right around the corner, and the evening slips into beery insobriety.

"A drunkness unforetold!" my friend says, and she and I nestle back into the bar's atmosphere of gentrifying hipster-kid bonhomie.

Out of which emerges the conversation of a table of women beside us, who are in town from all over the country, on what they call "business," though of what sort they don't say in much detail. ("Consulting, basically.") They thought to visit Brooklyn, they thought to visit Williamsburg, and so here they are.

We all get talking, and get drunker.

I remember that, at some crucial juncture, a track from my beloved '90s heroes Helium comes juddering into the speakers—"Trixie's Star," which features Mary Timony rocking these drony jagged licks and breathing out lines about *"cruising and shooting and fucking like some kind of movie."* It is weird and dirty and loud and it is also, to a certain kind of '90s-tuned sensibility, *perfect.* Or so I am busy saying to one of the women, whose name she tells me—ha-*ha!*—just happens to be Mary.

My friend, who has one of those jobs that requires showing up to, needs to call it a night. With a long look and one arched eyebrow, she encourages me to stay.

The beer has become bourbon, the talk has grown blurry and intricate, and all this combines somehow with the thudding drive of the guitar rock—*"Ba-aaaaby,"* the next track is saying, *"is going underground"*—to send a familiar rushing jolt through my blood. Yes. Yes, I think I will stay.

Eventually Mary asks me if I want to go outside and smoke with her. *Ah, cigarettes,* I think. *Is there nothing they can't do?* Suspecting what this means, and talking with her in an unceasing flow about what was best and what was worst about 1995, I follow her out to the sidewalk, and there, against an unlighted patch of wall, we commence making out. Presently, after a taxi ride of streaked bridge lights and minor groping, we are in her hotel—or, I should say, her *unbelievably luxe* Midtown hotel, where some very few hours later I am taking a shower in a chamber of steam and sleek wood and mirrored glass that feels so expensively architectured and curated I find myself imagining the names of the lifestyle magazines in which it might appear. *Habitus*, maybe, or *Cell. Danish Intimacy.* There is a practiced sociability to these morning-afters, and Mary and I hit our marks fluently. We thank each other. We part amicably.

Nothing about any of this feels bad. It does not seem to me sordid, shameful, or really much of anything that is not a spirit-lifting kind of good. ("Do you know what's great about sleeping with strangers?" Jordan will say to me later. *"Everything."*) And it does not stop feeling this special kind of good—a warming little ember of memory—which makes only the more confusing the thought that, all that morning and then all afternoon and all week, comes bounding directly across it.

The shortest version goes like this: *What the fuck are you doing?* Really, really, really: what the fuck are you doing?

IN A HENRY JAMES novel I'm teaching I stumble into a phrase. He talks of one character's "instinctive aversion to cheap raptures." I read this and think, once more, *Dear God, is that not me.*

Nothing about rapture feels cheap to me and when, in the cavernous quiet of my house back in Maine, I ask myself why this is, I've got an answer. It's pretty simple, really. Raise yourself on pop songs—like a lot of us do, out of need or circumstance or opportunity—raise yourself on pop songs, tilt huge quantities of life toward them, and you, too, will bristle when someone calls those raptures "cheap." Cheap? My first inclination is to respond with a resounding *GO FUCK YOURSELF*, though I have acquired by now many better words.

I need only think of the best, the least frantic and desperate hours of these past few years. Think of what's filled them. Many have involved talk, conversation in extravagant disputatious extension, in bars. A few have involved dancing. Some slender but nonnegligible quantity have unfolded, with luminous indelibility, in the bedrooms of strangers, acquaintances, springtime girlfriends, erstwhile intimates.

These have been good hours.

But the far vaster quantity of better hours has transpired in the company of songs. They have been made of music.

And I have found there every kind of unlikely replenishment. Songs have been company in solitude, the promise of connection in conditions of terrible isolation—the steadying reminder of vibrant loves in the midst of desperate loneliness. They've made me thoughtful when I couldn't think, and happy when happiness was something unrecoverably lost, a tingling phantom limb. Elation by elation by elation, they brought me out of those deserts of ruinous misery, so unfalteringly I've come to think of them as, like love, something of a human miracle.

Of course I think that. I was that kind of boy and now, ongoingly, am that kind of man. Here I am, returned to my workaday life in Maine and making this suburban house shudder with the sound of Dylan's twirling romp "The Man in Me," spinning out on repeat and at unnecessarily obliterating volume. (You probably remember it from the opening sequence of *The Big Lebowski*.) The faint hoarseness of Dylan's voice, the carnival organ, the giddy delirium of a song by rock's most revered poet that begins, *"La-la-la-la-laaa-la-la-la!"* If there are mice in these walls, they are feeling this song like an earthquake, or perhaps engaging in mouse debates about the underappreciated genius of midperiod Dylan . . .

And yet, just here, in the puzzled aftermath of this latest bar-to-bed encounter, with residual exhilaration running up against something less jubilant, new congruities assert themselves, with a force they've not yet had.

I keep saying, to anyone who asks—to Beth, Dana, John, Henry, anyone—that I know what it is that I *want* from my life after Evany. And it's true. The long months of sorrow have distilled it into clarity, into words I can say right off.

I say: I want an impassioned love capacious enough to build a fucking life around. I want to fall in soul-racking love with someone, and I want to turn that love into a *world*, filled with sex and noise and people, books and songs, the girls, a clamoring multitude of other loves in all their range and variety. I want this so badly—exactly this—and with such fevered intensity, that it shakes me awake some nights.

This is what I want.

But what I am seeing, in the disquiet that visits me after my otherwise untroubling city tryst, is that what I want seems at some point to have come unstuck from what I go looking for. What it is I *want* is indeed now starkly mismatched to what it is I want, evidently, to *feel*.

I remember saying to Beth, of a little romance undertaken after my intoxicated months with Theo, that this new thing didn't seem to me radiant enough, large enough, to stick with.

"What does that mean to you?" she wondered.

I thought about it.

"It means that when I'm with her," I said, "I don't feel like I'm standing in a house that's on fire."

A little river of silence flowed between us for a moment, and then, more sharply than I'd expected, at something only a little less than a shout, she said, *"I want you to listen to the words you have just said to me."*

A marriage is not an affair. You do not, I suppose, build a world inside a burning house. I *know* this. And yet if recovery has any signature, any resonant mark in and through my body, it can only be elation: captivation, delirium, an exhilarated dissolving bliss.

What are affairs but long-playing elations, passages of delight you live inside until they corrode, grow dulled by their repetitions, their gradually dawning intractabilities?

I know by now that the entanglements I've pursued, the heedless microromances, might reasonably be described as the ones likeliest to be, let's say, self-detonating. And worse: anything that has gathered into itself some inertial direction, a listing toward unwritten futures, I have *fled*. Anything tinged with even the least ambivalence, the least premonitory flash of uncertainty, I have endeavored to badger and cajole and fret myself right the fuck out of.

What I want to feel, evidently, is winning absolution from any such human uncertainty. What I want to feel, again and again and again, is rapture: an ambivalenceless rush of joyous captivation.

How could it be otherwise? Tilt the whole of your life toward pop songs, allow them to be your rescue and your companion, your true north in the deepest fogs, and you, too, might incline to mistake elation for recovery, confuse it with the very best of love.

Because this, too, is the thing about songs. They tell you, with a repetitiveness that should grow boring but somehow does not, that rapturous love is by its nature duplicitous, unstable, uncertain, a struggle with intractability, in others and in ourselves. *Desire*, songs will tell you, is perhaps our least pejorative word for an impulse to infinite self-confoundment.

Mistrust desire, in all its forms: it is the gateway to beautiful harm!

Songs *tell* us this.

But because of what songs often are—shocks of joy, dilated passages of pure captivation—they *convince* us otherwise. Again and again.

This must be why we love them, some of us, in the lunatic and indefensible way we do.

Dylan is still rhapsodizing—*la-la-la-la-laaa-la-la-la!*—riffing on a joy too grand and too silly for ordinary speech, and it's such a circus of sound you want to laugh out loud. But I am not laughing. I am thinking instead that I'm going to need to devise some way to encounter frontally the ordinary facts of what people are: *not* pop songs but, contrarily, occasions for uncertainty, ambivalence, love without guarantee. I'm thinking that I will need to devise some way to absolve myself of the urge to hide away inside four-minute pop deliriums, one after another, despite the fact that these are indeed spectacularly reliable, if what you want is to banish these more halting parts of being in love, and of being a person.

The idea that Helium won't help me here, or Superchunk, or Prince—it fairly buckles me. They have rescued me, as I've said. But it's maybe also true that they have been providing me obscurer instruction as well, a kind of miseducation.

People are not songs, I remind myself.

Obvious, right? But because of who I am, I will need to keep saying it.

MEANWHILE, THOUGH, WHATEVER IT is I have lost and whatever it is I have mislearned, I am reminded each day a little more forcefully that there are *other* worlds of love—quite apart from these incendiary little dalliances—to which I do, in some fashion or other, belong even still. They have in them, these worlds, a good deal more uncertainty and fear, which must be what has made it hard for me to enter into them quite as heed-lessly. Nevertheless, I'm trying. We are, the girls and I, making our way.

The season rolls along and in our little sojourns together I continue to offer, along with unneeded fashion commentary, ca-reening bits of romantic counsel to Amelia and to Lucy, largely in the form of inside jokes and phrases set in heavy rotation. We tell each other we are elaborating a taxonomy, detailed and pre-cise, of (as we put it) "the many varieties of Terrible Dude." It is labor undertaken largely in the key of silliness, though this doesn't quite make it unserious. How better to equip teenage girls for their entanglements with a world growing wider for them each day?

The days are now stretching out toward warmth and bright-ness, so we take walks, the three of us, over bridges, down the main drag, across the campus where they passed so many little-girl hours. One sun-swept afternoon we walk among the huge branching oaks that line the paths around the redbrick building where my office is. We sit a moment on the grass beneath one of these and, because it becomes suddenly vivid to me, I remind Lucy of the memorable game of catch she and I had played maybe five years before, exactly here.

Evany had taken Amelia on a mother-daughter trip to Boston for the weekend, leaving Lucy and me to fill the time together as we would. There were soccer practices to attend (of course), homework to get done, and later that Saturday a little backyard barbecue to attend at a colleague's house. In the gap of time be-fore the party, with hours to kill, we made our way to cam-pus, mitts under our arms. Students lie about like photogenic extras in a portrait of sylvan collegiate tranquility. We find a space not too crowded and throw the ball back and forth, over distances that dilate and contract. I throw grounders, fly balls, knuckle-curves. I throw and throw and throw to this indefatigable kid until, at last, wheezing and arm-sore, I plead for a break. Lucy gives a body-long shrug of exasperation and trots over. We lie side by side on the grass and, there, on my back, I start throwing the ball straight up and down to myself, bare hand to gloved hand. I tell Lucy I can't begin to quantify the number of childhood hours I passed, on my back in the yard or the basement or my bedroom, doing exactly this. Up, *clop*. Up, *clop*. It's a little hypnotic.

Lucy wants to try it.

"Oh, sweetie, I don't know. It's kind of weird—you're not really throwing it *to* anyone, you know? And you're on your back so it's an awkward kind of catch."

Lucy wants to try it.

"I'm not sure that's a good idea, sweetheart, honest."

Lucy *really* wants to try it.

Stop being pissy, I tell myself. I hand her the ball.

Exactly one throw later Lucy is pealing with hiccuping giggly laughter, grinning and grinning, and has, also, a face full of spattered blood. One throw: straight up and—oh, yeah—straight down, bashing her right in the mouth, though giving her a nosebleed, too, for good measure. I am, for a frozen instant, purely horror-struck. And then, in a beat, spasms of panic. *Ohmygod ohmygod are you alright? Did you lose a tooth? Should we head to the ER? Sweetie?* Lucy won't stop laughing, though—not shock laughs: hilarity laughs. She is laughing and laughing and when she does there's this fine pink mist of blood.

Ohmygod ohmygod.

My pulse seizes and rattles but then, sensibly, begins to decelerate. She is not frightened. She is not damaged. I have not harmed her with stepparental negligence.

"Nice catch," I say, and she collapses again into giggles.

Lucy, now a stylish teenager, does indeed remember this, and in fact remembers better than I do the punch line. She recalls going to that barbecue and arriving to a notable quantity of fuss. "Yeah," I say, *"maybe because you were covered in blood."* And it's true. I remember my colleagues' responses to her, and how they followed quite exactly the curve of my own, from a little jolt of shock to concern to a dawning sense of the comedy of it. *"Chief,"* Henry is there to observe, *"a bravura performance of solo parenting!"* And the mirth is general and teasing and kind. I remember watching Lucy for the rest of the afternoon, as she circulated among the kids and grown-ups, making chatty conversation, eating her hot dog, absorbed, wonderfully unperturbed.

And here are these two teenaged girls walking beside me under the leafless branches, griping at each other in sisterly style, stretching toward an adulthood no longer so inconceivably distant. They are much like they've always been: grouchy, funny, tedious, unreasonable, flashing with anger or annoyance, unpoliceably vivacious. No, assuredly they do not need my wise counsel, though they receive it with impressive equanimity. As happens I guess to parents, I am seized by a quick gasping sense of how beautiful these girls are, how radiant with everyday grace, and how measurelessly precious to me. *You are miracles of awesomeness,* I think to say, but don't.

It comes over me that I have been, in the strangest way, enveloping them in a kind of mistake.

All these months I have been delighting in them, but also watching them, seized, fearful, awaiting the advent of some sign of the harm that's come to them, the damage I have done. I wonder if I have once again been misrecognizing, as *injury*, something that is maybe not so dire. Look at them. There they are, unbloodied. Battered maybe, knocked around by the last years and feeling their way into angers they will need a long time to work themselves back out of, and yet, ongoingly, themselves.

We walk back down the hill, past the ice cream stand that's not yet open, past the green, the gazebo. We get gelato. We listen to mixes on the ride back, and consider the kinds of douchebag we suspect Bono might be, and these we debate.

And it's here, in the midst of this familiar scenery and time-passing chatter, that another microrevelation, long kept right on the trembling edge of disclosing itself, comes tumbling out over me. I am thinking about these mixes, these many, many years of specially curated songs, and it comes to me that they are not keepsakes or archives of parental wisdom, and never have been—and even less are they, I don't know, road maps to the byways of Cool. The girls haven't much need for any of these things. It occurs to me at last that they have always been something else, something stranger. They are nearer, I think, to *prayers*—the wishes you make, unutterable in any other form but this, for their future selves. That they be vibrant and fearless. That they be joyous and tough and, in the teeth of all that is broken, loved. And loved and loved and loved.

I drop them off up north, kiss them good-bye, tell each girl that I love her, though I'm beginning to gather that the little language we've been making together, of old phrases and loose taxonomies and shared delights, has been built to say almost nothing else.

They go inside. I slide back into the car, drive back along the rutted seaside roads, and cry and cry and cry and cry and cry.

18

Midnight Train

"WILL YOU BE here the weekend after?" Lucy asks.

"You mean the weekend of the spring dance thing, the big show?"

"No. The weekend *after*. The weekend after the recital, I mean."

"Oh—oh, no. I'm not."

"Are you going to your *salon*?" Amelia adds and gives a side-long grin.

"Dude, I wish. I'm giving a talk, at this, uh—at a conference."

We're having a quiet dinner in town, the three of us. Their schedules have grown dense with obligations, so I'm grateful to have stolen this little slice of time from the calendar.

"Where is it?" Lucy asks.

I tell her the name of the town, of the university.

"Isn't that where you got that job? Where they wanted you to go?"

These girls: they are a constancy of surprise. I'm flummoxed that she remembers this, though this I do not say. I tell her it is.

She sips contemplatively on her soda. "Will your friends be there?"

"Yeah, actually, a lot of my friends. I'm looking forward to it."

Another contemplative pause. "Do you want your fries?" she says to her sister, who stares back at her, wordless.

"Sister Amelia! Are you gonna eat those?"

"Uh—*yeah*." An expressive eye roll, comprising her entire face.

"Do *you* want your pickle?" I say, defusing, or trying to. "Because I am always ready for the unwanted pickle."

"You so are."

"Did I tell you about that band I was in in college? We were called the Unwanted Pickle. Girls, we knew how to rock."

"Uh-huh."

"You know who *else* knows how to rock?" Lucy asks, beaming.

A ripe little silence. Amelia looks at me expectantly.

"Nope!" I say. "Nope, nope, nope. Not falling for it, my dears."

Another beat of silence, a grin, a stifled giggle.

"Fine," Lucy says at last. "So *rude*!"

And then, Amelia, under her breath, "Your *mom*'s rude."

And with that, a tableful of sputtering teenaged laughter.

There was a time, I know, I would've found it all tedious, trying. I'd have struggled for patience. But now? I confess I find it irresistible. I'm laughing too.

"Well played, dude," I say to Amelia, who knows. "Seriously, though: do you want that pickle?"

THERE ARE SO, so many ways for the brokenhearted to shamble into haphazard self-punishment, so many ways to transform the necessities of recovery into ruinous little habits. These range from the involved and intricate—fidelities and infidelities, affairs overlapping and ill defined, etc.—to those as simple as stone. Think of them all! You let the pain of whatever's happened scare you out of the possibility of reencountering it, in any guise at all, no matter how unlikely to harm. Or you gather up the coins of your sorrow and, like a miser, count them out in hoarded solitude. Or maybe you grieve what you've lost so devotedly that to turn your heart toward something else, anything, comes to seem somehow traducing, *unnatural*: a betrayal of something obscure but precious. You decide to stay forever true to what's wounded you by refusing to let it be supplanted, freezing it in the alembic of your grieving, and in this way transform your sorrow into a sad kind of preservative.

Or, or, or.

All these familiar genres of battered self-sabotage.

But our follies, like our mix tapes, are as distinct as fingerprints—and no algorithm is going to convince me otherwise. If my own clumsy efforts at recovery bear the mark of all of these, they light out nevertheless into territories of their own. I can see by now that mine have involved an unwillingness to surrender some cherished fantasies about the redeeming force not only of love, but of *my* love, *my* attention, *my* devotion and ardor and care. It is I suppose a kind of grandiosity—*the world can be remade by love!*—that made me tremendously enticing to Evany, if also, finally, a kind of intolerable. What to do with the remains of that impulse, I have no idea.

But I know also, or am starting to know, that if loving songs the way I have has in several nonmetaphorical senses saved me, it has not made the question of what remains any more soluble. What are lovers supposed to be, if not occasions for these fear-annihilating bursts of joyousness? Records have less to tell me about this than I might wish.

And yet, as afternoon by afternoon the Maine winter recedes north and spring comes sashaying in, gaudy and fragrant and late, I do not wean myself from the intoxications of rock records, as maybe I should. *I do not break up with music.* How can I? If making myself better is to involve a great deal of letting go, there are some things I cannot, evidently, forswear. It seems there are impulses within in me that, if they're not hardwired, have been networked so deeply into my sensorium, stamped into the buzzing tracery of all my nerves, that jettisoning them seems at this point as unlikely as getting taller or sprouting a pair of wings.

A life is not likely to be rebuilt through the banishing of fearfulness in a series of heart-seizing elations. *Got it,* I think. *Yes.* The records I pour myself into both confirm the truth of this and, in the space of that confirmation, unravel it, because, as I am coming finally to grasp, *this is how songs work.* And yet I can no more do without them, these lifelines not only to exhilaration but to a cavalcade of people who are *not* Evany and to the worlds we have made together around them, than I can make it true that I've never lost Evany, or our little house, or our life there with the girls . . .

. . . the girls who are not, in fact, lost to me, or so it pleases me sometimes to hope. We are making something together, certainly. There's a circuitry here, lights flashing and wires alive with signals running at every frequency, but none of us knows yet what to call it. We do our things. We make our way. I am, for them, the man who used to be their semistepdad, became their stepdad, and then . . . no longer lived with them even part of the time. I am the man who was married to their mother and then, one day, wasn't. I am the person they meet up with for dinner and gelato, for walks, for low-octane silliness and easy talk. Dessert and boys and bands. I am Pete.

And the girls, for me? I miss them when I don't see them. I text them, unobtrusively I hope, and learn from them excellent new idioms of praise and dispraise. (Our uncontested favorite term of appreciation: *totes adorbs.*) I worry, in pointless unending spirals, for their well-being, their nights and days, their happiness. I know this: they are as much my children as anyone ever has been or will be. I think of that long-ago afternoon, when I heaved out sobs in the bathroom at Amelia's school after she'd taken her little spill in the recess gymnastics show. Now as then, I think: there is no use pretending—they are my daughters.

Except: I never, ever say this aloud. Not when the three of us are waiting to be seated at some overcrowded sushi place in Portland, not in company, not in private, not to them—never to them—not *ever*. I call them "the girls" or I call them "Lucy and Amelia." Like a person with poor command of a foreign tongue (like myself in Italy, actually), I scramble my syntax, flip phrases and reconjugate, to avoid the necessity of any designation besides *the girls* or *Lucy and Amelia*.

I hardly notice it, but Henry does. We are at a tavern down the block from his house and mine, returning to an old springtime ritual from years back and watching the Sox and the Yanks slog their way through an early-season blowout. I've joined him here for the late innings, after gelato with the girls. "I'm not trying to press," he says, noting that the words *my daughters* never pass my lips. "Just wondering. If you've thought about it."

As with not a few other of my acquired habits of postdivorce living, it is a kind of mystery to me. There is the long-brewed stepparental wariness of overstepping, of course. Then, too, there are what you might call the "facts" of the matter, of which virtually every fucking thing—school, the state, the offhand commentary of strangers and even friends—offers me stark reminders: I am *not* their father, not in any binding or worldly sense that appears on anybody's radar. If for that reason alone I ought not to go around calling them my daughters. When the world speaks, what it says isn't unclear: they are not.

I tell Henry the story of a Father's Day years and years before. A neighbor had come by looking for Evany and found only me, basking in the enjoyment of a scene of maximal suburban luxuriance: reading, beer in my lap, and gently a-sway in my brand-new family-sized white rope *hammock*. This was a gift from Evany and the girls. The neighbor had laughed at the spectacle and I laughed at being caught. "I *know*," I said. "Have you ever seen a better Father's Day present?"

And then, brightly, in immediate reply: "But—you're not their father!"

A sentence that had the indisputable virtue of being, in a strict sense, true.

She was not trying to be ungracious, honestly. She was not by any human measure an unkind person, and I knew that. So I fumbled through some smoothing reply, and on went the day, unbroken. It wasn't terrible, I tell Henry, just a small-scale reminder of the order of familial things.

Even as I rattle it off, though, I can hear the false note in this little barroom anecdote. It explains nothing. Why should I give even the first fuck about what the bourgeois parents of small-town Maine do and do not think of my parenthood? Something else is stopping up my words, making a phrase like *They are my daughters* stick in my throat. I cannot place it. But it takes up residence, this little puzzlement, alongside the equally mysterious tendency to cry myself dehydrated on each and all of these return treks down the coast after dropping off the girls. Nothing quite explains these, either. They are all such pleasing, equable times. The girls are with me. I am with them. We make of our small hours together almost nothing that is not warming and bright. They are unbroken.

Why, then, these weepy onslaughts? Why their persistence?

I don't know what to make of these little insolubilities, or their shape-shifting persistence. But I have, you could say, a place to put them. I continue to make the girls mixes—now for Valentine's Day, now for spring break, for study hall, for *my* birthday— and I find, in these, something at once analgesic and steadying.

They are solacing, and I try to take that solace as it comes.

≈

"HE IS *NOT* EIGHTEEN," the oldest says.

"No—listen! I think he is. Emma said so."

"*Amelia.* He is—*not*—*eighteen*. He's not even seventeen."

"Older than you are."

"Duh."

"Don't say it's not a great song. It is."

"It's a stupid song but it's a good song. It's the cheesiest thing humans have ever made."

"I don't think it's stupid. It's sort of stupid. I mean, it's *totally* stupid, but it's also, like, it's not?"

"He's just exactly seventeen."

"What?"

"He turned seventeen, like, last month."

"How do you know that?"

"How do you think?"

"Your mom."

"Aaaaaand here we go," I say.

"*Your* mom."

"Wait," I say, retracing. "Lucy—wait. You were the *same age*? For most of the past three months?"

"Yep."

"Yep."

"Sweetie, that's . . . that's kind of crazy."

"Right! Me and the Biebs. Sweet Jesus!"

"Lucy!"

"*Amelia.*"

If they are waiting for me to be the policeman of language, they'll wait to no purpose. I'm willing to let *sweet Jesus* stand and, also, it makes me laugh, as does driving in a car with exactly these teenaged girls listening in on—and getting to take part in!—a pop disquisition this unfettered and exacting. We are listening to Justin Bieber's first megahit, which is called "Baby," and there is no mystery whatsoever in why it has sold by now tens of millions of copies. It's like chirping tween heroin, laced here and there with R&B, hip-hop flourishes, trace elements of doo-wop and its boy-band afterlives, and polished into gleaming by some truly virtuosic work in the studio. It is pop product so pure and generically note-perfect that resisting it seems an exercise in churlishness, so I don't, and anyway in the midst of it there's Ludacris—fucking *Ludacris!*—dropping this rap tuned up for the middle school set.

"Don't need no Starbucks—WOOO!" Amelia and Lucy warble out in unison.

"What do you think Luda is *doing* on a song like this?"

"Killin' it."

"Yeah, but."

"Maybe he's friends with Usher."

"I'll tell you what he's doing," I say, buzz-killing. "He's making *bank*."

"Oh, whatever, dude."

On we roll, under stands of pine, past trees in first flower, roadside markets, lobster shacks.

ANOTHER RETURN: EXACTLY THREE years before—three impossible years—I had come to this busy, ruralish, pretty university town, back when Evany and I were considering the possibility of relocating our lives here for that offered job, that potentially newly made life. We came out, in fact, together, and had been treated with solicitude, kindness, and a truly expansive hospitality. So much so that I'm nervous to be back again—this time attending an academic conference—trailing behind me so much dingy catastrophe.

As it proves, there is no cause for it whatsoever. The handful of folks who know me from my previous visit greet me with a warmth uninflected by anything that is not an easy tactful kindness. One senior colleague, who was especially understanding through every stage of my candidacy, runs into me outside one of the sessions.

"Peter," he says and holds me with a steady gaze. "We're all very, very happy you've come back."

With that, my flinching disquietude floats up out of me and dissolves.

Soon enough a handful of us are at the bar, enjoying this brief restoration to one another's company and turning the night toward louder and louder enjoyments. There is talk and talk and talk, and it's all you might wish for by way of bar fighting: noisy, affectionate, filled with invective and exaggeration and a rapid-fire hilarity that keeps doubling down on itself. It makes of the evening—and, of all things, of this *conference*, of fucking *academics*—a special kind of abundance. It shouldn't be so joyous, and yet, indisputably, it is. Here is Beth, here is Dana, here is Jordan, here is Mark, each of whom has been on the receiving end of so many tearful calls, so much of my clinging desperation. But here is also Ivy and Gus and Glenn and Sarah . . . Here we all are, riding out the pleasures of all these funny ways of being together.

And it is exactly here, with the wonderful crystalline clarity proper to drunkish bar nights, that something snaps back into place for me. This talk, this making together of a language of disparagement and joy: this is how people like us, people marooned from the more ordinary languages of devotion—marriage, couplehood, family—contrive to build for ourselves a habitable little world. It is the language these ardors invent for themselves, the preserve we make for the sorts of love that don't have a lot of nearer-to-hand terms for what it is that makes them nourishing, and durable, a thing to cherish.

The night is stretching on to the smaller hours, and my wonderful friend Hester, in high ironic style, and also *totally meaning it*, has begun taking me to task for my unrenounced love of the 1973 Gladys Knight classic "Midnight Train to Georgia," which I have in fact, for no especially good reason, been making a point of contentious pride. (*A masterpiece!* I say; *Misogynist wish-fulfillment!* she says.) Soon enough we are all of us going back and forth with it, singing it, shouting it, kicking it round and round. Phones come out, the Internet gets involved, there is invective that reverts to laughter and gears itself back up.

I find enough space in consciousness to recognize that I am, in the moment, very, very happy.

I can't say if what we're doing ought to be called bar fighting. I can't say if it's a kind of practical criticism, or midlife indolence, or just some sustaining silliness, burning through the words the bunch of us tend to have too many of anyway.

Whatever you call it, I know I am correct when, at some blurry point in the evening, I make my stand.

"Dudes," I say. "Dudes! Listen. This is a *love* song."

SUCH AT ANY RATE are the glowing pop rhapsodies I carry back with me to Maine and out into a long dinner with the girls, this one up north in a casual little hole-in-the-wall-ish place nearer where their mom and dad now live and so far from the downtown gelato joint where we've become familiars. Just down the hill from us is an old mill bridge that looks out on a vista of genuinely breathtaking Maine scenery, a thing of postcards and tourist pictures, complete with colored buoys, high-prowed lobster boats, squadrons of squawking gulls, an osprey or two rising in the thermals.

To the degree that we three could be said to have access to such things, it is an ordinary night—as ordinary as two girls out with that fatherlike man in their life who is not their father but was married to their mom, for a while, when they were little. Nothing about the evening is exceptional, save perhaps this Kodachrome sky and the almost obscene redolence of the long late-April dusk. I remember taking a picture of our three pairs of sneakers, side by side by side: all of them hipsterish, striped, in grays and greens and reds. I remember Lucy asserting her age in the microcalibrated big-sisterly tones she sometimes directs at her sister, who darkens with resentment when these become too strident. The virtues of vegetarianism are discussed, the neighborhoods in New York it seems likeliest I'll end up in this summer, the gossip proper to their respective grades. I am right now in the midst of a brief happy fling with one of what would soon be many '90s-throwback bands—this one called Sky Larkin, who are the most Sleater-Kinney-sounding band striding the earth who are not Sleater-Kinney—and this I try to press on them, in my apparently never-ending quest to induce in them a burning affection for guitar-toting women who shred.

"They're a little like Pavement"—a familiar touchstone—"but they rock more."

But the conference, the bar talk, the bright sense of being part of an expansive word-built world—this is all vivid to me still, as the girls and I eat and chat and eventually stroll down the hill and toward the mill bridge. I am walking with them, and talking, but my thoughts are in an eddying little drift. I am thinking, still again, that the world is not overfull with names for what it is that we are devising together. There are not ready-made languages to describe the scene we three make, and are. And I am thinking, as we meander around the docks and moorings, that this will never not be a heartbreak to me. The want of words for my attachment to them, and theirs to me, will forever be a kind of wound—the mark left behind when something has been cut away. I will suffer that absence, mostly in insignificant ways, though as they accumulate they will hurt. I will never not be just on the outer edges of the charmed circle of real family. Pretending that's not a sorrow seems, at this point, futile—another consoling fantasy probably best done without.

But in the unhurried drift of this evening—the school year nearly over, the day flushed and lingering, "all sense / Of being in a hurry gone," as the wonderful Philip Larkin poem says—I find I cannot quite place why this namelessness matters. It is here, standing in the middle of talk about dances and DJs and Bieber and who likes who and who doesn't and why, on an evening exactly as ordinary and lovely as the one on which I met their mother, that I understand this heartbreak is, finally, my own.

It belongs to me, and not to the girls.

We walk down to the wharf and the sky above the water is a latticework of reds and silvery whites. If I have been crying after seeing them, it is not, as it was so often with Evany, a matter of happiness overspilling its narrow channels and turning itself to tears. If I have been crying it has been, I think, in the fear that the heartbreak I feel is only an echo of something much, much worse, something that I have inflicted upon them. I have been crying because I know they love me—I know it by their faces, and their voices, and the words they say, and the words they take such care not to say. I know it by the astounding grace with which they set to the task, the awful arduous task, of remaking a world together out of the fragments of a life blown apart, a life I could not preserve but, somehow, *should have*, should have known how to.

Who else was going to? Their sorrowing mother? Their feckless father? The two of them? They were *children*.

I tried so hard, girls, I want to say, *I tried so hard and everything I did was wrong,* and because I will never, ever say this, I have been crying. I have been crying because, without ever saying such a thing to myself, I have believed that I have done something terrible to them, these children who are not my daughters and whom I love. I have believed that they would eventually come to find in themselves such indignant justified *fury* about it all, the awful collapse, the failures of repair, the unhappy endings entangling us.

I have been crying to think of how much they will have to forgive to keep loving me.

Listen to them, though. Look at them. Listen to the melody of their talking, and griping, and gossiping, and turning back to me, and to one another. Do they seem in the grip of some smothered blindsiding anger?

And then the day changes.

Something arrives to me, something they have been making plain to me with every hour poured out in low-octane silliness and easy talk. The possibility that they have never thought of me as a person in need of their forgiveness—the possibility that it has never yet occurred to them to be furious at me for what's happened, and *never will*—settles around me like falling light, like the pollen gathering in pink and yellow pools. It might be that they just love me. With ordinary sturdy unofficial love, beyond the need for titles, proper names.

Who needs names? Listen to them.

"Lucy, who told you that?"

"What?"

"Stop it! You know."

"Oh, that. Your mom."

"*Your* mom."

"Oh, Sister Amelia."

"Oh, Sister Lucy."

"Is that my belt?"

"Who said it's yours?"

"You *wish*."

"Girls—be nice."

"Wait, Pete—what's that song called?"

"Which one, sweetie?"

"The one that goes, '*I wish warm weather on your upturned . . . faaaaaace!*'"

"It's called 'White Noise.' It's by Superchunk."

"Oh, yeah. You *love* them. It goes, '*Well, it's white noise and wishes that held us together, I know . . .*' I-I-I-I-I remember them. Keep wishing, Sister Amelia."

"Whatever, dude."

"Don't 'dude' me, girlie."

"Fine."

"Sing it with me, Sister Amelia: '*I wish warm weather on you . . . !*'"

Here, I like to think, is our happy ending.

You don't have to be driving around with a fifteen-year-old on her first-ever trip to California to fall in love, abruptly and defenselessly, with "Call Me Maybe." You remember "Call Me Maybe": the bit of mass-cultural ubiquity to which for the rest of human time lazy producers of VH1-ish "documentaries" will turn when they need to signify, in one decisive burst, "back in 2012." Such a setting is not required, nor is such a young person—let's call her Amelia, and let's say she's your youngest stepdaughter, though let's say, too, and with some sorrow, that you are no longer married to her mother—but I will tell you that they help.

Talk to me all you want about Carly Rae Jepsen and the new dynamics of pop distribution (from forgotten single to Bieber tweet to astoundingly winning Bieber home video to marginless aural hegemony), or about the confectioner's delight that is the song's layering of genial club beats and catastrophically catchy hooks with bright bubbles of electronic counterpoint, all of them twinkling like a prom date's starry eyes . . . None of it quite touches the indelibility, to me, of this coltish, paradigmatically teenaged, insupportably beautiful kid interrupting her passages of touristic rapture—Golden Gate Bridge! Muir Woods! Stinson Beach!—to scan through the rental car's FM dial, certain she will come upon "Call Me Maybe," and proving herself, again and again and again, absolutely correct. Watch that kid sing along, full throated and besotted, so she can teach you the words. Then tuck this away, safe from any imaginable harm or deterioration, as the very image of joy.

≈

Here's the thing about "Call Me Maybe": it's almost impossible to talk about what makes it so delight-giving without stumbling into varieties of overstatement that are antithetical to the particular charm in question. It certainly pleases, the way it's a song less about the tingly anxiety a girl feels giving her number to this hella-cute boy than about how the rich, the positively galvanic thrill of doing so exceeds, by many powers, the fear. And oh, the compressed brilliance of it! Before you came into my life, I missed you so, so bad! *In all the annals of pop you won't find many better single lines about what it's like to fall in love and to discover, in one culminating rush, that every love song you've ever heard or sung or committed to memory has been about a certain kind of protagonist and, now, that protagonist is you.*

Resist it if you must. Amelia and I don't much care.

But to say even this is already to misapprehend the winningest aspect of "Call Me Maybe," which is just the profound effortlessness of it. There is in the song no self-pleased brattiness, no wooden, weary striving after "scandalousness" or "edge." You hear in the track nothing straining and nothing strained, no on-brand reverse engineering. Over these three-plus minutes of pop domination, you hear, I think, something else: nothing but the possibility, shimmering into momentary sonic fact, of an unbelabored joyousness.

Another name for this, of course, is youth.

Is there something unseemly about a middle-aged man so loving, all in a jumble, his kid's transporting pleasure in this most un-stepped-on specimen of pop product, as well as the product itself? Maybe. But then pop songs have never been at their strongest when instructing us in how best to obey the relevant proprieties. And anyway, separating those loves would be, for me, like trying to unmix paint. Why bother? Better I think to leave Amelia there in the passenger seat, fifteen and hilarious, radiant with all these new and frightening pleasures, and singing herself elated in the high throes of a delight that nothing—not the lameness of boys, the darker clouds of adolescence, the bewilderments of adult sorrow—can diminish in the least.

Acknowledgments

SOME OF THE FIRST PASSES at what would become this book appeared in *Avidly*, under the stewardship of Sarah Blackwood and Sarah Mesle. Everything here has been improved by their scrupulousness, their brilliance, and their care.

I've been very fortunate in counselors and readers. My thanks to Willing Davidson, Beth Freeman, Jordy Rosenberg, Gus Stadler, Pam Thurschwell, Nate Vinton, and Sandy Zipp. At J's and elsewhere, Brock Clarke and Justin Tussing did a lot of advisory heavy lifting; it pleases me to be ongoingly in their debt.

Elda Rotor, for any who don't know, is heaven's dream of an editor, exacting and far-sighted and fantastically giving. I am lucky beyond measure to get to work with her, and with her sterling team at Penguin. Speaking of luck: Chris Parris-Lamb saw, from the first, a different, ampler, and altogether better book than the one I kept thinking I was writing. And then, draft by draft, he coaxed it into the world, in a labor of patience and imagination for which I will never stop being grateful.

Then there's Julie Orlemanski, who consoled and encouraged me during the worst of the writing. Her openheartedness, the unmatched agility of her mind, her world-shifting joyousness—the shorthand for all this is: her love—fomented all that's best in these sentences. But not only in these sentences.

As probably goes without saying, this book is one person's account of a series of tangled-up months and years. It is, in that sense, far, far, far from authoritative. To everyone who lived through those seasons of upheaval as well, to those named and unnamed and renamed, remembered and misremembered: my all-at-once gratitude and apologies and more-than-thanks.

Two final and unrepayable debts: to every member of every band whose songs buoyed and sustained me, and to the two girls who gave me new ears to hear them.